Security Integration in the Post-Soviet Space and Collective Security Treaty Organization

Ramakrushna Pradhan · Sukanya Kakoty

Security Integration in the Post-Soviet Space and Collective Security Treaty Organization

Roadmap for Future Cooperation

Ramakrushna Pradhan
Department of Political Science
School of Social Science
Guru Ghasidas Vishwavidyalaya
(A Central University)
Bilaspur, Chhattisgarh, India

Sukanya Kakoty
Omnify, Inc
New Delhi, Delhi, India

ISBN 978-981-97-6444-0   ISBN 978-981-97-6445-7   (eBook)
https://doi.org/10.1007/978-981-97-6445-7

Cover illustration: © Melisa Hasan

This Palgrave Macmillan imprint is published by the registered company Springer Nature Singapore Pte Ltd.
The registered company address is: 152 Beach Road, #21-01/04 Gateway East, Singapore 189721, Singapore

If disposing of this product, please recycle the paper.

Acknowledgements

Writing of this book gives us this opportunity to express our profound gratitude and deep regards to a number of people without whose continual support and motivation this book would have reached its fruition. We owe our extraordinary debt of acknowledgement to our Professors/Mentors late Prof. Arun Mohanty and Prof. Phool Badan of Centre for Russian and Central Asian Studies, School of International Studies, Jawaharlal Nehru University, New Delhi for their inspiration in excelling our academic journey through enriched research culminating in write-ups, article and books. This book is one such result dedicated to their unconditional love, affection and support.

A plenty of other people to whom we owe our gratitude for their exemplary guidance, monitoring and constant support throughout the years are the Vice-Chancellor of Guru Ghasidas Vishwavidyalaya, Bialaspur, Chhattisgarh Prof. Alok Kumar Chakrawal, Prof. Atanu Mohapatra, Dr. Siba Sankar Mohanty, Prof. B.B. Mohanty and Smt. Namita Mohanty among others. The blessing, help and guidance given by them from time to time shall carry us a long way in the journey of life on which we are about to embark.

We would also like to take this opportunity to express a deep sense of gratitude to our friends, seniors and juniors for their cordial support, valuable information and guidance, which helped us in completing this book through various stages. Special thanks are due to Somnath, Milli, Ruma and Nirmal for their active help and support.

We are obliged to staff members of Central Library, Jawaharlal Nehru University for the valuable informations and services provided by them. We are grateful for their cooperation during the entire period of writing of this book.

Lastly, we thank almighty, our parents, brother, sisters and other unnamed friends for their constant encouragement without which completion of this book would not be possible.

Prof. Ramakrushna Pradhan
Dr. Sukanya Kakoty

ABOUT THIS BOOK

This book aims to examine the role of CSTO in ensuring security of the region. It analyses the evolution of the cooperation between post-Soviet states since the demise of the Soviet Union first under the framework of the CIS, and later under the framework of CSTO. The book focuses on the purpose of the establishment of the CSTO as a regional organisation since 2002 with six out of 11 members of the CIS. This book tries to fill the gap in the existing research on the security paradigm in the post-Soviet space. It has to be borne in mind that not much study has been done so far regarding the security paradigm in the post-Soviet space in general and collective security mechanism of CSTO in the post-Soviet space in particular. The importance of multilateralism as a unique strategy taken up by the former Soviet republics and Russia's foreign policy particularly to sustain security measures in this area has not been understood by many western scholars. Many western scholars admonish CSTO to be just an instrument of formally institutionalising Russia's position and influence in the former Soviet space. At times, CSTO has also been referred to as a 'paper tiger'. CSTO as an important collective security organisation has also been devalued and many studies have paralleled Russia with CSTO. This book we are sure will be an informative handbook on regional integration, Eurasianism and CSTO for the students, scholars, readers, academicians and researchers working on this area.

CONTENTS

About the Authors

Prof. Ramakrushna Pradhan (b. 1982) is a Professor of Political Science, Head of the Department of Political Science, Dean, School of Social Science, Guru Ghasidas Vishwavidyalaya (A Central University), Bilaspur, Chhattisgarh, India. Previously worked as an *Assistant Professor* in Political Science in the Department of Social Science, Fakir Mohan University, Balasore, Prof. Pradhan also served as a Visiting Professor at L. N. Gumilyov Eurasian National University, Astana, Kazakhstan. He holds a Ph.D. from Centre for Russian and Central Asian Studies, School of International Studies, Jawaharlal Nehru University, New Delhi. Prof. Pradhan also worked as the *Associate Editor* in *Eurasian Report*- an area study research journal and *Research Associate* in *Eurasian Foundation*, New Delhi between February 2007 and February 2011. Currently he is working in the position of *Managing Editor* in *Eurasian Report*, New Delhi and *Joint Editor* of The Third Voice: Reality and Vision Journal published by Voice for Voiceless, Cuttack, Odisha. The author has authored/coauthored five books on '*Geopolitics of energy Security in Central Asia: India's Position and Policy*' (Routledge 2020), '*Geopolitics of Energy and Pipeline Diplomacy in Central Asia: Policy options for India*' (Masters Publisher, Kazakhstan, 2018), '*Geopolitics of Central Asia: China-US Engagement*' (2010), 'Geopolitics and Energy Diplomacy' (2016) and '*State Politics in Odisha*' (2016). He has also edited and co-edited several books prominent among them are: *Contemporary Odisha: Realities and Vision* (2011), *Clean Energy Options and Nuclear Safety: An Indian Perspective* (2013), *Women's Rights as Human Rights in India: Problems and Paradoxes* (2013), *Swami Vivekananda: The Man and His Message (2013), Emerging Odisha: Problems and Prospects (2014), India's Globalisation-Issues of trade, development and environment (2016), India and the Emerging World Order (2016).* Along with this, he has written several research papers concerning his area study. He has his expertise on the topic of Geopolitics, Energy Security, Strategic Studies, Central Asia, India and International Relations. In various capacities he is associated with many research organisations and academic institutions.

Dr. Sukanya Kakoty has a remarkable academic background in International Relations, holding a Ph.D. from the prestigious Jawaharlal Nehru University (JNU), India. Fuelled by her passion for research and writing, she ventured into the world of content creation and found herself in a fulfilling role as a Content Writer for Omnify, a prominent US-based SAAS company.

Through her dedication and skill, Sukanya's journey evolved as she rose to the position of Content Strategist, becoming an instrumental force in driving the company's marketing endeavours. Her expertise in crafting compelling narratives and her penchant for strategic thinking have led Omnify to new heights in the digital realm.

With an unwavering commitment to both her family and career, Sukanya cherishes her role as a loving parent, spending moments with her 4-year-old toddler. Additionally, she embraces her wanderlust spirit, exploring diverse landscapes whenever she gets a chance. Her interests majorly include international studies, security dynamics of Russian and Central Asian states and the region's energy policy. She hails from Sivasagar, Assam.

Acronyms and Abbreviations

BSF	Black Sea Fleet
BTC	Baku-Tbilisi-Ceyhan oil pipeline
CDM	Council of Defence Ministers
CENTO	Central Eastern Treaty Organisation
CFM	Council of Foreign Ministers
CIS	Commonwealth of Independent States
CORF	Collective Operational Reaction Forces
CRRF	Collective Rapid Reaction Force
CSC	Collective Security Council
CSSC	Committee of the Secretaries of the Security Council
CST	Collective Security Treaty
CSTO	Collective Security Treaty Organisation
EEC	Eurasian Economic Community
EU	European Union
GUAM	Georgia Ukraine Azerbaijan Moldova
IAEA	International Atomic Energy Agency
IMU	Islamic Movement of Uzbekistan
MAD	Mutually Assured Destruction
NATO PfP	NATO Partnership for Peace
NATO	North Atlantic Treaty Organisation
NRC	NATO-Russia Council
NSC	National Security Concept
OSCE	Organisation for Security and Cooperation in Europe
PF	CSTO Peacekeeping Forces
RATS	Regional Anti-Terrorist Structure
SCO	Shanghai Cooperation Organisation

SEATO	South East Asia Treaty Organisation
SES	Single Economic Space
TCS	Treaty of Collective Security
UN	United Nations
UNO	United Nations Organisation
US	United States
USSR	Union of Soviet Socialist Republics

LIST OF FIGURES

CHAPTER 1

Eurasian Regionalism: An Introduction

Abstract Eurasianism, a quasi-political and intellectual movement, emerged in the 1920s as an anti-Bolshevik movement. It emphasized Russia's unique blend of Slavic and non-Slavic cultures and ethnic groups, and the corporate nature of the Russian state. Eurasianism was a precursor to post-Soviet Russia's ideology, blending Marxism with nationalism. Historians have considered alternative options for the Soviet regime, including Trotsky, Bukharin, Mensheviks, and Peter B. Struve. The past is dependent on the present, with historians examining the past to understand the present political trends.

Keywords Regionalism · Eurasianism · Post-Soviet states · Russia and New Regionalism

1.1 INTRODUCTION

The single most striking feature of globalization has been unprecedented mushrooming of regionalization process leading to the formation of diverse regional communities or territorial conglomerations of different sizes based on certain internal cohesion such as historical, political, cultural, economic, geographical and civilizational among other factors.

© The Author(s), under exclusive license to Springer Nature
Singapore Pte Ltd. 2024
R. Pradhan and S. Kakoty, *Security Integration in the Post-Soviet Space and Collective Security Treaty Organization*,
https://doi.org/10.1007/978-981-97-6445-7_1

1

Such regionalization manifested at both domestic and international level can be seen at least from two perspectives. These are namely "de jure" and "de facto" regionalization. "De jure" regionalization generally manifests in the regions with similar political and geographical orientations while "de facto" regionalization are not formed deliberately but due to certain historical factors. Hence, de jure regionalization leads to easy control and operation largely attributing to their deliberate creation while the de facto regionalization results into weak control or no control attributing its imposed nature. Nevertheless, both types of organizations are conditioned by certain historical factors of regionalization. If one look at the feature and mechanisms of the regionalization process two interrelated trends comes to the picture: disintegration and integration. While disintegration trend takes place when new countries formed out of a single geographical entity come together after their independence either due to fear of decay or threat for survival whereas integration type of regionalization takes place when territorial and political actors come together to form a community for mutual benefits. The formation of new regionalism 'geospace' in the post-Soviet space after the disintegration of the Soviet Union in this direction would offer an interesting read with the combination of the factors discussed above through historical development process taking place in the Eurasian space. In this context this book certainly offers vivid nuances to understand the process of regionalization and its journey through varied geographical space and political attributes with the single most agenda focusing on the regional integration process in the post-Soviet space – then and now.

1.2   A Prelude

As the book goes to press, two interesting coincident that knock our mind is that the disintegration of the Soviet Union on December 2021 marked 30 years while the formation of the Soviet Union marked Centenary in December, 2022. Exactly thirty-two years back, three Slavic states of Ukraine, Belarus and Russia met at Malta on 8th December, 1991 without informing and consulting other members of the Union, to discuss the fate of the former Soviet Union. The unilateral declaration of these three Slavic states formally marked the disintegration of the Union of the Soviet Socialist Republics (USSR). As a result of the disintegration, the largest political landmass of the World was divided into fifteen newly independent, sovereign, and territorially fixed units that have led to an astonishing geopolitical event in the twentieth century World order.

Nevertheless, after the fall of the Soviet Union in December 1991, Russia emerged as the largest and most powerful of the newly independent post-Soviet states (NIS). Its post-communist officials originally appeared eager to abandon the remnants of the 'empire', such as worthless subsidies to other NIS. However, the consequences of the disintegration, particularly the breakdown of the former Soviet Union's unified economic complex, were no less destructive to Russian national interests than they were to the national interests of smaller NIS. Transitioning to new types of political and economic interactions amongst these governments required a new, multilateral approach. The Commonwealth of Independent States (CIS) was envisioned as a transitional arrangement.

The establishment of the CIS, along with its Interstate Economic Committee (1994–1999), Inter-Parliamentary Assembly, and a set of preferential trade agreements, carried the promise of progressing far beyond the initial stage of a civilized break-up and distribution of assets among the constituent republics of the former USSR. While declaring the former Soviet Union's legal norms null and void, the agreement on the establishment of the CIS committed the parties to developing cooperation in politics, economics, culture, and education; foreign policy coordination; and cooperation in the formation and development of 'all-European and Eurasian markets' (Article 7). Apart from Russia, Armenia, Belarus, and the Central Asian states, Kazakhstan appeared to be the most enthusiastic about the CIS project and economic reintegration.

The first CIS customs union was formed in 1994 by Kazakhstan, Uzbekistan, and Kyrgyzstan. Kazakhstan's President Nursultan Nazarbayev suggested the formation of the Eurasian Union of States. The draft document titled 'Establishment of a Eurasian Union of States' was officially submitted to the Heads of State of the Commonwealth of Independent States in June 1994 and disseminated at the UN General Assembly's Forty-ninth session the following month (Molchanov 2015). However, the notion could only come to reality if Russia joined in and led the process known as Eurasian regional integration.

The 'Eurasian' label draws on the tradition of Russian émigré thinkers of the early twentieth century, who posited the existence of a specifically 'Eurasian' core to the Old World continent, which is neither Europe nor Asia as such, but represents the 'Old World's centre', the continental 'torso' of the Eurasian landmass, consisting primarily of its three largest plains—East European (Russian), West Siberian, and Central Asian—and their adjacent peripheries to the east. This Eurasia proper, *Eurasia sensu stricto*, differs from the traditional geographic definition of a continent that encompasses both Europe and Asia in its entirety, *Eurasia sensu latiore* (Molchanov 2015).

The concept of the continental 'trunk', which bears a striking resemblance to Halford Mackinders (1904) Heartland, has had significant geopolitical implications: a historical mission of Eurasia proper, according to classic Eurasianists, was to be a unifier of the entire continent, the true'middle' world bridging both European and Asian 'peripheries of the Old World'. Eurasia has been regarded as a naturally integrated organism predestined to remain whole and indivisible: in one formulation, 'the nature of the Eurasian world is least conducive to 'separatisms' of any sort - whether political, cultural, or economic' (Savitskii 2007: 247).

Eurasianism, historically a post-monarchical Russian imperialism, has been revived in Eurasian regional integration in the late 20th and early twenty-first century. It focuses on voluntary processes of economic cooperation, social, political, administrative, regulatory, and normative exchanges among post-communist states like Belarus and Tajikistan.

Post-Soviet Eurasia's regional integration is a response to global economic challenges and security dilemmas. New regionalism scholars view this as a complex process that involves cultural, political, and security aspects of societies. The process involves structure and agency, with foreign policies focusing on region-building and establishing regional coherence and identity.

Studying post-communist regionalism is a novel endeavour. It could be categorized as part of the global regionalisms that are referred to as the "third wave." This is in contrast to the first "wave," which is typically linked to closed regional trade agreements and import substitution tactics, and the "second wave," which is also known as "open regionalism," which placed an emphasis on regional integration that is compatible with non-discriminatory trade liberalization and openness to outsiders. According to this plan, the "third wave" is an effort to revive previous preferential trade agreements through selective, negotiated openness; this process has gained traction in reaction to the recent two decades' global financial crises (Bonapace 2005).

Some analysts, however, contend that there are only two types of regionalism: old and new. The latter is thought to have been sparked by the US's support of regional integration in the Americas, the Single European Market's early successes, and the GATT/WTO's seeming inability to resolve long-standing trade disputes. Undoubtedly, the narrative and institutional spread of regionalist principles borrowed from the European integration discourse have informed regionalization attempts throughout Eurasia. Conceptual borrowing was also inevitably impacted by the 2008–2009 financial crises, which brought down the neo-liberal globalization paradigm and the Euro zone's subsequent protracted recession.

1.3 Eurasianism Supranational Identity

The Eurasian region is witnessing perhaps the bloodiest war of twenty-first century and most devastating war since World War–II. No doubt the war sparked fierce debates on several issues ranging from military to political and ideological. Numerous theories and varied narratives were developed to support Putin's action in one of its closest 'Near Abroad.' The most important discourse around which the debate centred around is Eurasianism which developed in early 1990s after the disintegration of the Soviet Union. In several political and cultural circles an idea was flourished reshape the post-Soviet space with a Russian identity after the dissolution of the great USSR. Although many claim the Russian identity to have its roots in the 1917's Bolshevik revolution, yet the core of the concept is to preserves the multi-ethnic nature of the wide Eurasian region by a 'symphonic personality' link diverse ethnic people by geography. The idea was to reject the old imperial practices and to accept and promote Russian as the greatest of the Slavs and their brotherly as the basis of overall Eurasian ideas. This was in fact to promote with intent to create a 'sui generis'—a supranational identity named Eurasianism with Russia at the apex. Based on this premise, a Neo-Eurasianism philosophy was developed to support the Russian foreign policy with slight deviation from the 'idea of brotherly nations' to the idea of Russian supremacist. And not to be surprised 'Eurasianism' has been used as a cultural idea, political doctrine, an ethno-genesis theory, a historical globalist philosophy and a geopolitical principle at the behest of Russia to promote the interests and ideas of Kremlin. Any deviation from this economic, political and geostrategic goal of Russia has to meet with serious military and economic ramifications. The current Ukraine Crisis is one such deviation on part of Kiev to move away from the Russian sphere of influence to the western sphere of influence through joining EU and NATO. The genesis of this crisis can be found in the failure of Ukraine and Russia to stay together in greater Eurasian world. Nevertheless, the regionalism proposed in the post-Soviet space needs an elaborate analysis to understand the crisis at hand resulted because of the failure of the Eurasianism in the hinterlands of Russia. Let's have a broader understanding of how regionalism was formed in the former Soviet space at first place. However, no understanding of Eurasianism would be complete without understanding the dissolution process of the Soviet Union.

1.4   Aftermath of the Dissolution of the Soviet Union

To be precise, three Slavic states of Ukraine, Belarus and Russia met at Malta on 8th December, 1991 without informing and consulting other members of the Union, to discuss the fate of the former Soviet Union. The unilateral declaration of these three Slavic states formally marked the disintegration of the Union of the Soviet Socialist Republics (USSR). As a result of the disintegration, the largest political landmass of the World was divided into fifteen newly independent sovereign, territorially fixed units that have led to an astonishing geopolitical event in the twentieth century World order. The comparison of which can be made only with that of the collapse of the great empires of 'Habsburg' and 'Ottoman' during the First World War. A massive chunk of territory has been torn away from the biggest geographical and political landmass of the World into diverse directions only to be territorially demarcated into several, unique, political units. Perhaps the 'civilized divorce' of its republics from the Union has been formally completed with the formation of the Commonwealth of the Independent States (CIS). Although the Commonwealth was purely a symbolic organization without any concrete steps following the foundation in early 1990s, it's role, structure and functions in a while increased manifold. Russia's sudden rise from the disintegration slumbers and assuming the role of true and sole successor of the former Soviet Union during the mid-1990s have resulted in shifting the dynamics of the CIS. The growing Russian presences and active involvement in the post-Soviet space with its foreign policy connotation of 'near abroad' following with the consequent events in late 1990s such as incursion to Kyrgyz south and attacks in Tashkent by Islamic Movement of Uzbekistan (IMU), the eastward movement of NATO, growing US involvement and penetration into the Post-Soviet space, instability in Afghanistan, sporadic violence in the aftermath of disintegration of the USSR and security vulnerability of the regional countries has led to the formation of the new regional security organization—Collective Security Treaty Organization (CSTO) among the seven members of the Commonwealth of Independent States under the leadership of Russia. Further the tragic event of 9/11 has strengthened the idea of CSTO as a military, military-political, and military-technical organization for ensuring better regional security and unification among the former Union members.

Notwithstanding, Russia's neighbourhood crises and challenges especially with Georgia and currently the war Moscow has been fighting with its erstwhile close ally Ukraine since 2022 put serious question marks over the Russian idea of 'space without borders' with its neighbours making Russia sole responsible actor guarantying the security of its neighbours. Now Russia's near abroad consists of a community of independent states that cannot ensure their own security and survival by relying only on their own forces. From Estonia in the west to Kyrgyzstan in the east, the existence of these countries in a competitive international environment is ensured by their link with one of the nuclear superpowers. Moreover, such connections can only complement each other with great difficulty. As the recent developments in Kazakhstan have demonstrated, they are not limited to the threat of an external invasion; even internal circumstances can become deadly.

Thus, Russia needs to take the lead to preserve the independence of these states surrounding it and direct all its efforts to ensure that they become effective powers, eager to survive. This desire for survival is seen as the main condition for rational behaviour, i.e. creating a foreign policy, which considers the geopolitical conditions and the power composition of Eurasia. In other words, CSTO can be the best mechanism led by Russia in protecting and preserving the territorial integrity of the Eurasian countries within the framework of the CSTO charter. However, the recent actions of Kremlin to develop the Eurasian space and its integration process as an alternative political order challenging the Liberal World Order taking place under new conditions and taking full control of its neighbours with which, it shares a single geopolitical space could offer a very different analysis then what the CSTO charter offers to us. The rule book of CSTO and the action of Russia in the Eurasian space and new dynamics taking place in the regional order offers an interesting debate of regional integration process in the post-Soviet space this book proposes to look into in details.

1.5   SCOPE AND OBJECTIVE

The purpose of this book is to investigate how CSTO contributes to regional security. It examines how post-Soviet collaboration has developed since the fall of the Soviet Union, initially inside the CIS and then under the CSTO frameworks. The goal of the CSTO's formation as a regional organisation in 2002—along with six of the eleven CIS members—is the main subject of the book.

At the start of the twenty-first century, Russia's top focus has been integration within the frameworks of the CIS and CSTO. Russia preferred the democratic growth of the West after the fall of the Soviet Union, and it had long since lost interest in the "near abroad." However, Russia's policy shifted to post-Soviet republics in an effort to appease the country's politicians and regain its status as a "superpower." The CIS, which was created as a rival to the USSR, has been a mechanism for member integration. That being said, the Commonwealth accomplished nothing particularly noteworthy until the late 1990s. The Islamic Movement of Uzbekistan (IMU) invasion of southern Kyrgyzstan and the vehicle attacks in Tashkent in 1999 presented the CIS countries with the problems of the modern world and brought the topic of regional security to the forefront of the organization's agenda for its meetings.

Members decided to create the Collective Security Treaty Organisation (CSTO) in order to fight terrorism, illicit drug trafficking, illegal immigration, and organised crime after the 9/11 terrorist assault highlighted the significance of this issue for both national and regional security. The CSTO foundation elevated member relations to a new plane.

The prerequisites for integration within the CSTO framework and its efficacy in guaranteeing regional security are covered in this book. Since two of the Organization's seven members are directly bordered by Afghanistan and four of the members are Central Asian nations, the influence of Afghanistan is also covered in greater detail within the framework of the book.

So, this book focuses on the challenges to the security of the region, and also discusses the growing role of the CSTO and Russia in the region. At last, CSTO member states' relations and cooperation with other international organizations on the territory of the CIS will be discussed.

1.6 ARGUMENT

The proposed book tries to fill the gap in the existing research on the security paradigm in the post-Soviet space. It has to be borne in mind that not much study has been done so far regarding the security paradigm in the post-Soviet space in general and collective security mechanism of CSTO in the post-Soviet space in particular. The importance of multi-lateralism as a unique strategy taken up by former Soviet republics and Russia's foreign policy particularly to sustain security measures in this area has not been understood by many western scholars. Many western scholars rebuke CSTO to be just an instrument of formally institutional-izing Russia's position and influence in the former Soviet space. At times, CSTO has also been referred to as a 'paper tiger'. CSTO as an important collective security organization has also been devalued and many studies have paralleled Russia with CSTO.

However, it has been seen that Russia's hegemony has indeed been a binding factor in the post-Soviet area; as Gleason puts in, "A situation in which a cooperative regime is established through the imposition of the will of a single, dominant co-operator." Militarily, Russia's power is overwhelming; hence CSTO being fundamentally a military alliance and Russia-led is of definite significance. CSTO has successfully conducted number of military exercises, cooperated in the issues of security, crime and narcotics, deployed peacekeeping forces under the UN mandate. Considering all these, the proposed work will be a relevant contribution to the security studies because no significant and proper academic work has been done specifically on the security integration process in the post-Soviet space particularly on the CSTO. Moreover, this study attempts to be a pointer towards future research in this direction. The main focus of the book however is confined to and around:

- To examine the security parameters of the post-Soviet space consid-ering the swift and domino-effect transitions after the disintegration of the Soviet Union and also after the '9/11 attacks' that marked foreign policy shifts on part of the former Soviet republics.
- To analyse Russia-led CSTO's potential as a relevant collective security mechanism aftermath the Cold war era.
- To examine and study the Commonwealth of Independent States and its approach to Regional Security for ensuring better unification and stability in the post-Soviet space.

- To study multilateralism as a foreign policy dimension of Russia to address security issues.
- To study CSTO, its structure, activities, and role in maintaining collective security in the region.
- To understand the level of competitive security cooperation taking place in the post-Soviet space which witnesses the presence of other security organisations apart from CSTO like the SCO and the NATO.

1.7   Scheme of the Chapters

This book has been clubbed into eight different chapters excluding the introduction and conclusion. The scheme of the book is as follows:

Chapter 1: Eurasian Regionalism: An Introduction has been curated deliberately to provide a brief background about the relevance of the book and contextualising the Eurasian region from the Russian perspective after the end of Cold War that has cumulated in formation of the CSTO. This chapter while providing a background of this book argues in favour of Eurasian Regionalism as the vortex of Russian philosophy since antiquity and Russian assertion of opposing any deviation from this Russian worldview delineating the current Ukraine War as the by-product of such deviation by Kiev on the behest of the west and America.

Chapter 2: Regional Integration and Eurasianism: A Theoretical Interrogation provides a historical background, philosophical underpinnings of regionalism crediting the unprecedented rise of globalization behind mushrooming of regional organizations attributing to various factors. This chapter has broadly been divided into three pertinent sections: theories of regionalism, forms of regionalism and Eurasianism. To understand the phenomenon of regionalism, this chapter incorporates the theoretical aspects of international relations to understand the philosophy of regionalism. Taking this debate further, this chapter discusses various forms of regionalism ranging from unilateralism to multilateralism. After thorough interrogation of theoretical aspects of regionalism, it discusses the Eurasian regionalism through its journey from Classical Regionalism to Global Eurasianism depicting the Russia's worldview as inseparable from Eurasianism.

Chapter 3: Concept of Security: an introduction while providing a brief background of the concept of security in international politics delve into fill the gap in the security paradigms so far discussed in relations to the post-Soviet space. It has to be borne in mind that not much study has been done so far regarding the security paradigm in the post-Soviet space in general and collective security mechanism of CSTO in the post-Soviet space in particular. The importance of multilateralism as a unique strategy taken up by former Soviet republics and Russia's foreign policy particularly to sustain security measures in this area has not been understood by many western scholars. Many western scholars proclaim CSTO to be just an instrument of formally institutionalizing Russia's position and influence in the former Soviet space. At times CSTO has also been referred to as a 'paper tiger'. CSTO as an important collective security organization has also been devalued and many studies have paralleled Russia with CSTO remain thrust of this chapter.

Chapter 4: Commonwealth of Independent States (CIS): An Emerging Model of Regional Security largely focuses on the origin and formation of CIS, institutional bodies of CIS and their activities, performance of CIS in dealing with security challenges in the region.

Chapter 5: Russia's Security Policy in the post-Soviet Space begins by an understanding of the security environment in the post-Soviet space followed by the patterns that Russia followed in pursuing a foreign and security policy in the post-Soviet space, the motive and attempts for security integration and military cooperation.

Chapter 6: CSTO: Structure, Activities and Role in Maintaining Collective Security in the post-Soviet Space covers the origin of the CSTO, its evolution, the legal basis of its foundation, the military-technical components of the CSTO and the way it works towards security integration in the region. Altogether it contains almost every step that the CSTO has taken in action and in relation towards individual CSTO members.

Chapter 7: Increasing Diversity in the Threat Perception of the CSTO Member States discusses the emerging transnational security challenges in the aftermath of the Soviet disintegration; terrorism and instability in Afghanistan; efforts for promoting regional security in Central Asia for strengthening stability, security, peace and order in the region.

Chapter 8: Competitive Security Cooperation in the post-Soviet Space: A Comparative study of CSTO presents an increasing penetration of other regional security organizations such as SCO, OSCE and increasing influence of NATO and PfP Program in the post-Soviet space. It also tries to draw out a picture of competitive cooperation among similar security organizations like SCO and NATO having its presence in the post-Soviet space. It further tries to understand what equation the CSTO shares with these two organizations.

Chapter 9: Russia's Eurasian Strategy: A Way Forward focuses on the strategies Kremlin has been adopting since the end of Cold War to keep the entire Eurasia in its geopolitical orbit and debates the change in policies to readjust Russian approach towards the member states in the wake of the Russia-Ukraine war taking place since 2022 in the Eurasian space. This chapter provides a blueprint about Russia's Eurasianism approach to understand Moscow's philosophy and practice of regionalism with regards to Eurasia and analyses the policy approach amidst war to cope up with other member states of the region gripped under the fear of domino effect of the Ukraine war.

Finally, the Conclusion chapter thoroughly elaborates the findings of the book and recommends certain policy measures to be taken for further strengthening the organization after carefully going through the problems and prospects of the organization for the member states. It also sheds light on how to use CSTO as an opportunity to ensure security in the region and to achieve desirable unification among the member states as far as security issues are concerned.

References

Bonapace, T. 2005. Regional Trade and Investment Architecture in Asia-Pacific: Emerging Trends and Imperatives. *Economic and Political Weekly* 40 (36): 3941–3947.

Mackinder, Halford. 1904. The Geographical Pivot of History. *The Geographical Journal* 23 (4): 421–437.

Molchanov, Mikhail A. 2015. Eurasian Regionalism: Ideas and Practice. In *Power, Politics and Confrontation in Eurasia: Foreign Policy in a Contested Region*, ed. R.E. Kanet and M. Sussex, 135–160. New York: Palgrave Macmillan.

Savitskii, P. N. 2007. Geographical and Geopolitical Foundations of Eurasianism. In *Geopolitika*, ed. B.A. Isaev, 235–242. St. Petersburg: Peter.

CHAPTER 2

Regional Integration and Eurasianism: A Theoretical Interrogation

Abstract Regionalism is an international political effort by nations to increase collaboration and support in various governmental operations, including military, political, economic, and social-cultural exchanges. It often results in regional integration among governments within a specific region. A process or a situation, driven by historical experiences, economic circumstances, geographic proximity, cultural similarity, or a common sense of threat from a dominant power, regionalism has been seen from various theoretical perspectives in this chapter.

Keywords Regionalism · International relations · Theories of regionalism · Functionalism and neo-functionalism · Systems Theory and New Eurasianism

2.1 Introduction

In international politics, regionalism denotes an endeavour by nations within a given geographic area to pursue increased collaboration and backing in several domains of governmental operations, including military, political, economic, and social-cultural exchanges. Occasionally, the

R. Pradhan and S. Kakoty, *Security Integration in the Post-Soviet Space and Collective Security Treaty Organization*,
https://doi.org/10.1007/978-981-97-6445-7_2

desire for the establishment of regional organisations is a gradual manifestation of the necessity for such cooperation. Another name for this process is regional integration. Therefore, regionalism frequently results in regional cooperation and integration among the governments that make up a certain region. Nearly every place on Earth has encountered this phenomenon, and since the 1990s, there has been a greater focus on its advancement. In this context, it's crucial to consider whether regionalism is a 'process' or 'condition'.

Regionalism can be thought of as both a process and a situation. In the world of ideas and emotions, it is a condition when nations in a region feel a sense of affinity and belonging because of things like historical experiences (like colonialism in Asia and Africa), economic circumstances (like economic underdevelopment in Latin America), geographic proximity, cultural similarity (like linguistic or tribal affinities), or a common sense of threat from a dominant power. These are a few of the circumstances that support emotion and affinities inside the region, which eventually lead to the creation of a regional organisation.

Regionalism may also be defined as the process of creating a blueprint for regional organisation by focusing specific efforts within an area on identifying and strengthening the latent affinities among the participants in order to advance the cause of tighter collaboration and integration. In the 1950s, Latin America adopted the import substitution industrialization (ISI) model of development, which persuaded all of the continent's nations to pursue greater economic integration. Therefore, regionalism as a phenomenon refers to both a state and a process that both result in ties of belonging and collaboration.

2.2   Evolution of Regionalism

It's interesting to note that neighborhood-based regional collaboration is not a recent development. Since the beginning of organised political life, we have witnessed instances of regionalism. But its most well-known avatar has only been dating back to the seventeenth century. It began with regional trade agreements involving colonies, provinces, and states, leading to political and commercial unions. However, regional integration developed after World War II with the creation of the European Economic Community. The Soviet Union's Council for Mutual Economic Assistance (CMEA) in 1949 stifled regional economic integration. The first wave of regionalism began with the European Community in 1957 and the European Free Trade Association in 1960, promoting regional integration in Latin America and Africa. The second stage of regionalism began in the mid-1980s, with the European Community deepening its integration (Galiakberov and Abdullin 2014).

In the post-Cold War era and the current stage of globalization and regionalization reflects the growing interdependence of states and the close relationship between international and national laws. Sustainable regional integration systems use the goodwill of participants to protect common interests (Farhutdinov 2005). Immanuel Kant viewed the supra-state as a transitional stage towards world peace, advocating for cosmopolitan norms independent of the state. Legal integration processes and harmonization of systems are evident, with the European Union's law being an interesting example. Economic integration involves business entities and other public life spheres. The evolution of international integration processes has occurred through basic steps such as free trade areas, customs unions, common markets, and economic unions. The ultimate goal is the harmonization of domestic legal systems to ensure free movement of production factors like goods, services, labor, investment, and finance. This can only be achieved if the state transfers competence to the economic integration system organs. Harmonization and unification strengthen supranational regulation methods and make it easier to control the integration process. Regional integration involves the development of third-party relations through treaties, followed by the expansion of direct economic relations. Supranational law is formed through the interaction of international and domestic laws, forming a legal superstructure. Regional integration can be achieved through a special legal regime that focuses on economic and political integration.

The Agreement on the Customs Union and Common Economic Space aims to create a single economic space for the parties' territories, ensuring the free movement of goods, services, capital, and labour force. The unification of law aims to harmonize the interaction of different legal systems and national legal systems. Regional integration systems provide various benefits to members, with international courts serving as the institutional basis for integration. In Latin America, international courts are established within integration associations, providing uniform formation, interpretation, and application of law based on their competence. The "law of integration" is a part of international economic law, and successful integration requires economic development. The regulation of interstate association rights involves the constitution of each state and international law, as well as the acts of interstate organizations. Interstate unions express a greater degree of integration due to historical commonality, reflect the structure of member states' institutions, and have judicial institutions to resolve disputes and conflicting procedures.

Similarly, the collapse of the CMPEA in the 1990s led to the establishment of linkages between Central and Eastern European states and the EU, with about a third of new Regional Trade Agreements (RTAs) involving transition economies. Japan joined the trend, signing an FTA with Singapore in 2002. The South has seen a revival of RTAs, with 30–40% of RTAs currently in force being among Less Developed Countries. Southern RTAs are more open to global market forces and have long transition periods. The formation of GATT after World War II supported multilateral trade liberalization, but regionalism emerged as a significant force with the creation of regional agreements. Regionalism is now seen as a policy and project aimed at pursuing common goals in one or more issue areas.

2.3   Theories of Regionalism

Theory is a crucial tool for understanding international relations and regionalism. Understanding and building theories of regionalism helps us understand the phenomenon itself. This collection aims to reveal the pluralism and richness of theories, with divergent meta-theoretical and conceptual points of departure, different ways of producing knowledge, and diverse research questions. Recognizing and embracing a variety of theories helps clarify differences and similarities between concepts and theories.

2.3.1   Theory of Functionalism and Neo-functionalism

Conceptually, a model for cooperation was laid out by David Mitrany in his 1943 book A Working Peace System. In it, he suggested collaborating in what he refers to as "functional" areas—technical areas of interdependence—in order to promote closer ties and increased interaction between member states. He thought that these exchanges would eventually lead to cooperative behaviours and a better understanding among the involved states, which would create system interdependencies and connections in other domains as well. He believed that doing this would create the groundwork for the state system to function peacefully.

His strategy for achieving peace became known as the functionalist strategy. It implies that the formation and persistence of rising interdependence in technical and trade-related exchanges among the states is one of the primary reasons responsible for the evolution of regionalism and regional cooperation. Member states gradually expand their collaboration to other domains when they discover that it is advantageous to work together in certain "functional" areas. We call this the spill over effect. After World War II, the functionalist approach gained the most popularity in Europe due to the continent's post-war reconstruction challenges and need for economic cooperation. What started off as functional area collaboration gained more traction and value throughout the European region, evolving into a regional organization.

The European Coal and Steel Community was the first to be formed, and it led to the creation of the regional European Economic Community. A concerted effort was made in the 1960s to tailor the functionalist approach to the unique requirements of Europe by incorporating political cooperation within the framework of trade and economics. The redesigned Mitrany functional cooperation programme was defined by a group of regionalists under the direction of Ernst B. Haas. Their method, which became known as "neofunctionalism," emphasised how political participation in the regional cooperative plan was a necessary component for regional integration.

Theories of functionalism and neo-functionalism are umbrella terms for a variety of studies conducted in this area. The mechanism by which authorities of distinct nation-states now make decisions is the focus of international integration, according to P. E. Jacob and J. V. Toscano. The process through which particular tasks (functions) are now carried out by international organisations as opposed to independent nation-state authorities is the focus of international functionalism (Onuf 1989). The study of international organisations has greatly benefited from the theories of functionalism and neo-functionalism in a number of ways. The theory's proponents contend that in order to address global economic and social issues, organisations founded on functions rather than borders are essential. As in non-political, economic, social, and other technical domains where national differences would be minimal, the idea implies that functional cooperation among nations could start there. The idea that a state will never inevitably lose its sovereignty is supported by this method. It contends, therefore, that the major concerns in the developing global society outweigh the sovereignty debate.

2.3.2   Theory of Complex Interdependence

The international system's structure and the underlying issues with collective action and collaboration provide the motivation for international cooperation. The latter are predicated on interdependence (Hurrell 1995: 350; Keohane 1984: 51), while it is supposed that there is a neo-realistic view of an international system that is anarchistically constructed and devoid of any kind of global coercive mechanism or hierarchical order. In light of this, nations would be well advised to protect their existence and well-being by pursuing their objectives egoistically and without regard for others (Waltz 1979). But anarchy in the international system does not always mean the hostile and conflict-ridden world portrayed in Hobbes' Leviathan; rather, it permits even selfish, utility-maximizing agents to look for mutual assistance in particular difficult circumstances.

Complex interdependence in international relations implies that policies, actions, and returns of one individual state are not isolated events but rather interlaced and a function of its counterparts' behaviour and action. According to this understanding, interdependence is certainly not exclusively confined to the economic realm but occurs in virtually every issue area of international relations, such as security, infrastructure, climate, and environment. The existence of complex interdependence between various actors, i.e. states, in various specific issue-areas is the primary cause of prevalent problematic situations in international relations (Keohane and Nye 1987). In light of this, policies aimed at cooperation and coordination, depending on the circumstances, may aid in achieving Pareto-superior results for all actors, provided that the benefits of the (expected) related actions outweigh the costs of maintaining the status quo in an uncoordinated manner (Zürn 1993: 9–10).

2.3.3   Theory of Neo-liberal Institutionalism

Neo-liberals reject the more expansive integration drive cultivated by globalisation, and view regionalism as a form of new protectionism. The neo-liberal interpretation of regionalism opposes globalisation and increasing market integration because it is a type of political intervention used by state regulators to offset the state's loss of centrality. The central claim of neo-liberalism is that as market integration increases, political integration inevitably rises as well, ensuring greater political, legal, and economic standards both within and between nations in the "international society of states (Barbieri 2019)."

Neo-liberal institutionalism an offshoot of neoliberalism offers a very likely and broadly applicable explanation for the rise of regionalism. Norms, regulations, and establishments are created to aid governments in resolving shared issues and to improve welfare. Furthermore, neo-liberal institutionalism is strongly statist, focused on how to coax cooperation from governments that are thought of being rational egoists. The state is seen as the efficient gatekeeper between the domestic and the international, in contrast to the pluralist networks emphasised by the neo-functionalists.

2.3.4   The IPE Theory

According to IPE, new regionalism is qualitatively novel insofar as it encompasses a wide range of participants and is influenced by sociological, cultural, and organisational elements in addition to market dynamics. For IPE academics, the essence of regional dynamics is what neo-liberals consider to be regionalism's second-best quality. As per IPE, regionalism possesses an entirely own ontological content; it functions in tandem with globalisation, complementing it by tackling problems that globalisation neglects to tackle. When viewed in this light, regionalism serves to promote both free trade and global openness rather than acting in opposition to them. Because of this, the term "new regionalism" frequently alludes to the idea of "open regionalism," which is perceived as an alternative way of implementing the globalisation process (Barbieri 2019).

2.3.5   Structural-Situational Theory

The sine qua non and independent variable that gives states incentives to engage in cooperation and the establishment of accompanying institutions is a problematic situation based on complex interdependence in international relations, which can be modelled and illustrated by means of various game types (Taylor 1987: 19). The scenario structural approach identifies multiple ideal categories of problematic situations that imply varying degrees of conduciveness to collaboration and the establishment of common regulative institutions, against the backdrop of game- and cooperation theory: Cooperation is relatively simple to attain in challenging circumstances that correlate to coordination and assurance games, but it is more challenging in scenarios that resemble dilemmas, and it is most challenging to attain in so-called "Rambo-type games.

Consequently, the likelihood of an international cooperation realisation, the strength of the need for regulatory institutions, and the relevance and influence of potential context variables all rely, in principle, on the nature and structure of an underlying problematic situation, or the kind of game (Zürn 1993: 69–70). Regionalism, or the states' codified response to a particular problematic situation in international relations on a regional level, is therefore regarded as a dependent variable that shall be explained. This institutionalised international cooperation with its design and inherent set of rules at its core. Furthermore, the scenario structural model makes the assumption that contextual variables that intervene may have an impact on the likelihood of institutionalised regional cooperation.

They have special significance in mixed-motive games like Rambo-type scenarios or dilemmas since the latter kind of collective action problems lack obvious answers and rational utility-maximizing agents are unlikely to adopt a cooperative strategy from the outset. Since power is a crucial component of international relations, it is considered to be the most relevant and important context variable, even though the number of potentially applicable context variables is arbitrary and elastic (Keohane and Nye 2001; Stein 1993: 319; Zürn 1993: 70–71). As a result, it will be given particular consideration when developing the theoretical foundation for the task (Zürn 1993: 70–71).

2.3.6   Theory of Constructivism

In his investigation of international relations norms, Nicholas Onuf employed the word constructivism. According to his theory, constructivist ideas emphasise what has been dubbed "cognitive regionalism," shared feelings of belonging to a specific regional group, and regional consciousness and identity. They emphasise how much mutual response, real community, and a high degree of what may be called cognitive interdependence are the foundations of a long-lasting feeling of community, which is necessary for regional cohesion. Constructivists emphasise the value of shared knowledge, learning, ideational forces, moral and institutional structures, rather than only material incentives. They contend that by comprehending inter-subjective structures, we can track the ways in which identities and interests shift over time and how new kinds of community and cooperation can arise.

Further, Constructivism had much greater success in finding application outside of the European experience in addressing regional dynamics in a non-Western world. Through Alexander Wendt's major work, it advanced our understanding of emerging regional processes. Constructivism introduces the importance of identitarian, normative, and ideal components in the study of regionalism, putting open opposition to the neo-liberal and neo-functionalist concentration on material and rationalist elements with its reliance on ideational and normative content. Constructivism has given these factors more weight in explaining why a regional process emerges and has offered an interpretive framework in which material factors, such as the degree of free trade or the efficacy of collective defence agreements, are subordinated to norms and ideas when evaluating the performance of a regional institution (Barbieri 2019).

2.3.7   Convergence Theory

Converging domestic policy preferences among regional governments are the basis for the idea of convergence theories, which explain the dynamics of regional cooperation and, in particular, regional economic integration. As a result, revisionist accounts of the European community have highlighted how seriously false the political mythology surrounding European integration was. It was undertaken as the best way to shield or preserve a specific domestic agenda centred around Keynesian economics, social welfare, and corporatist social arrangements rather than as part of a grand project to move "beyond the nation state." Unquestionably, domestic policy convergence has played a significant role in the comeback of regionalism, particularly in light of the broad adoption of market-liberal policies that prioritise trade liberalisation and export growth in the developing countries. Furthermore, regional integration can occasionally be used to strengthen market-liberal policies.

2.3.8   Theory of Neo-realism

On the one hand, neorealism has frequently appeared to directly contradict realism in the context of regional cooperation. In the 1950s, a lot of people believed that the emergence of an island of cooperation and peace in a world where power struggles predominated and war was a natural occurrence, which realism could not account for. Actually, a large portion of the early research on regionalism and regional integration can be understood as an effort to explain this seemingly oddity. Neo-realism, however, can actually teach us a lot of crucial lessons about regionalism. There are many similarities between the politics of alliance formation and the neo-realist movement, regionalism, and the rise of regionalist alignments (Walt 1987). Political and economic regionalism is essentially the same; regional groupings emerge in response to outside threats. Thus, economic regionalism can be viewed as a tactic in the context of neo-mercantilist rivalry. The US's growing interest in economic regionalism in the mid-1980s was a response to its declining competitiveness and its relative loss of economic power in comparison to Europe and Japan. It was also used as a negotiating ploy or bargaining tool, with NAFTA acting as a stick to increase pressure on Japan to open its markets and APEC as a means of applying pressure on the EU in the final stages of the negotiations on the Uruguay Round of GATT.

The policies of smaller governments outside of Europe can also be explained by the same neo-realist reasoning. According to this theory, a lot of regionalist organisations are essentially the normal reaction of weak governments that are imprisoned in the strong world. The Structural Interdependence Theory Regional globalisation and structural interdependence: One of the most persistent and insightful critiques of neo-realism has been its distortion of the global order. According to this perspective, systemic variables are crucial, but neo-realism gives an incredibly simplistic explanation of the structure of the system and ignores how the system's competitive dynamics evolve over time. Specifically, their depiction of the international system completely ignores the ways in which shifts in the global economic system impact the character of political and economic competition as well as the ensuing definition of state interests (Neuman 1992). Regional interdependence and regionalism are closely related, according to a second cluster of ideas that perceive this vision of outside-in approaches that begin with the system as a whole. The first two variations emphasise the crucial role that institutions play in promoting and strengthening regional cohesion and see regionalism as a useful response by states to the issues brought about by regional interdependence. Their emphasis on rationality, welfare objectives, scientific and technological knowledge, and their usually pluralist vision of international society place them squarely in the liberal camp.

2.3.9 Theory of Hegemony

Despite a great deal of analysis, the general relationship between regionalism and hegemony is still poorly understood. It is obvious that attempts to create inclusive regional agreements encompassing all or most of the governments within an area may be hampered by the presence of a strong hegemony within the region. A possible interpretation of regionalism is an attempt to impede the unrestricted exercise of hegemonic authority by means of regional institutions. Sub-regional alliances frequently form in reaction to the presence of a real or imagined hegemonic force. Therefore, sub-regional organisations have a propensity to emerge in many regions of the world in an effort to improve the balance of power in relation to a state that is either locally dominating or threatening.

2.3.10 Theory of Federalism

In addition to the functionalists and neo-functionalists, federalists also backed regionalism as a workable agenda. The federalists gave various justifications for their regionalism-supporting thesis. For them, decentralisation and integration were satisfied by regionalism and regional cooperation. The European Federalists, in particular, discussed the idea of pooling sovereignty, or allocating a portion of sovereignty to the establishment and maintenance of regional institutions in order to facilitate the creation of a more expansive federal entity and closer union that would be modelled after the European Economic Community. Therefore, three significant theoretical stances of the time—the functionalist, neo-functionalist, and federalist approaches—provided legitimacy and support for regionalism as an idea and project.

But for the first thirty years, the European Economic Community (EEC), which gave rise to the concept of European regionalism and later made it a reality, was primarily focused on trade and economic matters. Later, it embarked on a more ambitious journey towards a single currency and harmonised immigration and travel policies (Schengen visa), along with a change in name from EEC to European Union.

Similarly, the United States Constitution, which established both the federal and state levels of government, provided the administrative framework that allows for two levels of administration. General Powers of authority are, in the broadest sense, the provinces', unless specifically delegated to the federal government. Regional governance organisations as well as national or local governments are not mentioned or covered under the Constitution. These are things within the state's purview and are its prerogative. It seems sense, then, that when encouraging the coordination of governmental operations at the urban level, the federal government takes great care and caution. According to William Dodge, a lecturer on regional governance issues, regions are the new communities of the twenty-first century (Dodge 2003).

2.3.11   Theory of Typology

Despite being an overlapping conceptual theory, the typology of regionalism is commonly acknowledged as a unit for the evolution of regionalism types. Based on that, three primary forms of regionalism can be conceptualised. The first kind of regionalism is known as supra-state regionalism, and it is an expression of several states' shared group identity. This kind of regionalism involves a group of states banding together to take a unified stance on matters of mutual interest with respect to another group of states, or occasionally against the union. The resulting negative group identification is predicated on a particular issue or issues. This is not a case of state identities permanently merging into the communal identity. Intergroup rivalry, tensions, and conflicts may occasionally continue to exist alongside their collaboration. This may very well apply to the EU, SCO, SAARC, and CIS as examples.

Inter-state regionalism, which is coterminous with provincial areas and pits the identities of multiple states against one another, is another sort of regionalism that may be called that. Additionally, it is issue-specific. It is brought to light because it undermines their interest. For instance, because both Russia and Ukraine were a part of the former Soviet Union, disputes between them may be interpreted as interstate regionalism.

The third kind of regionalism is called intra-state regionalism, which is interpreted positively because it occurs within a state where a segment of the population aspires to self-identity and self-development. In other words, it works against the nation's and the state's common interests. For example, in international relations, there is always a sense of an eastern and a western zone (Bela 1961).

2.3.12   Theory of Economic Integration

Fawcett and Andrew (1998) described economic integration as the elimination of discrimination within a region. Furthermore, economic integration, in the words of W. J. Ethier (2005), is the process of gradually eliminating discrimination that takes place at national borders (Richards 1969). Therefore, actions that only lessen national discrimination are regarded as forms of cooperation rather than integration from a scientific standpoint. J. A. Scholte (2005) asserts that the meaning of economic integration varies for almost everyone. Allen contends that the well-known Balassa book's ability to define integration and distinguish it from cooperation is one of its many valuable features. The Economic Union, whose member states' fiscal and monetary policies are sometimes even fully aligned, is the most developed form of economic cooperation. It's commonly known as policy integration. A Monetary Union would be the most extreme form of an Economic Union (MU). The EU's member states, which share the Euro as their common currency, are excellent examples of the former.

2.3.13   Theory of Eurocentrism

The practice of emphasising European (Western) interests, culture, and values over those of other cultures—whether consciously or unconsciously—is known as Eurocentrism. Eurocentrism frequently entailed labelling non-white or non-European cultures as such or outright denying their existence. According to Breslin and Higgott (2003), regional names all across the world are named after European explorers and reflect a Eurocentric perspective. A self-sustaining notion that Europe and Europeans are fundamental to and most significant in all significant areas of global social values and cultural legacy is produced by the consequences of Eurocentricism. The Western narratives of mathematics' history, which are frequently regarded as Eurocentric because they downplay the significant contributions of mathematics from other parts of the world, including Chinese, Islamic, and Indian mathematics, are an example of Eurocentrism. However, it is also possible to view as Eurocentric university courses on the history of human thinking that focus on Aristotle, Kant, and Marx but ignore Confucius, Buddha, and the Upanishads, among others (Breslin and Higgott 2003).

The philosophy and practice of European integration has dominated the study of regionalism. In most of the theoretical and comparative discourse on comparative regionalism, eurocentrism still holds sway. Asia is not the only location in the globe where regionalism is studied in relation to European integration theory and practice. Two general perspectives about regionalism and European integration philosophy and practice can be distinguished, albeit somewhat simplistically. While one school of thought favours stronger European integration, the other is far less certain of the benefits of Eurocentric ideas and generalisations. Whether we discuss Asian, African, or Latin American regionalism, these two points of view are comparable. These two viewpoints are counterproductive to the advancement of regionalism theories.

The primary focus of the first perspective, which includes realist, intergovernmental, liberal, and institutionalist views, is on explaining why some situations differ from the typical European scenario. According to this perspective, alternative forms of regionalism and regional integration are typically viewed as unsuccessful (in Africa) or loose and informal (in Asia), reflecting a teleological prejudice based on the notion that the development of regional organisations is measured in terms of institutionalisation along EU lines. Due to a lack of awareness when comparing regions that hold unequal positions in the contemporary world order and have drastically different state forms, many comparisons and generalisations that stray from the European context and the European welfare state are warped. One related issue with this kind of Eurocentric bias is the way views of regionalism in other regions of the world are shaped by underlying assumptions and understandings about the nature of regionalism in Europe. Furthermore, a certain interpretation of European integration that lays a strong focus on the political and economic course of the EC/EU is the source of numerous recommendations. Hurrell rightly points out that "theories of regionalism," which are little more than the conversion of a certain set of European experiences into more esoteric theoretical language, have undoubtedly hampered the study of comparative regionalism (2005).

2.3.14   Social Network Theory

The study of how ideas and behaviours are influenced by the social structure of interactions surrounding an individual, group, or organisation is known as social network theory. Social organisation is inherently subject to fundamental pressures. A collection of techniques for identifying and gauging the intensity of the stresses is called network analysis. Every network method operates under the tenet that, rather than focusing on the characteristics of the units themselves, authenticity should be conceptualised and examined largely from the perspective of the relations between and within the units. It's a relational strategy. Individuals, groups or organisations, and societies are the social units used in social and communication research (Berkowitz 2003).

2.3.15 World-Systems Theory

Immanuel Wallerstein (1974) has pioneered the World-Systems theory in his work on the global economy, which characterised capitalism's unrelenting rise as a market force. The world systems approach, which has been further developed and enlarged by Andre Gunder Frank, Samir Amin, Giovanni Arrighi, Christopher Chase-Dunn, and others, sees the dynamics of the global economy as the defining factor that forms the global governance and world order (Martin 1994). The world-systems theory uses the concept of a system as its fundamental analytical unit. Wallerstein has defined and explained the idea in a number of ways. In a nutshell, he describes it as a socioeconomic group whose members are interdependent on one another and have a single division of labour.

Wallerstein expounds upon the global system in opposition to smaller systems. He claims that minisystems have a single division of labour and a common culture. Minisystems include simple agricultural or hunter-gatherer communities. There is no economic exchange between these and the outsiders. Earlier global systems, on the other hand, are distinguished by a single division of labour that unites disparate civilizations. They entail interactions and commercial networks that transcend political boundaries. The world system analysis focuses on world systems as operational units of social reality whose norms have a restricting influence on people and society, reflecting on mini-systems as features of the past, a bygone era.

Additionally, Wallerstein concentrates on the world economy and world empire. A world empire is a massive bureaucratic organisation with a single political core founded on dominance via conquest, such as the Roman and British empires in antiquity and contemporary times, respectively. On the other hand, the global economy is distinguished by a variety of political systems and cultural norms. It lacks a unified political framework. Wallerstein's primary focus is the global economy. Rather than political interests, he claims that a unified capitalist economy characterises the modern era. The global capitalist economy is primarily organised by economic interests and networks, rather than by governmental structures.

It goes on to explain that the emergence of market capitalism and the global economy started to take shape in the sixteenth century. With the increasing specialisation and diversification of agriculture, along with the growth of manufacturing industries such as metals and textiles, North Western Europe emerged as the centre of the birth of the global economy. The expansion of the manufacturing sector created a need among merchants and recently emerged entrepreneurs for specialised workers, raw materials, and new markets. The groundwork for meeting these demands was created by the later colonialism and the expansion of commerce networks. Expansion was justified more by economic factors than by political ones (Wallerstein 1974).

World-Systems theory indicated that to successfully gain economic growth you must go through these reflected steps in Fig. 2.1.

Geographically speaking, the core states are located in North America and Europe. Through taxation, government procurement, research and development sponsorship, funding infrastructure development (such as sewers, roads, and airports—all privately built but publicly financed—and upholding regional social order to reduce class conflict, these core states foster internal capital accumulation. Additionally, core states encourage capital accumulation throughout the global economy. These regimes possess the military, economic, and political clout to impose uneven

Fig. 2.1 Wallenstein's World-Systems Theory Model (P. P. Prajeesh. 2018. Theoretical Perspectives on Regionalism. International Journal of Creative Research Thoughts. Vol. 6. Issue. 2. April)

Wallerstein's World System Theory Model

exchange rates between the centre and the periphery. The few, the capitalist regional world system, are able to amass substantial wealth due to the economic, political, and military might of the core.

2.3.16 Semi-Peripheral States

Being both exploited by the core and contributing to the exploitation of the peripheral areas, the semi-peripheral areas act as a kind of intermediary. They have been manufacturing more in the last few years, especially for goods that core nations no longer feel to be very profitable. States in the Periphery The core states, semi-periphery areas, and peripheral areas comprise Wallerstein's division of the capitalist regional world economy. The least developed regions are the periphery, which the core takes use of for cheap labour, raw materials, and agricultural output (1974).

2.3.17 Development Theory

The term "development" was first used in the United States to describe the country's economic expansion in the 1940s, coinciding with a major foreign policy issue for the country: how to ensure that the newly independent states are not drawn into the communist Soviet bloc in the future (Weber 1992). Driven by this worry, the US gathered social scientists to research and design strategies for advancing capitalism economic growth and political stability in the so-called developing countries. Governmental structures typically view development as very important and strongminded; development shapes and interprets governance. The majority of development theory views the state as the main agent of development and links it to growth in the country's economy. Understanding and elucidating the state's role in development and the structure of government-market relations is thus one of its main priorities. There is a close linkage between development theory and practice because these explanations link development results to the scope and nature of the state's engagement in development.

The development hypothesis is a product of multiple intellectual streams. The theoretical foundation for determining whether regional economies determine whether they become more similar or more dissimilar over time is provided by neoclassical trade theory and growth theory. Modern regional growth theory's spatial component comes from a number of places. Scene theorists offer a paradigm for comprehending how transit expenses affect regional development and decline. Scholars writing in the flexible specialisation tradition and more recent neoclassical theorists have rediscovered the literature on external scale economies, which started with Marshall. Finally, concepts from central place theory are found in many current structuralist methods and the growth pole literature, which are prominent in the literature on regional development.

Factors influencing the world economy are located outside the ring. They are grouped in this way to illustrate the outside factors that affect the economic climate of a country. The two internal rings stand for elements that affect an economy's internal state within a nation. The elements affecting the economic balance either support or restrict regional economic activity. The resources required for enterprises to operate are the aspects that contribute to regional economic development. They are affected by both domestic and international economic balance and global economic issues, with no differentiation in the relative weights assigned to each. The capabilities of the military, other governmental branches, and international organisations can all have an impact on these variables.

Because it results in operational capabilities, regional integration of organisational economic functions is significant. Common functions allow organisations to integrate more effectively. When two or more organisations perform identical tasks, their combined capacity is higher since they can more readily continue to work together towards shared goals. By combining certain organisations in the right way, regional integration also produces economies of scale and synergy. One direct correlation between the number of organisations needed to impact all the regional economic issues and the challenge of sustaining unity of effort is this.

2.4   Forms of Regionalism

2.4.1   Unilateralism

Unilateralism is the word used to characterise a foreign policy approach in which a nation does not submit its objectives or course of action to the desires of other nations or the limitations imposed by international accords. There is controversy regarding the extent to which a nation (especially a hegemon like the United States) should pursue its foreign policy alone, even though few would support abandoning all multilateral commitments. Any philosophy or plan that encourages one-sided action is considered unilateralist. Such behaviour could be shown as disrespect for other people or as a commitment to a course of action that other people would deem acceptable. The term "unilateralism" in international political-economic relations more precisely refers to trade policies—many of which were implemented by the United States in the 1980s and 1990s—that entail imposing sanctions on nations whose markets are thought to be closed to foreign goods. Advocates of this strategy contend that pressure alone has the power to unlock previously closed markets; as a result, unilateralism may boost global welfare and boost overall levels of international trade. Specifically, they contend that nations like Japan, who are known for their informal or structural trade barriers, frequently, do not comply with multilateral regulations and hence need more robust approaches, like results-oriented managed trade, in order to enter their markets (Nye 1968).

2.4.2 Bilateralism

The political, economic, or cultural ties that exist between two sovereign governments are referred to as bilateralism. It stands in contrast to unilateralism and multilateralism, which denote the opposing approaches to diplomacy taken by one state and several governments. States that acknowledge each other as sovereign nations and decide to establish diplomatic ties exchange diplomatic envoys to help with future discussions and collaborations. It is a mutual agreement that affects or is undertaken by two parties.

2.4.3 Multilateralism

Multilateralism is the collaboration of several nations on a particular problem. According to Miles Kahler (1992), multilateralism is the international governance of the many. Its fundamental tenet is the rejection of bilateral discriminatory agreements that, in the view of the proponents, strengthen the power of the powerful over the weak and fuel global strife. Multilateralism is the process of coordinating national policies in groups of three or more governments, according to Robert Keohane (Keohane & Nye 1985). Multilateralism is the term used to describe cooperative solutions to global issues. More than two states confer and address a foreign policy issue together rather than taking independent action. Contrarily, unilateralism describes a circumstance in which one state, either out of necessity or choice, takes independent action to address a foreign policy issue.

This is distinct from unilateralist posturing, which happens when a nation pretends to reject international organisations, conventions, or customs without simultaneously eschewing the ideals of international consultation and cooperative behaviour with other governments. Multilateralism is both embodied in and promoted by international institutions. The larger discussion in the field has focused on unilateral versus multilateral tactics or internationalism versus isolationism. The end of the Cold War has brought about many changes, but neo-realists would expect this pattern to continue. For instance, they would expect the policies of the major powers acting unilaterally or of the macro-regional groupings that those powers will inevitably come to dominate to be necessary conditions for the success of subregional cooperation. For instance, in the Asia-Pacific region, the future of established sub regional alliances like ASEAN and more comprehensive cooperative initiatives like the APEC Regional Forum ultimately depends on the changing nature of the Chinese-Japanese-US balance (Fawcett 1998). In summary, the argument has been made that discussions on the resurgence of regionalism are closely linked to the larger theoretical discussions that have dominated the field of international relations and that there is significant value in identifying and delving into the nature of these linkages. Additionally, it is argued that understanding modern regionalism is only partially possible through the notions of regional integration that have dominated analyses of the European Community.

2.5   Theoretical Debates of Regionalism

Regionalism can be described in various ways, depending on the observer's perspective. Realism and structuralism are important for understanding regional endeavors, but regionalism is limited by national authority and security demands. Core and peripheral regions concepts from structuralism help establish prevailing agendas in politics, economy, and security, while liberal theories of interdependence like neo-functionalism and institutionalism are valuable for analyzing patterns in areas like Europe where security communities and economic integration are well-established. Social constructivism theories offer insights into the political nature of identity, which often becomes apparent during the regional process. The rise in American unilateralism and the pull towards bilateral rather than multilateral or regional understanding between the US and its allies point to the disposability of regionalism and the demise of any liberal global or regional order. Selective unilateralism has the potential to decrease but also increase regional options and autonomy.

It is no longer feasible to discuss regionalism's future with unrealistic optimism or frame it as an alternative to any kind of state-led or global system. A stable regional structure is not necessary for regionalism, and states can benefit from the assistance and experience of others. International cooperation and support are vital, and lessons learned from the past are still useful in these areas.

Regional organizations created to address regional problems can be categorized into technical organizations, conventional intergovernmental organizations, and politically legitimated bodies. Understanding modern regionalism is only partially and imperfectly guided by regional integration theories that have dominated the analysis of the European Community (EC).

2.6 THE RISE OF EURASIANISM

Eurasianism is an intellectual and quasi-political movement. Russia, according to its proponents, is a distinctive fusion of Slavic and non-Slavic ethnic groups and civilizations. Eurasianists also highlight how the Russian state is corporate in essence, setting it apart from the West. In the 1920s, an anti-Bolshevik movement called Eurasianism was born. However, as Eurasianism has developed, it has been more and more similar to the Marxism of the Soviet Union. One of the forerunners of the current post-Soviet Russian ideology was Eurasianism, which combined Marxism and nationalism.

2.6.1 Classical Eurasianism

Russia's location, race, and religion, along with its Slavic ethnicity and nationalized Orthodox Christianity, have been argued to separate it from European and Western values. Russia's Slavic race connects it to Eastern and Southern Europe, while remaining separate from other Slavs. These unique aspects have influenced modern-day Neo-Eurasianists, including Russian Messianism, Slavophilism, and Classical Eurasianism. Eurasian proponents argue that Russia's unique societal aspects, such as Cyrillic script and food, justify its rejection of European and Western values and its continued authoritarian rule (Molchanov 2009).

Classical Eurasianism emerged as a political theory in the 1920s, influenced by ideals of creating the Russian state. Eurasianists sought unique concepts of Russia, such as Moscow as the "Third Rome," and amalgamated them to create a positive role for Russia in global affairs, aiming to create a unique Russia (Stafford 2015).

- *Moscow as Third Rome*

The concept of Moscow as the "Third Rome" in Russia originated from the belief that the Byzantine Empire, led by Constantinople, continued the Christian Church's traditions after Rome's fall. The Ottoman capture of Constantinople in 1453 led to the burden of Christendom falling on the Muscovite empire. In the early 1500s, Orthodox Monk Philotheus of Pskov claimed Moscow as the Third Rome, claiming its prosperity and holiness as proof of the Russian Empire's holiness (Cao 2023). This idea later evolved into a state ideology that legitimized Russian tsars through the amalgamation of Russian Orthodox doctrine.

The Third Rome ideology, while not directly revealing Eurasianism's trappings, demonstrates the beginnings of Russians' moral and metaphysical separation from Europe. It emphasizes Russia as a separate state and challenges easy classification as European. This concept continues to play a pivotal role in Classical and Neo-Eurasianism. However, the Third Rome ideology's religious argument is not crucial to Eurasianism's modern arguments, as it sees religion and Orthodox values as part of a larger whole.

- *Turning towards and away from Europe*

Peter the Great aimed to Europeanize Russia by reforming education and forbidding beards in court. He did not view Russia as inferior to Europe, but his reforms forced Russian elites to question their cultural heritage. European influence led to genuine reforms and imitation, but it also damaged Russia's uniqueness. By demonstrating European knowledge and culture, Peter created a desire for Russia to become more European at the cost of its own heritage. He sent Russian elites and military officers to Europe for education, exposing them to European technology and knowledge. These actions unintentionally undermined the Russian state's perceived divine mission and set a precedent for Europeanization efforts in Russia (Stafford 2015).

In the nineteenth century, Russian Messianism emphasized the Tsarist Empire's uniqueness and contributed to Eurasianism. It viewed Russia as a "Third Rome" that saved Europe from itself, based on its victories over France, Mongol rule, and the Ottoman Empire. The Napoleonic Wars, which saw Russia defeat Napoleon and overthrow Mongol rule, solidified Russian Messianism's religious tenets. The suffering Russia experienced justified Russians as both saviors of Europe and separate from it. Tsar Alexander believed in a holy mission to defend Europe from liberals and revolutionaries.

Slavophilism emerged in nineteenth century Russia as a new ideology, arguing for the unique role of the Slavs in shaping Classical Eurasianism. The Slavophiles opposed Western Europe's focus on individualism and regarded the peasant and rural lifestyle with high esteem. They promoted the Russian village, or mir, as the highest form of moral conscience, justifying peasant traditions and their revisionist history. They criticized Peter the Great's closeness to Europe and saw the period as a discontinuation of Russian heritage (Stafford 2015). Slavophilism influenced Eurasianists to promote Russia's uniqueness beyond its religious aspects and see morality tied to its cultural traditions.

- *War's further Influences*

The Crimean War in 1877 led to Russia's perception of a separate identity from Europe, as it was viewed as a powerful but backward country. The alliance of France, Great Britain, and the Ottoman Empire against Russia fueled this desire for expansion (Evans 2023). Despite cultural and religious differences, the strongest European states defended the Ottomans to prevent Russia's expansion. This led Russia to look more towards the East than the West for expansion.

The Russo-Turkic War of 1877 saw Russian Messianism return to national consciousness, as Russia sought to demonstrate its power to Western Europe. Russia gained independence for Serbia, Montenegro, and Romania and nearly captured Istanbul, legitimizing and defining messianic ideology. This war transformed Russian Messianism and Slavophilism into a distinctly Russian form of nationalism.

For future Eurasianists, the war defined Russia's role in international affairs through its efforts to free Slavic states and fight the Ottomans. However, it also showed Eurasianists that Russia could never be a truly European country. The Treaty of San Stefano ended the war partly due to British Empire interventions to prevent Russian expansion. Eurasianists used this to justify seeking growth beyond Europe.

2.6.2   The Birth of Eurasianism

Eurasianism, a movement primarily formed in European academic circles, aimed to create a functional ideology that justified the perceived backwardness of their homeland while accounting for the Soviet Revolution (Pizzolo 2019). The movement argued against the preeminence of European culture and the use of European ideas and progress to gauge Russian development. The Eurasianists believed events and cultural identities, such as the Mongol Horde, Orthodox Church, and Far Eastern land, contributed to a uniquely Eurasian culture, different from that of the rest of Europe (Stafford 2015).

The Eurasianist ideology sought a separate path from Europe, using new means to justify their beliefs. Slavophiles, Pan-Slavists, and Russian nationalists argued for a divergence between Europe and Russia, arguing that one cannot judge Russia in relation to Europe. Russian novelist Dostoyevsky made a separation from "European Europe" a central theme, arguing that European civilization is based on soulless materialism and that Russia's cultural differences prevent it from fully separate from Europe. Eurasianists saw these differences as a means of salvation in Russia's conservative moral and physical geography.

- *Nikolai Trubetskoi*

Nikolai Trubetskoi, an exiled Russian Prince and phonologist, is credited with the origins of the Eurasianist movement. He argued against the European model of liberal development, arguing for a separate path of development rather than a special place for Russian or Slavic traditions (Stafford 2015). Trubetskoi set the Eurasianist precedent by gauging Russian civilization based on intangible ideals such as religion, conservatism, and geographic expansion. He used the mixing of Russian blood with Central Asian and Steppic peoples to show the divergence between

Russians and European counterparts. Trubetskoi believed that the proximity of Russia to Turks and Fins created a unique state entity, and only through the creation of a Eurasian state could the successor to tsarist Russia survive. He also believed that ethnicity played a smaller role than geography and the closeness of the Great Russians to Turks and other peoples.

- *Petr Savitskii*

Petr Savitskii, along with Trubetskoi, played a significant role in creating a standardized Eurasian ideal. As a geographer, Savitskii argued that Russia's vastness and diversity led to a "Third Way" outside Europe and Asia, and that any grouping with either continent or cultural tradition fails to account for Russian realties (Voytek 2012). As the world's largest country, Russia occupies a significant portion of both Europe and Asia, but its population remains largely relegated to Europe. Savitskii also argued that Eurasian nationalism based on Russia's vastness does not allow for European social ideals and shows Asian and Mongol influence. He dedicated his works specifically to Eurasianism and agreed with Trubetskoi on the need for authoritarian leadership in Russia. Savitskii continued to write on Eurasianism throughout his life, providing enough material for Neo-Eurasianists to revisit when formulating their own doctrine.

- *Lev Gumilev*

Lev Gumilev, a prominent figure in the development of Eurasianism, continued to write until his death after the fall of the Soviet Union. Despite facing difficulties in Soviet universities and gulag, Gumilev earned a lecturing position at Leningrad state in the 1960s, allowing him to further his writing and develop his own Eurasianist theories. His writing focused on ethnicity, unlike Savitskii's geography, but he maintained a correspondence with him, which helped coalesce his ideas on Russia's third way. Gumilev brought Eurasianism into the mindset of post-Soviet Russians and remained a functional bridge between Classical and Neo-Eurasianists. He created a theory of ethno-genesis, or biological determinism, which placed ethnicity at the center of an individual's identity and claimed that true personal growth, may only come through the development of one's ethnic group as a whole. Gumilev's insistence on using ethnicity as a means to elevate Russians and the Soviet Union over Europe led to his classification as either Neo or Trans-Eurasianist (Stafford 2015).

Gumilev, a Soviet citizen, significantly influenced modern Eurasianist thought by focusing on ethnicity and his attitude towards Communism and the Soviet Union. He actively sought to incorporate the Soviet Union's role into Eurasianist doctrine, unlike other émigré Eurasianists who were at odds with the Soviet Union's official Socialist ideology. Gumilev lived long enough to see the fall of the Soviet Union and lamented its demise, while Classical Eurasianists were at odds with the Soviet Union's official Socialist ideology but still promoted a Russia-led empire across the steppe. The reliance on geography to justify Russian authoritarianism forced Eurasianists to see the need for Russia to maintain an empire as part of its identity, and the Mongol occupation of Russia in a different light. Gumilev's status as a Soviet citizen allowed him to actively lament the fall of the Soviet Union.

Gumilev, a prominent figure in Eurasianist thought, gained immense popularity in Russia after the fall of the Soviet Union. His ideas, particularly in relation to ethnic relations, helped create the post-Soviet Discourse. His emphasis on ethnic Great Russians emerged as Russia's population remains predominantly Russian, unlike the Soviet Union's diverse population. Gumilev's revisionist and ethnocentric history of Russia is now taught in schools and textbooks. However, his theories of ethno-genesis and "passionarity" have little scientific value, leading to a dangerous perception of them as fact, further increasing his popularity as an ideologist.

Classical Eurasianism is an inconsistent model that lacked a defined set of ideological ideals but was adaptable to the post-Soviet environment. It aimed to justify the lack of Russian development and perceived backwardness to the West. The Eurasianists used geography to justify a lack of development, setting a precedent for authoritarianism and allowing Russian expansion to Asia's edges. The Eurasianism of Savitskii and other classical Eurasianists hybridize Russian Messianism through geopolitics, placing Russia's geography as the central component. They created an idealized Russia based on superiority to Europe, using the expansion as proof of the superior developmental characteristics of Imperial Russia and its Slavs. Russia never developed a specific ideological role for its Far East and Siberian territories, but Eurasianism provided such an ideology.

2.6.3   Modern Eurasianism

Modern Eurasianism emerged after the Soviet collapse, aiming to express divergence from the West and counter anti-Western sentiments in Russia. Alexander Panarin and Alexander Dugin sought to control the "Third Way" dialogue in post-Soviet Russia. The Russian people's identity reverted to the primordial Russian ideal of Orthodoxy and conservatism, contrasted with liberal reforms and a more Westernized identity. Despite democratic principles, the state is no longer democratic (Stafford 2015). Eurasianists sought to justify Russia's rentier economic model and authoritarian proclivities, combining traditional Russian ideals with a degree of messianism to "rescue" Russia from the forces of liberalization, Europeanization, Atlanticism, and the globalized economy.

This section discusses Alexander Dugin, the most prominent proponent of Eurasianism, and his role in the Neo-Eurasianism movement. Dugin is prominent in Russian political and intellectual life, publishing in major newspapers and regularly attending top-notch conferences. He is also a prominent figure in the field, appearing on talk shows, maintaining websites, and supporting politicians. Dugin's Eurasianism differs from that of Trubetskoi and Savitskii in the 1920s, which aimed to justify Russia's perceived backwardness to Europeans and the West. The current wave of Eurasianism aims to gain support primarily among Russians and the Russian elite.

2.7   Differences Between Classical Eurasianism and Neo-Eurasianism

Classical Eurasianism, originating outside the Soviet Union, differs from Neo-Eurasianism due to its focus on Russia. Modern Eurasianists, who write primarily in Russia, face two forces: the state and Russians as a whole. The Russian state controls media and uses it for its own needs, influencing Eurasianists. They support the Putin regime and are more political than earlier Eurasianism. To remain relevant, Eurasianists must abide by Russian zeitgeist and be open to state influence. Classical Eurasianists aimed at Europeans and themselves, while modern Eurasianists prioritize the needs of the Russian state and its people.

2.7.1   Defining Modern Eurasianism

Modern Eurasianism, like Classical Eurasianism, is challenging to compile into a coherent set of ideas due to its lack of proponents and a scarcity of ideologues. It focuses on Russia seeking a "Third Way" apart from Europe or Asia and the messianic idea of Russia's duty to save Europe. The West's varying academic views on Eurasianism have not helped clarify its meaning, with multiple naming conventions that confuse the new ideas and serve multiple purposes rather than a singular one.

- *Alexander Dugin and the Eurasianist Heritage*

Alexander Dugin, a prominent Russian politician, asserts his Eurasianist heritage, claiming it to represent the political-intellectual legacy of Classical Eurasianism. This legitimacy allows Dugin to maintain support from right-wing Russians and alter his Eurasianist vision to align with the regime's ideology. Dugin's Eurasianism differs significantly from Classical Eurasianism, covering topics like metaphysics, conspiracy theories, and traditionalism. He also seeks to establish and expand borders and alliances with other states like China, Japan, and India. Dugin's rhetoric often focuses on justifying Russia as a Great Power rather than responding to cultural and economic globalization (Dina 2014).

Dugin's Eurasianism, despite its use, is not entirely a product of Classical Eurasianism. In his 2012 book, The Fourth Political Theory, he argues that Neo-Eurasianism replaced Classical Eurasianism with ideas from traditionalism, geopolitics, structuralism, Heidegger's fundamental-ontology, sociology, and anthropology (Dugin 2014). Dugin traces Neo-Eurasianism to Classical Eurasianists through Claude Levi-Strauss, who's theories on structural anthropology influence Neo- Eurasianism. Dugin uses two separate areas of the humanities, structural anthropology and phonology, to argue for a classical origin to his Eurasianism. While Dugin's Eurasianism and Classical Eurasianism are not directly linked, his argument creates enough evidence to successfully bond Classical to Neo-Eurasianism.

- *Dugin and Global Eurasianism*

Dugin's Neo-Eurasianism differs from Classical Eurasianism in its portrayal as a global movement. Unlike Classical Eurasianists, Dugin aims to internationalize his theory to increase its popularity and legitimacy. He engages with anti-globalization movements outside Russia and maintains websites in various languages. Dugin sees Eurasianism as a global alternative to liberalism and a cultural destiny for Russia. However, his arguments for an international version have not gained widespread support, making it more relevant for legitimizing the Eurasianist movement in Russia. His followers maintain websites in various languages, showcasing his vision of the Indo-European Empire (Stafford 2015).

Dugin's Eurasianist rhetoric is relevant in areas like Central Asia, where Russia has strong ties and a history of authoritarian rule. Promoting Eurasianism in Central Asia would benefit Russia, as its pervasive Soviet academic heritage makes it a natural outgrowth. Turkey also has active Eurasianists who work to balance Westernization and traditional Islam. Turkey lacks the communist traditions of Russia, suggesting Eurasianist movements must form as a response to Westernism. Eurasianism in Western Europe forms alongside right-wing, anti-EU groups, but these alliances are often alliances of convenience.

Dugin's Eurasianism is a complex political ideology that aims to create a Russocentric antiWesternism that appeals to countries outside Russia. By expanding Eurasianism beyond Russia, Dugin removes cultural arguments used by Classical Eurasianism to differentiate Russia from the West. Instead, he relies on antiWesternism and his own geopolitics to create a universal movement. Dugin uses Russian Orthodoxy and culture to expand Eurasianism in Russia, while maintaining cultural arguments to appease ethnic Russians. This demonstrates that the primary purpose of expanding Eurasianism beyond Russia's borders is to maintain political legitimacy.

Dugin's anti-liberal views are undermined by his rapprochement with other states, such as Japan, Germany, and India. He encourages Russia's rapprochement with these countries, but this undermines his desire to limit Western influences. Germany, an EU and NATO member, remains dedicated to the West, while Japan and Russia still argue over the Kuril islands. Japan and India's cultural differences divide them from Russia more than Russia's own. Dugin also sees China as a potential enemy to Russia, not due to its rising economic and military might but due to the less likely possibility of joining an alliance with the United States. He believes that Japan will form a pact with Russia and aims to show China as a dominating force in East Asia. Despite China's opposition to the West, Dugin proposes a means to balance China without rapprochement with the US, despite the impossibility of creating a Russo-Japan security partnership. This particularism weakens the Eurasianism argument and shows his need to create a Russo-centric argument to account for Russia's rivalries (Dugin 2014).

Dugin's Eurasianism focuses on the inclusion of Europe and Asia, rather than a separate path for Europe or Asia. He believes that both Asia and Europe are destined to fall under Russian-Eurasian domination, with Russia eventually expanding its scope to cover larger portions of Europe and Asia. However, this argument fails to form a coherent Eurasianist discourse due to two main reasons. Firstly, it becomes an expansionist and imperial argument, excluding Europe from the focus. Secondly, Dugin must account for cultural differences alongside expansionist rhetoric, which he fails to do. This makes Neo-Eurasianism less of an ideology with set precepts and more of a political theory that adapts to trends.

2.8   Conclusion

The Russian Federation experienced a severe cultural and functional vacuum with the collapse of Soviet ideology. According to Margot Light, "Soviet Ideology included a description of the past, a diagnosis of the present, and a blueprint of an ideal future, together with an indication of the means by which the future would be attained," in her essay "In Search of an identity: Russian Foreign Policy and the End of Ideology." Russians are currently experiencing a transitional identity crisis as a result of the weight of ideology and the loss that followed. Russia needs to fill this void in order to explain both its loss and the magnificence the Soviet Union instilled in each and every Russian person.

Dugin's growing popularity and his aim to establish a "Third Way" for Russia do not translate into widespread acceptance for his beliefs in Russia. The political and intellectual climate calls for less of the "Third Way" and more of a return to the idea of Russia as a Great Power comparable to the USSR and, to a lesser extent, the imperial state. Herein lies the real goal of the Russian state: to continue being viewed as a legitimate government by the people by continuing to be a Great Power. Anything less would suggest that Russia is not as powerful as the USSR. Eurasianism aims to support the government in this endeavour. The desire of Russians to see their country as a Great Power is the main factor supporting Eurasianism as a credible Russian ideology.

References

Barbieri, Giovani. 2019. Regionalism, Globalism and Complexity: A Stimulus Towards Global IR? *Third World Thematics: A TWQ Journal* 4. November.

Bela, Balassa. 1961. *The Theory of Economic Integration*. Illinois: Homewood.

Berkowitz S. D. eds. 2003. *Social Structures, A Network Approach*, 477–497. London: Jai Press.

Breslin, S., and R. Higgott. 2003. New Regionalism in Historical Perspective. *Asia-Europe Journal*, May.

Cao, Jiaqi. 2023. Religious Origin and Political Extension of the Idea of "Moscow— Third Rome." *Advance*, October 24. Retrieved from: https://doi.org/10.31124/advance.24306514.v1.

Dina, Newman. 2014. Russian Nationalist Thinker Dugin Sees War with Ukraine. BBC News, July 9. http://www.bbc.com/news/world-europe-28229785.

Dodge, William R. 2003. Regional Excellence: Governing Together to Compete Globally and Flourish Locally.

Dugin, Alexander. 2014. Letter to the American People on Ukraine. Open Revolt. Last modified March 8. Retrieved from: http://openrevolt.info/2014/03/08/alexander-dugin-letter-to-the-american-peopleon-ukraine/.

Ethier, W.J. 2005. Regional Regionalism. In *Regionalism and Globalization: Theory and Practice*, ed. S Lahiri. London: MIT Press.

Evans, Alexander T. 2023. Alternative Futures Following a Great Power War: Vol. 1, Scenarios, Findings, and Recommendations, RR-A591-1.

Farhutdinov, I. 2005. *Mezhdunarodnoe investicionnoe pravo. Teoriia i praktika primeneniia*. Moscow: Volters Kluver.

Fawcett, Louise, and Andrew Hurrell. 1998. *Regionalism in World Politics: Regional Organisation and International Order*. New York: Oxford University Press.

Galiakberov, Adel and Adel Abdullin. 2014. Theory and Practice of Regional Integration Based on the Eurasec Model (Russian Point of View). *Journal of Eurasian Studies* 5 (2). Retrieved from: https://doi.org/10.1016/j.euras.2014.05.004.

Hurrell A. 2005. Hegemony and Regional Governance. In *Regionalism and Governance in the America*, ed. L. Fawcett. Basingstoke: Macmillan.

Hurrell, Andrew. 1995. Explaining the Resurgence of Regionalism in World Politics. *Review of International Studies* 21 (4): 331–358.

Kahler, Miles. 1992. Multilateralism with Small and Large Numbers. *International Organization* 46 (3, Summer).

Keohane, R.O., and Joseph Nye. 1985. *Two Cheers for Multilateralism*, 148–167. New York: HarperCollins.

Keohane, Robert O. 1984. *After Hegemony. Cooperation and Discord in the World Political Economy*. Princeton: Princeton University Press.

Keohane, Robert O., and Joseph S. Nye. 1987. Power and Interdependence Revisited. *International Organization* 41 (4): 725–753.

Keohane, Robert O., and Joseph S. Nye. 2001. *Power and Interdependence*. New York: Longman.

Martin, William. G. 1994. The World-Systems Perspective in Perspective: Assessing the Attempt to Move Beyond Nineteenth-Century Eurocentric Conceptions. *Review* 17 (2, Spring).

Molchanov, Mikhail A. 2009. Regionalization from above: Russia's Asian vector and the state led regionalism in Eurasia. [Online: web] Accessed 5 May 2012. http://people.stu.ca/~molchan/Euras-regm-above.pdf.

Neuman, Ivar B., ed. 1992. *Regional Great Powers in International Politics*. London: Macmillan.

Nye, Joseph, ed. 1968. *International Regionalism*. Boston: Little Brown and Corporation.

Onuf, Nicholas. 1989. *World of Our Making Rules and Rule in Social Theory and International Relations*. Columbia: University of South Carolina Press.

Prajeesh, P.P. 2018. Theoretical Perspectives on Regionalism. *International Journal of Creative Research Thoughts* 6 (2, April).

Pizzolo, Paolo. 2019. Eurasianism: An Ideology for the Multipolar World. Thesis submitted to LUISS. Guido Carli. Retrieved from: https://iris.luiss.it/bitstream/11385/201069/2/20190626-pizzolo.pdf.

Richards, Kahnert F.P, eds. 1969. *Economic Integration Among Developing Countries*. Paris: Development Center of the Organization for Economic Co-operation and Development (OECD).

Scholte J.A. 2005. *The Sources of Neoliberal Globalization*, October. Geneva: United Nations Research Institute for Social Development. Program paper No. 8.

Stafford, Andrew. 2015. *Eurasianism: A Historical and Contemporary Context*. Thesis submitted to Naval Post-Graduate School. Monterey. California.

Stein, Arthur. 1993. Coordination and Collaboration: Regimes in an Anarchic World. In *Neorealism and Neoliberalism: The Contemporary Debate*, ed. David A. Baldwin, 29–59. New York: Columbia University Press.

Taylor, Michael. 1987. *The Possibility of Cooperation. Studies in Rationality and Social Change*. Cambridge: Cambridge University Press.

Voytek, Steven K. 2012. Eurasianist T asianist Trends in Russian F ends in Russian Foreign Policy: A Critical Analysis Policy: A Critical Analysis. Graduate Theses, Dissertations, and Problem Reports. 256. Retrieved from: https://researchrepository.wvu.edu/etd/256?utm_source=researchrepository.wvu.edu%2Fetd%2F256&utm_medium=PDF&utm_campaign=PDFCoverPages.

Wallerstein, Immanuel. 1974. *The Modern World System I: Capitalist Agriculture and the Origins of the European World-Economy in the Sixteenth Century*. New York: Academic Press.

Walt, Stephen M. 1987. *The Origins of Alliances*. Cornell University Press. https://www.jstor.org/stable/10.7591/j.ctt32b5fc.

Waltz, Kenneth. 1979. *Theory of International Politics*. Reading, MA: Addison-Wesley.

Weber, Steve.1992. Shaping the Postwar Balance of Power: Multilateralism in NATO. *International Organization* 46 (3, Summer).

Zürn, Michael. 1993. Problematic Social Situations and International Institutions: On the Use of Game Theory in International Politics. In *International Relations and Pan-Europe: Theoretical Approaches and Empirical Findings*, ed. Frank Pfetsch, 63–84. Münster: Lit-Verlag.

CHAPTER 3

Concept of Security: An Introduction

Abstract Security is a crucial aspect of neorealism, as it infers the primary motivation of states. The international system is anarchic due to uncertainty, lack of trust, and competition among actors. Cooperation between states is essential for achieving security goals, and neoliberal institutionalism argues that international institutions are more helpful in achieving cooperation and stability. Collective security theorists argue that collective security provides an effective mechanism and regulated institutionalized balancing against an aggressor or when necessary, banding together to stop an aggression. This chapter analyzes the threats posed by non-state actors with respect to the Eurasian Collective Security Treaty Organization (CSTO) and its comparisons with other organizations like the Shanghai Cooperation Organisation (SCO) and the NATO PfP.

Keywords Security · CSTO · SCO · NATO · Neo-Realism · Neo-Liberal Institutionalism and Constructivism

R. Pradhan and S. Kakoty, *Security Integration in the Post-Soviet Space and Collective Security Treaty Organization*, https://doi.org/10.1007/978-981-97-6445-7_3
47

3.1   INTRODUCTION

Security studies have been studied from ages, as long as human society itself, but as a subject of academic inquiry it came to prominence only after the Second World War (Booth 2005). The concept of security is very significant and is of great concern while doing in-depth study in international relations and it is one of the essential sub-fields in the study of International Relations. To quote Buzan—

> In the case of Security, the discussion is about the pursuit of freedom from threat. When this discussion is in the context of the international system, security is about the ability of states and societies to maintain their independent identity and their functional integrity. (Buzan 1983)

Barry Buzan in his book argues persuasively that security apart from being about states, relates to all human collectivities; and it could not be limited to focussing on military force. Instead, Buzan developed a structure whereby he argues that the security of human collectivities (not just states) is affected by five major factors, each having its own 'focal point' and 'way of ordering priorities'. These ordering priorities are *military* focused on military offensive and defensive capabilities of states and its understanding of intentions of other states, *political* that is focused on the organisational stability of states, classification of Government and ideologies bestowing legitimacy; *economic* refers to resources, finance and markets for welfare and state power; *societal* focused on development of national identity and custom and *environmental* concerned with the maintenance of the natural environment (Williams 2008).

> Most scholars within International Relations (IR) work with a definition of security that involves the alleviation of threats to cherished values. (Ibid)

3.2   THEORETICAL FRAMEWORK

Security is a matter of prime importance in neorealism, as it infers the primary motivation of states. The international system is anarchic because of the absence of a central authority to control states' behaviour. There is uncertainty of intentions and lack of trust among actors. Further, the problem of cheating and the problem of relative gains make cooperation among actors a difficult job. The sovereign states therefore develop offensive military capabilities for their own defence. As Kenneth Waltz observes:

> In anarchy, security is the highest end. Only if survival is assured can states seek such other goals as tranquillity, profit, and power. (Baylis 2007)

But contrary to the views of traditional neo-realist like Waltz and Mearsheimer who remain not very positive regarding the cooperation between states in a post cold war world, there are other group of neo-realist writers who present a more positive assessment. Charles Glasner, a Contingent Realist argues that in order to achieve security goals at best, cooperative policies become more useful than competitive ones. Hence security is also understood as 'contingent' or conditional to circumstances (Ibid).

Liberal Institutionalism also known as neo-liberalism argues that international institutions are much more helpful in achieving cooperation and stability. As cited by Keohane and Martin, "*Institutions can provide information, reduce transaction costs, make commitments more credible, establish focal points for coordination and in general, facilitate the operation of reciprocity (Ibid).*"

While, Liberal institutionalists argue that institutions can help build a system for cooperation which can work towards overcoming the possibility and crises of security competition among states. Hence cooperation between states helps massively in countering transnational security threats (Ibid). Neoliberal institutionalism intensifies on the role of international institutions in conflict mitigation. Therefore, institutions are so important because despite of various hindrances, they benefit states in different kinds of enforcement and conflict resolution methods. They are also durable. Existing regimes persist even in hard conditions '*because they are difficult to create or reconstruct*' (Keohane 1984). The question is: How suitable is neoliberal insitutionalism with regard to security issues? Jervis cites that, "*the realm of security has special characteristics that at the same time make regime creation more difficult and increase its need. Security regimes, with their call for mutual restraint and limitations on unilateral actions, rarely seem attractive to decision-makers under the security dilemma*" *(Jervis 1982)*. Neoliberal institutionalists believe in the idea of common interests of states. But what will happen if antagonists do not share common interests? According to Jervis, (Jervis 1999) '*states will establish an institution if and only if they seek the goals that the institution will help them reach'*. It does not seem, superficially, that institutions could do much to increase security.

Considering the subject of security integration process and moreover in connection to the Collective Security Treaty Organisation (CSTO) and security in post-cold war era which is the focus of this study, collective security theorists *Charles* and *Clifford Kupchan* cites that, *"collective security is a way of providing an effective mechanism and regulated institutionalised balancing against an aggressor or when necessary band together to stop an aggression* (Kupchan and Kupchan 1995).*"*According to Danchin, *"the concept of collective security is notoriously difficult to define, as the term is associated with a loose set of assumptions and ideas and its continued existence remains a contested concept (Danchin 2009)."*

Roberts and Kingsbury define *collective security as "an arrangement where each state in the system accepts that security of one of them is a concern of all, and agrees to join in a collective response to aggression" (Roberts and Kingsbury 1993).*

Collective security supporters argue that this mechanism has been more effective and successful in the post-cold war era and also in the post-Soviet space where newly independent states have emerged, and the security concerns are unlimited (Baylis 2007).

Moreover, it has been observed that in a chaotic world, in order to find peace and stability, international as well as regional organisations have become indispensable. Keeping in mind the theory of collective security, this chapter analyzes the threats posed by non-state actors with respect to Eurasian collective security organization especially the CIS Collective Security Treaty Organization (CSTO) and its comparisons with other organisations like the Shanghai Cooperation Organisation (SCO) and the NATO PfP.

As cited by Organski, there are five basic assumptions underlying the theory of collective security. These are as follows--

- *"In an armed conflict, member states will be able to agree on which nation an aggressor is.*
- *All member nation-states are equally committed to contain and constrain the aggression, irrespective of its source or origin.*
- *All member nation-states have identical freedom of action and ability to join in proceedings against the aggressor.*

- *The cumulative power of the cooperating members of the alliance for collective security will be adequate and sufficient to overpower the might of the aggressor.*
- *In the light of the threat posed by the collective might of the nations of a collective security coalition, the aggressor nation will modify its policies, or if unwilling to do so, will be defeated."* (Organski 1958)

Collective security arrangements and related phenomena such as arms control agreements are designed to enhance the security of their participants' *vis-à-vis* each other. According to Claude Jr., collective security rests on the proposition *"that war can be prevented by deterrent effect of overwhelming power of states that are too rational to invite certain defeat."* (Ibid).

The present work explores the concept and theories of alliances, paying special attention to the persistence of alliance system. In the chapters, an attempt has been made to explain the cause of CSTO's persistence and its future prospects. The research tries to make a comparative study of the activities of NATO and CSTO in the post-Soviet space. Alliances of states happen to be one of the most significant elements for advancing a state's interest. In particular, alliances are a primary instrument for improving a state's security in the face of external and sometimes internal threats. As Stephan Walt cites, *"An alliance is a formal or informal relationship of security cooperation between two or more sovereign states."* (Walt 1987) It also helps understanding the workings of the CSTO in relation with NATO. If CSTO is viewed as the extension of the Warsaw Pact following the dissolution of the Soviet Union, then alliance studies focus our attention as to how for several years, great powers, and many smaller ones as well, have regularly formed, acted through, and sometimes broken alliances, to understand the balance of power system, bandwagon etc., a major component of states' external security is by alliance systems.

Patricia Weitsman cites, *"alliances are bilateral or multilateral agreements to provide some element of security to the signatories."* (Weitsman 2004).

3.3   Historical Background

After the end of the World War II, almost for four decades, the United States and the Soviet Union were the two superpowers in a well defined bipolar international world order. These two superpowers belonged to antagonistic political, socio-economic and ideological blocs. Conflicts between Soviet Union and the United States were in the lines of ideological rivalry between capitalism and communism and difference regarding a democratic polity and market economy in case of the US and a totalitarian polity and a command economy in case of the Soviet Union. It displayed the central drama within the international system. This ideological divide was so grave that it drove for a very severe competition between them. Both the superpowers strived to possess armies and arsenals unmatched by the others, (Goldgeier 2003) seen as the primary application of the doctrine of Mutually Assured Destruction (MAD). Hence the cold war between the United States and the Soviet Union dominated the security environment from 1945 when the Second World War ends until 1989.

The end of cold war greatly changed European security scenario. The security environment and the international scenario before and after the demise of one of the superpowers also changed in a big way. Not only that in case of the international environment the changes were felt, like the global stage went from being a bipolar world to a unipolar world order but internally also in the Soviet Union, because of its collapse in 1991, it led to the appearance of fifteen independent republics.

After the disintegration of the Soviet Union, Russia and the former Soviet states found themselves in a drastically changed situation. It was totally different from the totalitarian era. The transition to democracy was a costly affair and with inconsistent economic and political situation. Not only that numerous other problems also cropped up in the region in form of territorial and ethnic tensions and socio-economic crises. Moreover, there were the attempts of the West to disrupt relations between Russia and the former Soviet states.

On studying the security aspect of an area like the post-Soviet space, the security paradigm has to be understood in the context of its historical background and the vivid and sudden striking transformations that it had gone through.

The ripples felt in the international relations after the dissolution of Soviet Union in 1991, very significantly transformed the geopolitics of the Eurasian continent. The major change seen in Russian foreign policy aspect was seen in its Eurasian focus. Other than complicated international situation, the demise of the Soviet Union also brought about new domestic changes. Regarding the aspect of security in the post-Soviet space, the commonly defined "new security challenges" include "the proliferation of weapons of mass destruction, the growth of ethnic nationalism and extremism, international terrorism, and crime and drug trafficking (Johnson 1999)."

The post-Soviet states had to handle immediately two contradictory challenges- that is the process of state building with a new national authority while at the same time wrestling with the 'sub-national' ethnic disputes, regional political mobilization and the demands for secession. Since the collapse of the USSR in the late 1980s there have been six violent ethnic and regional conflicts (Azerbaijan-Nogorno Karabakh-Armenia; Moldova-Transdnistria; Russia-Chechnya; Georgia-Abkhazia; Georgia-South Ossetia; Tajikistan civil war) and seven significant conflicts which did not occur (Hughes 2001).

The instability and conflict within states that threatened to spread over into the inter-state arena posing new adversities for the Russian army and the new post-Soviet states. As Flynn and Farell cited, *"States' efforts to check this new security environment resulted into exceptional arrangements like traditional alliances, great power concerts and community building and collective security* (Flynn 1999)."

As cited by Charles and Clifford Kupchan, "*Under Collective security, states agree to abide by certain norms and rules to maintain stability and when necessary, band together to stop aggression* (Kupchan and Kupchan 1995)."

In the post-Soviet space, the Commonwealth of Independent States (CIS) has been used for integration of former Soviet states just after 1990s. It was established to be an *"instrument of civilised divorce."* as Yeltsin put in (Libman 2007).

The CIS in reality was established *"to make the process of USSR's dissolution most civilised and smooth one, with the fewest losses in the economic and humanitarian spheres..."* (Kobrinskaya 2007).

The Collective Security Treaty organisation (CSTO) was formed after the collapse of the Soviet Union and it embraced some of the former Soviet republics. Originally formed in 1992 under the auspices of the CIS and the Collective Security Treaty (CST), CSTO is Russian-led with the primary goal of preventing civil wars in the post-soviet space, to handle new challenges such as terrorism and the spread of radical Islamic militancy which was the result of growing instability in Afghanistan and northwest Pakistan, to ensure the collective defence of the members, secure its independence, territorial integrity and sovereignty of member states and a range of other conflicts. The old traditional function of the

CSTO is to counterbalance NATO which is seeking continued expansion eastwards through NATO's Partnership for Peace program (PfP) (Mowchan 2009).

Regarding how CSTO is building up Russia's stand, the consolidating factors would hence be threats of terrorism and extremism, NATO interference in the CIS, apprehension towards American presence and a belief that Russia could be the sole counterbalance. In brief, as Weinstein cites, *"if anti-terrorism and suspicion of NATO brought the CSTO powers together the American invasion of Iraq firmly cemented CSTO relations on the basis of fear of American powers (Weinstein 2007)."*

CSTO serves as a means for Russia to continue its military relationship with many of the former Soviet republics. As it is, since 1991 relations with the post-Soviet states have become of increasing focus for Russian foreign policy terming it as *Near Abroad* and to be under Russia's *Sphere of Influence*. The year 2009 was significant for CSTO as Russia revived its attention on CSTO and created a new component i.e. the Collective Rapid Reaction Forces which increased the number of troops in the military security bloc from 1500 to 16,000. CSTO has strengthened Russia's position by providing Russia a less aggressive and more institutionalised platform to respond to security related events within the region (Chausovsky 2011).

3.4   TRADITIONAL SECURITY
THREATS AND MILITARY SECURITY

The end of the cold war led to the subsequent rise of new security concerns in the post-Soviet area such as terrorism, drug trafficking, organized crime, environmental degradation, economic problems, religious fundamentalism, ethnic crises and spillover effects of the failed states, etc. These transnational threats lead to the largest social, political and economic consequences following terrorism. Terrorism is a kind of issue that can threaten both hard and soft security of a region. Hans M. Kristensen argues about the traditional/hard security threats of Russia and the post-Soviet space. Threats have also been there with China having increasingly common ground with border agreement, joint exercises etc. (Kristensen 2006).

Niklas Swanstorm also cites that, "*there is an interconnection between traditional security threats and trans-national implications and traditional security threats like military threats to the government, follows the so-called soft security threats. A new network of militants in the southern part of Greater Central Asia, especially in Afghanistan, Tajikistan and Uzbekistan are posing soft security threats* (Swanstorm 2010)."

CSTO is the result of the process of achieving an effective collective security system and for that it works towards the coordination of military, security and foreign policy of the member countries. As already mentioned this post-Soviet region has such transnational problems that for any newly independent state it would be hard or a mammoth task to handle it alone. Hence cooperative strength is something which is indeed utterly necessary in an area like this. Abundant literature on the specific workings of the CSTO in such a troubled environment is difficult to find. Zhenis Kembayev argues the cooperation of CSTO in the sphere of military security and how the state parties to the organisation accomplish the composition of their own national armed forces and later on lead to a program of military security. CSTO also works under the framework of coalition groupings like 'Rubezh' for instance and conduct regular large scale military maneuvers. There is also military cooperation under CSTO in a way that the member states can buy Russian military equipment leading to effective control mechanisms against illegal export of Russian artillery (Kembayev 2009).

The CSTO in the post-Soviet countries is the single most consolidated military dimension institution demonstrating Russia's willingness to spread its wings in the post-Soviet space in a much more institutionalized manner.

Vladimir Paramonov and Oleg Stolpovski argue that Russia's willingness to further strengthen the CSTO is to create a kind of military and political bloc that is consistent with Kremlin's policy for the post-Soviet space. It even calls for the eventual withdrawal of US military bases. In practical military aspects, Russia has attempted to maintain elements of military integration like arrangement of military weapons and artillery, a common air defence system and joint training, etc.(Paramonov 2008).

Literature is abundant on describing the CSTO as a tool for Russian foreign policy designs while less mention has been made on the fact that apart from Russia there are other six members also which also play an active role in the CSTO decision-making and has close connections. The present work tries to look into the relations every particular member of the CSTO has with the organisation and actively plays their role.

3.5   NON-TRADITIONAL THREATS AND CSTO

After the disintegration of the Soviet Union in 1991 and coming up of the independent states of the Central Asian region and the Caucasus, the concept of security widened and led to the subsequent rise of new non-traditional threats; religious fundamentalism being one of the grave ones. It has to be borne in mind here that the post-Soviet space shares its borders with one of the most volatile regions of the world that is Afghanistan. Not to forget the mention of Uzbekistan that confronts the IMU and other extremists and radical elements that spread all over the Central Asian region and the Caucasus. Hence the security parameters should be very high.

> Niklas Swanstorm cites that, "*religious fundamentalism basically cropped as a very serious threat to all states of the region, Afghanistan is undoubtedly the natural sufferer because of its long-term instability and the dominant position of organized crime but the problem is more widespread. Much of the problem lies in the growing unemployment; weak government sponsored health care, social welfare at large, as well as a lack of belief in the future* (Swanstorm 2010)."

Terrorism is another serious threat perception in the post-Soviet region and arguably could be related to religious fundamentalism and the Muslim *Mujaheddin* targeting the post-Soviet space. Adam Weinstein argues about terrorism and cites the fact that the anti-Russian security policy in Central Asia and Eurasia receded after interstate terrorism showed up its ugly head. It was realised that the brutal conflicts like the secessionist movements of Chechnya, Tajik civil war, disastrous human rights record of Uzbekistan, the presence of IMU and the Taliban in Afghanistan etc., all of it also leading to the successive restructuring of the Collective Security Treaty from a convention to a full-fledged defence regime in the name of CSTO (Weinstein 2007).

CSTO's emphasis has always been on counteracting threats and challenges like acting against international terrorism and extremism, against practices of arms and drug trafficking, illegal cross-border migration and organized crime. Moreover, issues like drug trafficking and terrorism are serious transnational threats and hence a collective measure designed to counter the same is of utmost necessity. Zhenis Kembayev argues how CSTO has effectively from the very beginning of its formation has sought to fight the security problems of a complicated area like the post-Soviet space and mentioned about a eminent element of the anti-terrorist activities of the CSTO which lies in its operation of the Collective Rapid Reaction Forces (Kembayev 2009).

This book tries to fill the gap regarding the actions taken by the CSTO in countering these threats, on what specific steps the CSTO has taken; on how much it has succeeded in its attempts and on where the loopholes lie. It is in fact a modest attempt to study and explore the issues, problems and prospects of security integration in the post Soviet Space and the role of CSTO to materialise the process and efforts.

The CSTO was initially a Collective Security Treaty, which was upgraded to Collective Security Treaty Organisation (CSTO) only in 2002. Therefore, the mention and significance of the terrorist attacks of 11 September 2001 on US is of utmost importance. US's subsequent reaction to the 9/11 attacks in the form of the 'War on Terror' had led to its presence in and around Afghanistan and the post-Soviet area which has also prompted intensified post-Soviet states' cooperation in this area. The 9/11 attacks immediately transformed the global communities' priorities having profound influence on the future of Collective Security Treaty. CSTO acts as a counteracting force against the US owing to its Russian allegiance. Anatoliy A. Rozanov and Elena F. Dovgan argue how the CSTO has held the responsibility of dealing with a thematic threat like terrorism. Lena Johnson also explained the contours of a New Russian policy adopted post September 2001 examining Russia's policy response, the changing strategic and security situation in Central Asia and the evolution of the Russian policy in Central Asia in the light of the 11 September 2001 attacks. Russia continued its build-up of the Collective Security Treaty which nonetheless was sidestepped when US administration developed direct relations with the Central Asian Governments. However, in Kyrgyzstan, a Russian-military air base formally under the responsibility of the CST Rapid Reaction Force opened and a series of cooperation agreements on economic and security fields were developed (Rozanov 2010).

3.6   The Foreign Policy Perspective and CSTO

Considering the sphere of foreign policy also, the CSTO plays a crucial role. Russia holds multilateralism as its centrepiece of foreign policy and hails that it is the only legitimate basis for addressing problems of peace and security. Russia has a big brother or a guardian kind of attitude towards the post-Soviet region calling it also as its "backyard" and its "sphere of influence" which might be another reason why multilateral arrangement are often witnessed as a trait of its foreign policy. Here, Robert Legvold cites CSTO as *a multilateral umbrella for bilateral arrangements of individual member states with Russia in the field of security* (Legvold 2009). The CSTO member states cooperate closely on the international arena and coordinate their positions on key issues of the regional and global policy. All the member states are well aware of the security issues and recognise that these kinds of threats have to be dealt in a global level, hence cooperation and connection with the international community is mandatory for effective resolution. Anatoliy A. Rozanov arguing about the foreign policy component of the CSTO feels that evolving cooperation with other international organisations on countering common challenges and threats unites the efforts towards shaping the system of common and comprehensive security for Europe and Asia (Rozanov 2010). Elena F. Dovgan refers about the international legal assessment of the cooperation between CSTO and UN. Article 4 of the CSTO charter defines the right of CSTO to cooperate with other international intergovernmental organisations. It's one of the areas of CSTO foreign policy (Ibid). The CSTO not only works within the member states but is also active in maintaining an active relation with the other actors either bilaterally or with other international organisations like the NATO and the SCO primarily for the maintenance of peace and security in Eurasia. Zhenis Kembayev points out that CSTO's General Secretary Bordyuzha calls cooperation with NATO to be desirable yet not of utmost importance and that CSTO is a self-sufficient organisation. However, it has been clear that there are no anti-NATO feelings. While on the other hand, the author cites that the relations of CSTO with SCO seems to be less contentious. There is also a political willingness among these organisations to act as a single bloc regarding issues of military and security importance which happens to be the prime need of the hour (Kembayev 2009). Robert Legvold in his argument states that CSTO holds its central purpose to fill the security space and meet the security needs which NATO or other organisations might otherwise exploit and CSTO being a Russian led organisation, its foreign relations and throughout connections with other international actors are continually witnessed (Legvold 2009).

3.7   THE POLITICAL DIMENSION OF THE CSTO

CSTO has a very significant relationship with the United Nations (UN). Russia and its allies repeatedly call for attention of the CSTO capacity in the UN peacekeeping activities like in the case of Afghanistan in its fight against war and terrorism. Likewise, a similar peacekeeping mission under the UN mandate where CSTO has maintained peacekeeping forces explains this cooperative relation between the two. It is to be mentioned here that since 2004, CSTO has an observer status in the UN.

The literature in this topic is abundant. But what it lacks is the proper comparison of the CSTO with other collective security organisations in the post-Soviet space i.e. the Shanghai Cooperation Organisation (SCO) and the NATO's presence. The present work presents a comparative study of the CSTO with the SCO and NATO respectively.

Ingmar Oldberg points out Russia as being the undisputed leader in the CIS area and that an organisation like CSTO in the post-Soviet space has served to strengthen Russia's position not only in Eurasia but as a great power in the world. Russia has sought to bring together former Soviet Republics to such institutional arrangements that it is controlled by Russia itself. An evidence of it is how Russia leads the command, contributes to the strength of CSTO troops and supply weapons at favourable prices and how CSTO backed Russia in its war against Georgia in the year 2008 thus fulfilling Russia's political ambitions (Oldberg 2009).

3.8   THE ECONOMIC THEME
IN THE REVIEW OF THE CSTO

The CSTO does not deal with the issues of economic cooperation of member states. It is entirely a military and security organisation. But there is always a concept of economics or economic interest or at least a mild economic relationship as a prerequisite in any kind of cooperation and also for a fruitful economic cooperation a peaceful and secured intra-regional space is also very important. Niklas Swanstorm pinpoints the lack of economic growth in the region as one of the major threats against stability and stands as a reason behind other threats that are all interlinked. Social and economic deprivation has led to the dissatisfaction within the state resulting in major serious troubles. It also breeds the emergence of militant organisations (Swanstorm 2010).

The post-communist transitions presented the newly independent countries with all sorts of new problems. The majority of former Soviet republics lacked strong traditions of modern statehood. Hence a sort of re-integration process provided a balance with economic and political benefits- a possibility to rely on several states (as an organisation or in a collective framework) and an improved security system.

Mikhail A. Molchanov cites, "*the post-soviet space initially saw a decline in the share of intra-regional exports and imports after the dissolution of the Soviet Union. The post-Soviet space reflected a desire to find an optimal balance between security and development and with that energy trade has frequently linked the two together* (Molchanov 2009)."

The above literature gives enough solutions yet the history of attempts made over to understand the security paradigm and the security integration process in the post-Soviet space is not enough. The major questions to be addressed are—If the CSTO is 'Russia-led' then how does it tantamount to collective defence? Secondly, does the hegemonic character of the Russia hamper the working of CSTO smoothly in an unbiased manner? And thirdly, is it that the CSTO being an amalgamation of unequal member states pose any difficulty in the maintenance of security and peaceful cooperation? Another gap that has to be filled is regarding the thin membership of CSTO. Why is it that out of fifteen post-Soviet Republics only seven are member to it presently and why only those states? Moreover, does this minimal membership come in the way of meeting the security demands in the post-Soviet space? Considering all these, the proposed study will examine all the intricacies of collective security in the post-Soviet space with special emphasis on the activities of the CSTO. This paper will study in detail the nature of cooperation and mutual dependence and military collaboration between Russia and the other members of the CSTO and the problems and prospects associated with this. It will establish the linkage between different variables like foreign policy, military, security, geopolitics, strategic assets, the new 'Great Game' in the context of CSTO with Russia and post-Soviet space.

3.9   Conclusion

The study aims to fill the gap in the existing research on the security paradigm in the post-Soviet space. It has to be borne in mind that not much study has been done so far regarding the security paradigm in the post-Soviet space in general and collective security mechanism of CSTO in the post-Soviet space in particular. The importance of multilateralism as a unique strategy taken up by former Soviet republics and Russia's foreign policy particularly to sustain security measures in this area has not been understood by many western scholars. Many western scholars proclaim CSTO to be just an instrument of formally institutionalizing Russia's position and influence in the former Soviet space. At times CSTO has also been referred to as a 'paper tiger'. CSTO as an important collective security organisation has also been devalued and many studies have paralleled Russia with CSTO.

However, it has been seen that Russia's hegemony has indeed been a binding factor in the post-Soviet area; as Gleason puts in, "A situation in which a cooperative regime is established through the imposition of the will of a single, dominant co-operator (Gleason 2010)." Militarily, Russia's power is overwhelming; hence CSTO being fundamentally a military alliance and Russia-led is of definite significance. CSTO has successfully conducted number of military exercises, cooperated in the issues of security, crime and narcotics, deployed peacekeeping forces under the UN mandate. Considering all these, the proposed study will be a relevant contribution to the security studies because no significant and proper academic work has been done specifically on the security integration process in the post-Soviet space particularly on the CSTO.

References

Baylis, John. 2007. International and Global Security in the Post-Cold War Era. In *The Globalization of World Politics: An Introduction to International Relations*, Ed. Smith, Steve, John Baylis, and Patricia Owens, 4th rev. ed. USA: Oxford University Press. http://jerseylibrary.gov.je/items/293604.

Booth, Ken. 2005. *Theory of World Security*. Cambridge Studies on International Relations. Cambridge University Press. p. 5. https://doi.org/10.1017/CBO 9780511840210

Buzan, Barry. 1983. *People, States and Fear: The National Security Problem in International Relations*. NC: University of North Carolina Press.

Chausovsky, Eugene. 2011. *Dispatch: The CSTO and Russian Strategy.* [Online: web]. http://www.stratfor.com/analysis/20110706-dispatch-csto-and-russian-strategy. Accessed on October 8, 2011.

Danchin, P.G. 2009. Things Fall Apart: The Concept of Collective Security in International Law. In *United Nations Reform and the New Collective Security*, Ed. P.G. Danchin and H. Fisher. Cambridge: Cambridge University Press.

Flynn, Gregory, and Henry Farrell. 1999. Piecing Together the Democratic Peace: The CSCE, Norms, and the 'Construction' of Security in Post-Cold War Europe. *International Organization* 53 (3): 505–535. https://doi.org/10.1162/002081899550977.

Gleason, G. 2010. Russia and Central Asia's Multi Vector Foreign Policies. In *After Putin's Russia*, Ed. Stephen K. Wegren and Dale R. Herspring. UK: Rowman and Littlefield Publishers.

Goldgeier, James M., and Michael McFaul. 2003. *Power and Purpose: U.S. Policy toward Russia After the Cold War.* Brookings Institution Press. https://www.jstor.org/stable/10.7864/j.ctt1gpccth.

Hughes, James and Sasse, Gwendolyn. 2001. *Comparing Regional and Ethnic Conflicts in post Soviet Transition States: An Institutional APPROACH.* [Online: Web]. https://docs.google.com/viewer?a=v&q=cache:Erkdm5DPA1MJ:www.essex.ac.uk/ECPR/events/jointsessions/paperarchive/grenoble/ws2/hughes_sasse.pdf+&hl=en&pid=bl&srcid=ADGEESgMQ5ycYDBG9EdQDFO7fP6PDWZhrBJlPctRHknlK1x1pmTTReY_U0TdEVzU1fW8gvqEocXr093oRY_Mqq4seeuCUVdAQdAH07r0XHMTQuVFk4HJkC76IwZkLkXMl5UdJ06Idx&sig=AHIEtbR4bCbaUMwFNEmq1RjiUQ0UZwpI7g&pli=1. Accessed on September 14, 2011.

Jervis, Robert. 1982. Security Regimes. *International Organization* 36 (2): 357–378. https://doi.org/10.1017/S0020818300018981.

Jervis, Robert. 1999. Realism, Neoliberalism, and Cooperation: Understanding the Debate. *International Security* 24 (1): 42–63.

Johnson, Rebecca. 1999. *Post Cold War Security: The Lost Opportunities.*[Online: Web]. http://www.unidir.org/pdf/articles/pdf-art257.pdf. Accessed on September 9, 2011.

Kembayev, Zhenis. 2009. *Legal Aspects of the Regional Integration Processes in the Post-Soviet Area.* Verlag Berlin Heidelberg: Springer.

Keohane, Robert. 1984. *After Hegemony: Cooperation and Discord in the World Political Economy.* Princeton NJ: Princeton University Press. https://press.princeton.edu/books/paperback/9780691122489/after-hegemony.

Kobrinskaya, Irina. 2007. The Post-Soviet Space: From the USSR to the Commonwealth of Independent States and Beyond. In *The CIS, the EU and Russia: Challenges of Integration,,* Ed. Katlijn Malfiet, Lien Verspoest and Evgeny Vinokurov. New York: Palgrave Macmillan.

Kristensen, Hans M. 2006. *New and Traditional Security Threats to Russia, and the Utility of Nuclear Weapons*. Meeting paper on 12–13th October on emerging nuclear weapons policies: An opportunity to increase dialogue, FAS: Washington DC.

Kupchan, Charles A., and Clifford A. Kupchan. 1995. The Promise of Collective Security. *International Security* 20 (1): 52. https://doi.org/10.2307/2539215.

Legvold, R. 2009. The Role of Multilateralism in Russian Foreign Policy. In *The Multilateral Dimension in Russian Foreign Policy*, Ed. Elana Wilson Rowe and Stina Torjesen. USA and Canada: Routledge.

Libman, Alexander. 2007. Regionalisation and Regionalism in the Post-Soviet Space: Current Status and Implications for Institutional Development. *Europe-Asia Studies* 59 (3): 401–430. https://doi.org/10.1080/096681307012 39849.

Molchanov, Mikhail A. 2009. *Regionalization from Above: Russia's Asian Vector and the State Led Regionalism in Eurasia*. [Online: web]. http://people.stu.ca/~molchan/Euras-regm-above.pdf. Accessed on May 5, 2012.

Mowchan, John A. 2009. The Militarization of the Collective Security Treaty Organization. *Centre for Strategic Leadership* 6 (09): 1–6.

Oldberg, Ingmar. 2009. Russia's great power strategy under Putin and Medvedev. *Eurasia Daily Monitor (EDM)* 6 (108): 2–23.

Organski, A.F.K. 1958. World Politics. New York: *Alfred A. Knopf*, pp. Xii, 461. https://doi.org/10.1017/S000305540023325X.

Paramonov, Vladimir and O. Stolpovski. 2008. *Russia and Central Asia: Multilateral Security Cooperation*. [Online: web]. https://www.da.mod.uk/colleges/arag/document.../08(08)VP%20English.pdf. Accessed on April 30, 2012.

Roberts and Kingsbury. 1993. Introduction: The UN's Roles in International Society since 1945. In *United Nations, Divided World: The UN's role in international relations*, Ed. Adam Roberts and Benedict Kingsbury. Oxford and New York: Oxford University Press.

Rozanov, Anatolij Arkad′evič, Elena F. Dovgan′, and Anatolij Arkad′evič Rozanov. 2010. *Collective Security Treaty Organisation: 2002–2009*. DCAF Regional Programmes Series 6. Geneva: Geneva Centre for the Democratic Control of Armed Forces (DCAF).

Swanstorm, Niklas. 2010. Traditional and non-traditional security threats in Central Asia: Connecting the New and Old. *China and Eurasian Forum Quarterly* 8 (2): 35–51.

Walt, Stephen M. 1987. *The Origins of Alliances*. Cornell University Press. https://www.jstor.org/stable/10.7591/j.ctt32b5fc.

Weinstein, Adam. 2007. Russian Phoenix: The Collective Security Treaty Organization. *The Whitehead Journal of Diplomacy and International Relations,* VIII 1: 167–178.

Weitsman, Patricia A. 2004. *Dangerous Alliances: Proponents of Peace, Weapons of War.* Stanford: Stanford University Press.

Williams, Paul D. 2008. *Security Studies: An Introduction.* Routledge & CRC Press. https://www.routledge.com/Security-Studies-An-Introduction/Williams-McDonald/p/book/9781032162737.

Commonwealth of Independent States (CIS): An Emerging Model of Regional Security

Abstract Based on sovereign equality and the growth of friendship, interethnic harmony, trust, mutual understanding, and collaboration between nations, the Commonwealth of Independent nations (CIS) was established. Through the maintenance of unified command over military-strategic forces and nuclear weapon control, the CIS sought to assure international strategic stability and security. During the collapse of the USSR, Russia's Near Abroad foreign policy undermined the CIS. Nonetheless, the CIS offers tremendous advantages to its members, such as the ability to coordinate commerce, finance, lawmaking, and security.

Keywords CIS · CSTO · Russia · Regional security · Near Abroad

4.1 Introduction

The greatest political landmass on Earth, the Soviet Union, fell suddenly and unexpectedly, altering not just the geopolitical landscape of Asia but the whole world. With the appearance of these fifteen new, sovereign, and independent states on the global map. After breaking up into many

© The Author(s), under exclusive license to Springer Nature Singapore Pte Ltd. 2024
R. Pradhan and S. Kakoty, *Security Integration in the Post-Soviet Space and Collective Security Treaty Organization,*
https://doi.org/10.1007/978-981-97-6445-7_4

entities, the USSR came together to form the Commonwealth of Independent entities. This chapter is a meek attempt to examine how the post-Soviet republics are able to coexist peacefully inside the Commonwealth of Independent republics (CIS). It also concentrates on the establishment of the organisation, its institutions, and various entities that were created within it, such the Common Monetary Zone, EurAsEC, and Common Economic Space. It also covers how well the CIS has performed in handling security-related matters, including as the Collective Security Treaty, often known as the Tashkent Treaty, which was first negotiated under the CIS before evolving into a regional organisation in 2002.

4.2   Origin and Evolution

The "Viskuli" Belavezha Accords were signed on December 8, 1991 (Markedonov 2012). The heads of the three Slavic states—Boris Yeltsin, the president of Russia; Leonid Kravchuk, the president of Ukraine; and Stanislau Shushkevich, the chairman of the Supreme Soviet of Belarus— met alone and decided to dissolve the Soviet Union without telling the other partners (ibid.). Even though the assembly decided to dissolve the "Union," it was suggested that a "Commonwealth" be established in order to somewhat replace the Union. Consequently, the nations decided to dissolve the Soviet Union and replace it with the Commonwealth of Independent States. After two weeks, the CIS was established and Yeltsyn, Kravchuk, and Shushkevich were joined in Alma-Ata by eight other presidents. Mikhail Gorbachev resigned as President of the Soviet Union on December 25, 1991. The Soviet Union's red flag was taken down from the Kremlin (Belarus News, 2005).

The breakup of the Soviet Union in the early 1990s was most likely the catalyst for the foundation of the Commonwealth of Independent States. The fact that the Treaty of "Independent States Union," drafted by Mikhail Gorbachev's team, was in existence in 1991 as a means of resolving the Union's internal difficulties makes this quite clear (ibid.). Discussions also included the creation of the Commonwealth of Independent States, which replaced the USSR, based on the historical community of nations and their relationships with one another in light of bilateral agreements, as well as plans to strengthen ties based on mutual recognition and respect for state sovereignty. This seminar also covered the topics of geopolitical reality and international law.

The presidents of five Central Asian states—Kazakhstan, Kyrgyzstan, Tajikistan, Turkmenistan, and Uzbekistan—met in Ashgabat on December 13 and signed the Ashgabat proclamation, endorsing the formation of the CIS, a few weeks after the Minsk accord (Belovezh agreement) (Liberman 2011). The CIS declaration's formation stipulates that all member states of the Commonwealth of Independent States must be acknowledged as founders and designated in the test as high contracting bodies, and that the subjects of the former Soviet Union must participate equally in the process of finding solutions and creating documents for the Commonwealth.

The articles, resolutions, and agreements that were not up for discussion during the Commonwealth Agreement's development had to take into account all of the historical and socioeconomic circumstances of the Central Asian countries. Additionally, these states' leaders said that they were prepared to join the CIS as equal players who take into account the interests of all of its members (ibid.). In light of the favourable reception of the Ashgabat Declaration, the President of Kazakhstan proposed a meeting in Alma-Ata to deliberate on the designated themes and make decisions.

The Alma-Ata Protocol was signed on December 21, 1991, by the leaders of eight more former Soviet republics: Armenia (L. Ter-Petrosyan), Azerbaijan (A. Mutalibov), Kazakhstan (N. Nazarbaev), Kyrgyzstan (A. Akaev), Moldova (M. Snegur), Turkmenistan (S. Niyaziv), Tajikistan (R. Nabiev), and Uzbekistan (I. Karimov). This brought the total number of participating nations to 11 (Brzezinski et al. 1997). The Alma-Ata Declaration declared the assurances for carrying out the former Soviet Union's international commitments and reaffirmed the former republics' pledge to collaborate in a range of domestic and foreign policy areas. With Georgia's admission to the Commonwealth in December 1993, CIS now has twelve members. With the exception of three Baltic states, practically all of the former Soviet nations joined the CIS.

In accordance with the Declaration, democratic states governed by law will be established, and their relationships will be based on mutual recognition and respect for sovereign equality and state sovereignty, the inalienable right to self-determination, equality and non-interference in domestic affairs, rejection of the use of force, threats of force, and other forms of coercion, peaceful dispute resolution, respect for human rights and freedoms, including the rights of national minorities, diligent fulfilment of obligations, and other widely accepted standards and principles of international law; acknowledging and respecting each other's territorial integrity and the inviolability of the current borders; acknowledging their responsibility for maintaining interethnic harmony and civilian peace; adhering to the goals and tenets of the agreement that established the Commonwealth of Independent States; and believing that the development of friendship, good neighbourliness, and mutually beneficial cooperation, all of which have deep historical roots, serves the fundamental interests of nations and advances the cause of peace and security (Alma-Ata Declaration 1991).

The Charter, which outlines the rights and duties of the member nations as well as the objectives and guiding principles of the Commonwealth, was approved by the Council of Heads of State on January 22, 1993, and serves as the foundation for the CIS's operations. A multifunctional regional organisation with relatively close collaboration in the political, military, economic, social, and cultural domains is established under the CIS Charter (Danilenko 1999). The Commonwealth was established to promote and deepen the bonds of friendship, good neighbourliness, interethnic harmony, mutual trust, understanding, and mutually beneficial collaboration amongst its member nations. The objectives of the Commonwealth were articulated in Article 2 of the Charter;

    I. Cooperation in political, economic, ecological, humanitarian, cultural and other fields;

    II. Comprehensive and well-balanced economic and social development of the Member States within the framework of a common economic space, interstate cooperation and integration;

    III. Ensuring human rights and fundamental freedoms in accordance with the universally recognized principles and norms of international law and the documents of the CSCE;

    IV. Cooperation among the Member States in safeguarding international peace and security;

    V. implementing effective measures for the reduction of armaments and military expenditures, for the elimination of nuclear and other kinds of weapons of mass destruction, and for the achievement of universal and complete disarmament;

    VI. Promoting free communication, contacts and movement within the Commonwealth for the citizens of the Member States;

    VII. Mutual judicial assistance and cooperation in other spheres of legal relationships;

VIII. Peaceful settlement of disputes and conflicts among the States of the Commonwealth (ibid.).

It is clear to say that the Commonwealth was established on the foundation of each member state's sovereign equality and that each Member State was an equal subject of international law. The CIS promotes and strengthens interethnic harmony, friendship, mutual understanding, and collaboration between States, according to the Charter.

It was determined to maintain joint command of military-strategic forces and joint control over nuclear weapons in order to ensure international strategic stability and security. The parties also agreed to accept one another's inclination towards becoming a nuclear-free and/or neutral state. The Alma-Ata Declaration of 1991 reaffirmed the commitment to the creation and growth of a single economic area, as well as a shared European and Eurasian market (Alma-Ata Declaration 1991). The Union of Soviet Socialistic Republics was dissolved as a result of the creation of the Commonwealth of Independent States. The additional documents were created and approved during the Alma-Ata summit in addition to the Protocol and Alma-Ata Declaration. The "Agreement on coordinating institutions of the CIS" is one of the papers. The "CIS Council of the Heads of Government" and the "CIS Council of the Heads of States," the Commonwealth's supreme bodies, were also founded (ibid.).

While the process of transforming the Soviet Union into a Commonwealth came to an end at the Alma-Ata summit, CIS continued to function as a loose organisation since membership in the organisation was voluntary. In the early years of the breakup of the Soviet Union, Russia's Near Abroad foreign policy significantly undermined the CIS.

The CIS was seen as a "civilised divorce" and was said to be an organisation with no future during this time, since all of the newly independent republics were preoccupied with their own national reconstruction processes after the dissolution (Webber 1997: 1). The CIS's integration process was first recognised in 1994, but it has only been more evident since 1995, when member-state leaders started talking about collaboration at summits (ibid.). "The main tendency for the development of our countries has [now] taken shape," Russian President Boris Yeltsin declared during the January 1996 CIS summit. There is a trend towards the CIS member states' voluntary integration, according to Askar Akaev, the first president of the Kyrgyz Republic, who described it as a "dictum of time," and Nursultan Nazarbayev, the president of Kazakhstan, who described it as "an objective process, a historical necessity" (ibid.).

By the middle of the 1990s, the concept of integration had taken on a life of its own and had become the cornerstone of Russian foreign policy. It represented not only the country's military, economic, and political ties to its neighbours, but also the belief that Russia had "lost" its standing as a superpower (ibid..: p. 2).

The CIS is not a supranational organisation, though. Furthermore, the institution had performed atrociously due to a lack of agreement and conflicts of priorities between Russia and the other CIS member nations. The CIS's ability to function has been severely hampered by member state disagreements and national objectives, as well as by the organization's weak structure. The following list includes some effects of simple integration. Despite its claims of a "development of a single economic space" and a "joint military strategic space with poor development of major multilateral form," the Commonwealth of Independent States (CIS) falls short of certain requirements for an integrated association. The Commonwealth is not a supranational authority under the terms of its Charter, nor does it have a single currency, common citizenship, or unified armed forces. Conversely, the CIS undermines mutual understanding and cooperation among its member nations, leading to instances of overlap and conflict. It is the outcome of both bilateral and multilateral collaboration; the former has taken the shape of interactions within the Commonwealth of Independent governments (CIS), specific cooperation among a few governments, and regional associations. Nonetheless, the member states greatly benefit from the organisation. As an organisation, the CIS has the ability to coordinate actions in the areas of commerce, finance, security, and lawmaking. Along with taking part in UN peacekeeping operations, it has also encouraged collaboration on the democratisation of its member states and the prevention of transnational crime. The Collective Security Treaty Organisation (CSTO), often known as the Tashkent Treaty, has developed commercial cooperation between member nations of the CIS through the Eurasian Economic Community (EurAsEC or EAEC), Common Economic Space, and Common Monetary Zone.

Belarus, Russia, and Kazakhstan signed the EurAsEC Foundation Agreement on March 29, 1996. The organisation just welcomed Tajikistan and Kyrgyzstan on October 10, 2000. The group includes Ukraine,

Moldova, and Armenia as observers (ibid.). In Central Asia, organisations are primarily focused on creating a common energy market and investigating several cost-effective ways to utilise water. Meanwhile, the economic sector would entail an international commission on trade and tariffs and ultimately result in the creation of a single currency. With the intention of becoming a regional organisation that would be available to membership by other nations, it was founded by Russia, Ukraine, Kazakhstan, and Belarus (Mozaffari 1997b: 172).

An agreement to create a shared economic space under the framework of the Eurasian Economic Community (EurAsEC) was signed by Russia, Kazakhstan, and Belarus on January 1, 2010; the agreement was intended to be created by January 1, 2012 (Xinhuanet 2009). The decision to establish a shared economic space would "clear the way to the next stage of integration, a unified economic space," according to Kazakh President Nursultan Nazarbayev (Turkish Weekly 2009). Tajikistan and Kyrgyzstan have indicated their desire to become members of the Customs Union. However, according to Tajikistan's President Emomali Rakhmon, Tajikistan would participate as an observer (ibid.). As long as the CIS was primarily used as a regional platform, the member nations' efforts to integrate have often lagged. In addition, the member nations are a little irritated by Russia's monopoly and domineering stance towards the other CIS members. For instance, on August 12, 2008, President Mikhail Saakashvili of Georgia said that his country was leaving the Commonwealth of Independent States (CIS) due to Russian intervention in the conflict over Tskhinvali, the capital of South Ossetia's breakaway province (Georgia Finalises Withdrawal from CIS). Since the CIS's founding, Georgia is the first state to quit.

4.3   Institutional Models of the CIS

Early on in its development, the CIS saw conflict between two perspectives about its institutional framework: (1) the CIS was perceived as a powerful decision-making body; and (2) the CIS was seen as a loose forum that was just consultative, analogous to a "presidents' club" (Voitovich 1993). The Commonwealth's institutional growth aligned with its non-supranational coordinating character as established by its founding treaties. It seems that the CIS States were unwilling to revive the previous Soviet Union due to their extensive experience with extreme "supra-nationalism."

However, in order to lessen the agony of their "divorce," it was not possible to disregard the strong historical ties and high rates of integration and interdependence among the former Soviet Republics in almost every aspect of their lives. Furthermore, there was hope that the disintegration process within the borders of the former Soviet Union was a temporary effect of political disputes and mistakes in the previous integration practice, rather than a long-term trend, given the increasing integration in other parts of the world, particularly in Europe.

The most logical—though maybe not the most practical—development in that case was a slow transition from the most basic forms of bilateral and multilateral consultation and cooperation to a more complex institutional architecture consistent with modern international practice. In keeping with this attitude, the meeting's participants signed the necessary agreements to form the CIS's coordinating institutions on December 21, 1991 (CIS). 66 institutional entities were formed under the Commonwealth, with a focus on sectoral collaboration (Voitovich 1993).

Recent sectoral cooperation activities within the CIS have demonstrated that many of them have aided in the process of further integration within the Commonwealth framework and in resolving the issues outlined in the Conception of Further Development of the CIS and the Economic Development Strategies of the CIS till 2020 (SNG). About thirty intergovernmental organisations make up the CIS, an international organisation. These include the Inter-Parliamentary Assembly, the Council of Frontier Troops Commanders, the Council of Heads of Governments, the Council of Ministries of Foreign Affairs, the Council of Ministries of Defence of member states, the Council of Heads of States, and the Economic Court (CIS). The Executive Committee of the CIS, which consists of integrated standing executive, administrative, and coordination institutions of the CIS, organises the operations of all these institutions; develops Commonwealth strategies; conducts legal document examinations; evaluates the agreements and Resolutions' realisation process; and routinely updates the CIS's highest institutions. Since October 5, 2007, the Lebedev Sergei Nikolayevich (Executive Committee of the Commonwealth of Independent States) has served as its representative, and it is based in Minsk, Belarus. The Council of Heads of State (CHS) is the highest authority within the Commonwealth, tasked with deliberating and resolving any fundamental issues pertaining to the shared interests of the member states (Article 21).

In the economic, social, and other areas of their shared interests, the participating nations' executive authorities collaborate under the Council of Heads of Government (CHG) (Article 22). Both the CHG and the CHS approve decisions by consensus. This implies that any member state may declare that it is not interested in pursuing a particular issue, and that fact will not prevent a decision from being made (Baslar 2001: 97). The Decision of the Council of Heads of States of the Commonwealth from April 2, 1999, governs representation in the bodies of the Commonwealth.

President of the Russian Federation Dmitri Medvedev represented the CIS in 2010, while President of Tajikistan Emomali Rahmon represented it in 2011. The Council of Heads of Government of the Commonwealth of Independent States (CIS) was chaired by Turkmenistan in 2012 and Belarus in 2013. The collaboration of member states' executive powers in the social, economic, and other areas of shared interest is coordinated by the Council of Heads of Government (ibid.). In addition to carrying out the provisions outlined in the Agreement on the Establishment of the Economic Union and the operation of the free trade zone, the Council handles the matters assigned to it by the Council of Heads of State.

The development of transportation, communication, and energy systems; the adoption of cooperative business, agriculture, and other economic sectors' development programmes, as well as their financing; the establishment of Commonwealth bodies within its capacity; the selection of those bodies' managers; and the financing and dominance of those bodies' operations were all discussed during the twice-yearly meeting. One of the member nations initiates the extraordinary meeting, which is called. In addition, the Council refers issues to the Council of Foreign Affairs Ministers and the Economic Council of the Commonwealth, with the exception of issues sent to the Council by the Council of Heads of State (ibid.). The head of the Russian Federation government is the chairperson of the Council of Heads of Governments. The two Councils reach decisions by consensus. As the primary executive body responsible for coordinating the foreign policy efforts of the CIS member states on issues of shared interest, the Council of Ministers of Foreign Affairs adopts decisions between CHS and CHG meetings and on their orders (Article 27). On September 4, 1993, the Council of Heads of State made a decision that formed it (CIS 2011). It developed the Collective Forces Regulation on Peacekeeping in the Collective Security Area (CIS) and the Concept of Prevention and Regulation of Conflicts on the Territory of the

Member-States of the CIS in collaboration with the Council of Ministers of Defence.

The purpose of the Economic Court's operations is to guarantee that the economic obligations within the CIS framework are met (Article 32). Article 5 of the Agreement on Improvement of Accounts between Economic Organisations of the Participating States of the CIS (Information on the activities of the Economic Court of the CIS) stipulated its establishment on May 15, 1992. The primary goal of these organisations is to resolve global economic issues. Other Charter-based organisations include the Commission on Human Rights (Article 33), the High Command of the United Armed Forces (Article 30), the Council of Commanders of Border Troops (Article 31), the Coordinating-Consultative Committee (Article 28), and the Council of Ministers of Defence (Article 30) (Baslar 2001: 97). The most significant of them are covered in detail below.

The decision of the Council of Heads of States formed the Council of Ministries of Defence on February 14, 1992 (Citizen Information on the Council of Ministries of Defence of Member-States of the Commonwealth of Independent States). The Council was founded by the leaders of Armenia, Kazakhstan, Russia, Tajikistan, and Uzbekistan; Kyrgyzstan, Georgia, and Belarus eventually joined, while Moldova, Turkmenistan, and Ukraine were granted observer status. Georgia did, however, quit the Council in 2006 (ibid.). The institution's primary responsibilities include coordinating military cooperation, evaluating theoretical perspectives on matters of military organisation and strategy, and offering recommendations about governmental attempts to avert armed crises. Along with discussing defence and military organisation papers and making offers to the Council of Heads of States, the Council is also in charge of overseeing the operations of its branches (ibid.). The heads of state signed the agreement governing the operations of the General Headquarters of the CIS Armed Force in June 1992. In September 1993, it underwent a reconfiguration and became the CIS Military Cooperation Coordination Headquarters. Twice a year, the Council meets (ibid.).

On July 6, 1992, the Council of Frontier Troops Commanders was founded to address issues of security and stability inside the boundaries of the Commonwealth of Independent States. The members of the Council are: Armenia, Belarus, Kazakhstan, Kyrgyzstan, Moldova, Russia, Tajikistan, Turkmenistan, Uzbekistan, and Ukraine; Azerbaijan is an observer (The Council of Frontier Troops). The institution primarily addresses border defence and stability issues in the region, including coordination of efforts to defend external borders and the economic zone, fostering better friendly relations between the CIS member states' frontier troops, and strengthening and uniting the frontier troops (ibid.). Countering illegal migration and drug trafficking via the CIS's external borders are among the other duties of the service. On March 27, 1992, the Inter-Parliamentary Assembly was founded in accordance with the CIS framework (Inter-Parliamentary Assembly 2011). This organisation is only consultative. It talks about and looks over the projects of papers that are shared interests. Accepted on May 26, 1995, the Convention of the Inter-Parliamentary Assembly came into effect on January 6, 1996.

The Inter-Parliamentary Assembly of the CIS (2011) recognised the Assembly as an international organisation in accordance with convention. The Secretariat of the Inter-Parliamentary Assembly of the CIS, situated in St. Petersburg, is the Assembly's permanent entity. It convenes four times a year (CIS Inter-Parliamentary Assembly 2011). In addition to its duties, the Assembly handles peacekeeping missions. There are additional organs that were established on different dates. The Council of Collective Security is the highest political body of the states that are parties to the Agreement on Collective Security, which was signed on May 15, 1992. The agreement calls for coordination and cooperative efforts among the member states in order to carry out the terms of the agreement. The Interstate Bank was established in accordance with a special agreement that all ten participating states signed during the Minsk summit on January 22, 1993. Its functions include organising and carrying out multilateral interstate settlements between central (national) banks regarding trade and other transactions, as well as coordinating the monetary policies of the participating states (Baslar 2001). Numerous structures are within the purview of CIS. This chapter aims to focus exclusively on those structures that address security and military matters, as many of them are founded on commercial activity. Fig 4.1.

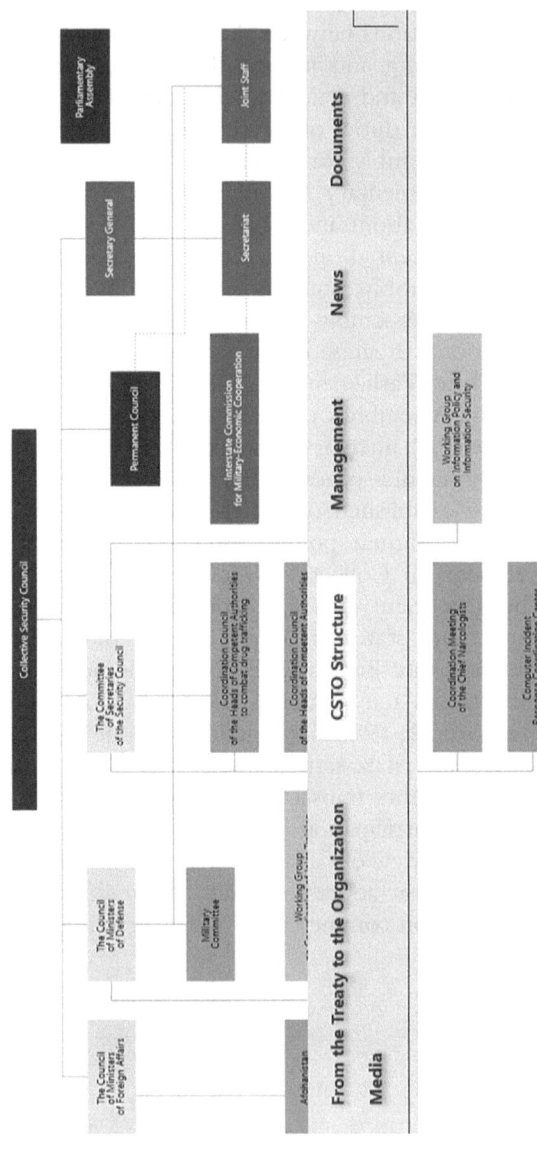

Fig. 4.1 CSTO Institutional Structure Available at: The CSTO Structure (odkb-csto.org)

4.4   Activities of the Commonwealth of Independent States

The Charter, which was approved by the Council of Heads of State on January 22, 1993, serves as the foundation for the Commonwealth's operations (CIS 2010). Prior to the Commonwealth of Independent States 2010's approval of the Charter, the Belavezha Agreement served as the organization's primary legal framework. The Commonwealth's objectives, guiding principles, and member nations' rights and responsibilities are outlined in the Charter.

4.5   Activities of CIS

Economic Cooperation: Encourages member nations to work together economically through joint ventures and trade agreements.

Political Dialogue: Promotes political debates and discussions on national, regional, and global concerns.

Cultural Exchange: Promotes educational and cultural exchanges to fortify relations between member countries.

Security Cooperation: Coordination of security measures, such as border control and counterterrorism, is known as security cooperation.

Humanitarian assistance: Offers assistance and support in times of emergency or natural disaster.

Legal Frameworks: Creates frameworks and agreements to control relations between member states.

Research and Information Sharing: Encourages data sharing, information sharing, and research among participating nations.

Sporting Events: Coordinates and manages sporting events, using athletics to promote unity.

Diplomatic Cooperation: Cooperation and diplomatic ties between member nations and the international community are facilitated by diplomatic relations.

Conflict Resolution: Conflict Resolution: Provides a forum for talking, negotiating, and settling issues and conflicts in the region.

4.6   ROLE OF CIS

These are some of the CIS's specialised responsibilities:

Economic cooperation: Through a variety of programmes, the CIS encourages member nations to cooperate economically. This involves standardising customs laws and establishing a free trade area.

Trade and investment: Among its member nations, the CIS promotes trade and investment. It offers a venue for corporate meetings and trade and investment agreements.

Military and security cooperation: Through a variety of programmes, the CIS manages member state military and security cooperation. This involves formulating uniform security standards and assembling a combined peacekeeping force.

Human rights and democracy: Among its member nations, the CIS works to further both of these values. It offers a conversation platform and keeps an eye on adherence to global norms.

Humanitarian aid: In the event of a natural disaster or other emergency, member nations of the CIS are eligible to receive humanitarian aid.

Cooperation in science and culture: The CIS encourages collaboration in science and culture among its member nations. This is accomplished by planning events and by giving initiatives financing.

Between December 1991 and July 2013, there were 45 sessions of the CIS Council of the Heads of State, 54 sessions of the CIS Council of Heads of Government, and 10 unofficial sessions of the Council of Heads of States. 1899 papers were adopted during this time once domestic processes were completed. During the aforementioned time frame, 21 documents were ratified but remained ineffective due to domestic ratification issue by the member states (CIS Minsk 2010). On December 30, 1991, the Heads of State convened for the first time and agreed agreements pertaining to border troops, strategic and military forces, and cooperative space research and utilisation (ibid.). Leaders of the member nations convened in Moscow in January 1992 to approve the Summit SNG 2000 Protocol on Temporal Provisions on the Coordinating Working Group and Protocol on Appointing Its Coordinator (Summit SNG 2000) (Figs. 4.2 and 4.3).

The primary topic of discussion at the early summits of the post-Soviet leaders was military matters: specifically, how the armed forces of the former Soviet Union should be divided among the newly independent states or should they be unified under the CIS (Brzezinski 1997). The other member states, however, rejected the notion of a Unified CIS Army during the subsequent conference because they believed it to be a danger to their independence. After these talks, CIS countries started to build their own national militaries and rejected the organisation as a single, cohesive security alliance. In spite of this resistance, six of the twelve CIS members signed the Tashkent Treaty on Collective Security (also known as the Collective Security Treaty) on May 15, 1992 (Mozaffari 1997a). Some states made the decision not to sign the treaty. The presidents of the CIS nations also inked several agreements concerning humanitarian ties, chemical weapons and WMDs, economic cooperation, and other topics during that time (CIS 2010). Additionally, agreements were reached on interstate TV and radio transmission and visa-free travel for nationals of the Commonwealth of Independent States (Brzezinski 1997). The Treaty on the Establishment of the Economic Union, which sought to provide beneficial conditions for the CIS states' economic cooperation, was signed

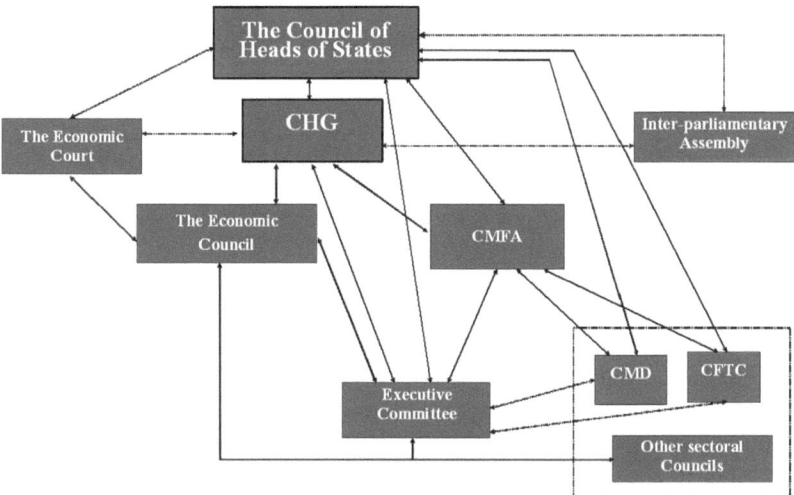

Fig. 4.2   Existing scheme of CIS' bodies

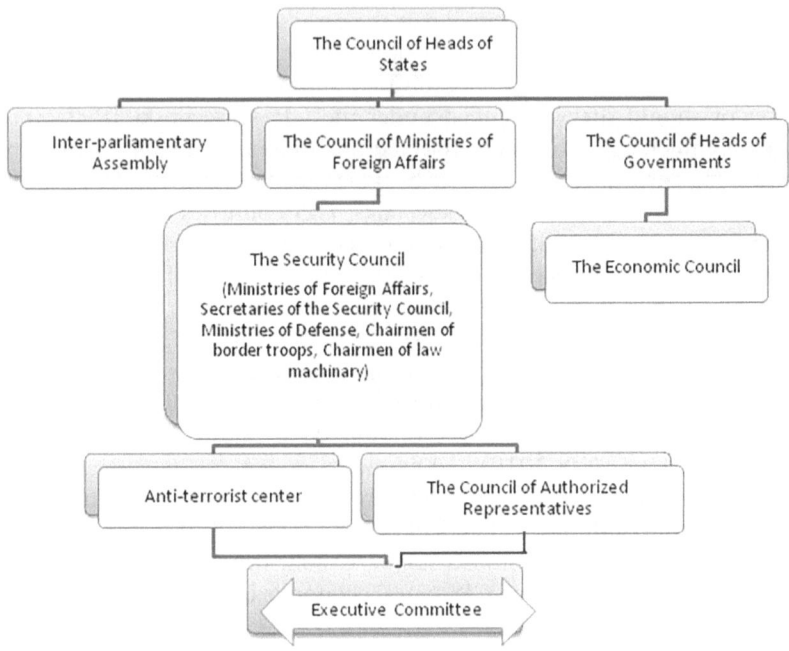

Fig. 4.3 Kazakhstan's proposal for reform in CIS' organizational structure from September 16, 2004

in 1993, making the year noteworthy (CIS Minsk). On December 9 of the same year, Georgia joined the Commonwealth. However, in 1993, nationalist leaders in Russia attempted to exert influence on post-Soviet state politics outside of the CIS (Goldman 2008).

The member nations of the Collective Security Treaty ratified it in 1994 for a period of five years, with the possibility of an extension. The signing of the CIS Free-Trade Zone Treaty was another important occasion that year (ibid.). In the same year, Russia was able to demonstrate its commitment to maintaining peace inside the borders of the Commonwealth of Independent States (CIS) by sending troops to Georgia and Tajikistan to assist in resolving the ongoing turmoil in those nations. But other CIS members rebelled against Russian policy after Russian soldiers invaded Chechnya, and by 1997 they were complaining that the CIS was being used as a tool to subjugate their own nations (Goldman 2008).

The next years included discussions on organised crime, peacekeeping, and resolving conflicts as well as economic cooperation. April 1999 saw the extension of the Collective Security Treaty for a further five years, and the expansion of military cooperation within the CIS until 2001 was deliberated (CIS Minsk).

Prior to the 1999 Batken invasion and the car explosives in Tashkent, the topic of international terrorism was not on the CIS agenda. Furthermore, in line with Russia's stance in separatist Chechnya, Putin emphasised the significance of fighting terrorism and the anti-terrorist battle following his appointment as acting president (Jonson 2004). Terrorism, drug trafficking, and the trafficking of weapons were seen to be the primary challenges to regional security, and the other CIS presidents agreed to strengthen multilateral security cooperation within the framework of the CIS and CSTO. With the signing of the Declaration on Maintaining Strategic Stability and the establishment of the joint CIS Anti-Terroristic Centre to combat international terrorism (CIS Minsk), 2000 was a remarkable year. This centre conducted summertime military drills in 2002, 2003, and 2004. Russia ratified the Anti-Ballistic Missile Treaty (Arms Control 2011) and the Strategic Arms Reduction Treaty (START-2) in the same year that the other members of the organisation backed them. On the other hand, it should be mentioned that by 2000, Russia had lost a lot of confidence in the CIS as its members had signed a number of agreements with western nations that avoided Russia: Azerbaijan and Georgia had agreed to build a pipeline with the US and Turkey, and other nations had started working with the US (Goldman 2008). The events of 9/11 marked a sea change in US-CIS ties. The CIS member states declared their readiness to work with the US to combat international terrorism in the wake of the sad terrorist acts. Dr. Minton F. Goldman highlights the three primary goals of this cooperation, which led to some members' scepticism about joining the Commonwealth: promoting democracy in post-communist nations; severing connections with Russia; and taking part in counterterrorism operations (ibid.: 51–52). Furthermore, by justifying its invasion of Chechnya, Russia has demonstrated its support for the United States in its war against international terrorism. To operate as a staging area for military operations in Afghanistan, it was decided to build US bases on the soil of Uzbekistan, Kyrgyzstan, and Tajikistan (Spechler 2002). All of these things forced Russia to try to strengthen the function of CST, which was renamed the Collective Security Treaty Organisation on May 15, 2002 (Marke-donov 2010). The Russians also established a base on Kyrgyz soil the next year, 30 km from the Manas air base (Radyuhin 2003). In 2004, Tajikistan established a second facility with 5,000 troops (Olcott 2005). The main topics on the meeting's agenda at the time included interna-tional terrorism, organised crime, illegal immigration, and border guard cooperation. UN Executive Directors of the UN Office of Drugs and Crimes, Antonio Maria Costa, Under Secretary General, and the Joint UN programme on HIV/AIDS, Peter Piot, Executive Director, partic-ipated at the September 2004 summit of the Heads of the States (CIS Minsk). Antonio Maria Costa emphasised that the UN supports the CIS's decisions on the matter, saying, "We are very aware of the fact that the leaders of the CIS countries are very much concerned of this problem and do their utmost to organise the struggle against drug-related crimes both on the national and international levels" (ibid.). In 2005, Turkmenistan left the Commonwealth as a full member and joined as "an associate member" (Goldman 2008). Later in 2006, discussions over Georgia's and Ukraine's exit from the organisation started, and in February of that same year, Georgia formally resigned from the Council of Ministries of Defence of the CIS (ibid.). This incident prompted the member states to emphasise the integration process once again and to talk about creating more effective organisations among CIS member states. The Council of Ministries of Defence decided to hold joint Comradeship-in-Arms exer-cises in June and September of 2010 after discussing military cooperation up until that point in 2007. On the agenda for the day were finan-cial concerns pertaining to the combined Air Defence System of the CIS. Throughout 2008, Russia tightened its soft security stance with the member republics of the CIS. The Roszarubezhsentr, a cultural and research centre with operations in 75 countries worldwide, was founded in six member nations (CIS 2010). These organisations' primary goals are to strengthen Russia's influence in "near abroad" and to provide a favourable picture of the country overseas.

Furthermore, 2008 was a remarkable year for Georgian-Russian ties in the wake of the five-day conflict in the breakaway province of Southern Ossetia (News ahead 2009). Georgia withdrew from the CIS in August 2009 after Russia acknowledged the independence of South Ossetia and Abkhazia in the same year. The following was said by Mikhail Saakashvili, the president of Georgia: "We definitely have to leave the CIS." The CIS was a complete failure as a global institution. It's a post-Soviet phenomenon that was essentially unable to stop this catastrophe from occurring. Furthermore, as you are aware, we are bidding the Soviet Union a last farewell by exiting the CIS (Georgia CIS 2011).

Georgia's primary source of dissatisfaction was its violation of the nation's territorial integrity, which is something that should be respected. Georgia was the first nation to leave the CIS after its 18-year existence and to completely distance itself from Russia. Another piece of bad news from Ukraine that year was that it refused to allow CIS anti-terrorist drills to take place on its soil. Colonel General Novikov, the head of the CIS Anti-Terrorism Centre, made the following statement on the incident: "The country's constitution, which forbids foreign military units from operating on its territory, was cited as justification for the refusal to hold the exercises in Ukraine" (Kyiv Post 2009). The year 2010 saw the reestablishment of ties between Russia and Ukraine following Yanukovych's election to office. Additionally, the Agreement on Common Economic Space was signed, with full implementation anticipated by January 2012. Nonetheless, the interethnic strife and crisis in the Kyrgyz South forced the CIS and CSTO to consider possible courses of action. It is not permitted to interfere in or stop interethnic disputes on the territory of its member states, as stated in the CIS Charter.

2013 marks the CIS's 22nd anniversary, and throughout that time, the organisation has had both highs and lows in terms of progress. Even among the member nations, there remain unresolved issues. One example is the conflict between Azerbaijan and Armenia over the Nagorno-Karabakh region. Since the fall of the USSR, several "hot spots" in Moldova and Central Asia remain unresolved and might resurface at any time, as in the instance of Osh (Kyrgyz-Uzbek relations). It should be highlighted, nevertheless, that Russia places a great deal of emphasis on its CIS strategy, which might lead to greater integration of former Soviet states.

4.7   Performance of CIS in Dealing with Security Challenges

When we discuss performance, we are referring to the commonwealth's advancement towards accomplishing the goals for which it was established. The very goals of the Commonwealth include: achieving cooperation in the political, economic, ecological, humanitarian, and other domains; ensuring that member states develop economically and socially in a balanced manner within the framework of a common economic space; fostering interstate cooperation and integration; guaranteeing individual rights and fundamental freedoms in conformity with internationally recognised norms and principles of international law and CSCE documents; collaborating among member states to maintain global peace and security; and implementing practical steps to reduce military spending and arms procurement, realisation of the following goals: mutual legal assistance and cooperation in other areas of legal relations; peaceful resolution of disputes and conflicts among the states of the Commonwealth; general and complete disarmament; promotion of freedom of communications, contacts, and travel within the Commonwealth for the citizens of its member states. The results of CIS have been inconsistent in this regard. As a functional regional organisation promoting political stability and economic development for the former Soviet states, the Commonwealth has had only patchy success. Its ability to reintegrate and coordinate its member nations over areas of shared interest is still elusive, despite having lessened the more severe repercussions of the Soviet Union's disintegration.

The organization's ability to continue as a viable regional organisation has been put in jeopardy by a consistent fall in cooperation and solidarity as well as in the number of signatory nations. Its ability to function as a mechanism to advance Russian interests within the "near abroad" has been undermined by this, as well as the emergence of new stakeholders (like the PRC) and the proliferation of various other international (like the Shanghai Cooperation Organisation) and regional (like the GUAM) organisations that conflict and compete with the CIS. However, the CIS still offers a political stage for forging closer sectoral and bilateral (as opposed to multilateral) connections with governments inside the Former Soviet Union as well as a diplomatic arena for maintaining communication and cooperation in that region (Abou 2012).

Politically, the Commonwealth of Independent States (CIS) has not been able to develop into a supranational organisation. Its inability to unite its members into a single political bloc and broaden its geopolitical influence is demonstrated by the Baltic States' rejection to join the Commonwealth, Ukraine's failure to ratify the CIS charter, and Georgia's 2009 exit from the CIS. This is a reflection of the CIS's failure to "mitigate inter-state tensions in the former Soviet Space and to promote good neighbourly relations with bordering states" (Libman 2007). Additionally on the economic front, the CIS has not yielded any notable outcomes. The Customs Union, which forms the foundation of Kazakhstan, Belarus, and Russia's shared economic area, is still badly designed and disorganised. The absence of an integrated single monetary system and disorganised investment, customs, and fiscal policies continue to be a problem for the common market, which was intended to increase productivity and reduce trade barriers (since the fall of the Rubble zone in 1993). Nevertheless, none of the aforementioned industries are of interest to us. This chapter will solely address the performance of CIS in the area of security because the research requires CIS ideas on bolstering regional security. Despite several setbacks, the CIS has yielded remarkable progress in the domains of military and security. States are forced to align militarily with Russia as a result of the post-Soviet security architecture established by the creation of the Collective Security Treaty Organisation in 2002. This has prevented its member nations from joining other military alliances, helping to countervail aggrandisement by other foreign military networks operating close to Russian borders. This has been especially helpful in disguising increased US participation and recent overtures in the former Soviet area (as shown by US outposts in Uzbekistan) and in gathering assets from the Soviet era. The Council of Ministers of Defence, which was founded in 1992 by the Council of Heads of State to develop a single military policy, is one of the two concurrent collective military structures within the CIS. It is home to the CIS Headquarters of Military Cooperation coordination as well as a permanent secretariat (Rianovosti 2010).

The other is the Tashkent Treaty, often known as the Collective Security Treaty, which was created inside the framework of the CIS and became a separate international organisation in 2002. Coordination of member states' policies on disarmament, weapons control, armed forces development, and security maintenance within the CIS is facilitated by the CIS charter (Burnashev 2002). Thus, the group approved a sizable amount of documents to govern collaboration in military security. The Collective Security Treaty, often known as the Tashkent Treaty, is a significant treaty that was signed on May 15, 1992 in Tashkent, Uzbekistan, by the Russian Federation, Tajikistan, Kazakhstan, Kyrgyzstan, and Uzbekistan (ibid.). With the accession of Azerbaijan, Georgia, and Belarus in 1993, the pact became operative on April 20, 1994. The three principal topics of discussion with the CIS prime ministers in October 1997 were organised crime, peacekeeping, and conflict resolution. Even though the topic of terrorism was heavily discussed in February 1999, it was not brought up on the CIS agenda until after the car bombings in Tashkent and the Batkent incidents in south Kyrgyzstan. Additionally, the leaders of Central Asia accepted Putin's plan for fostering multi-lateral security cooperation within the CSTO and CIS. Furthermore, the Council of Frontier Troops, another CIS supreme entity, deals with member state border disputes (Toktogulov 2007). This organisation also oversees the illegal migration and drug trafficking over the CIS's exterior borders. The Inter-Parliamentary Assembly contributes to the Common-wealth's peacekeeping effort in addition to the CFT. The Assembly works on maintaining peace in the "hot spots" of the CIS (Allison 2003). Since then, transnational issues including drug trafficking and weapon smuggling have been prioritised by the CIS agenda alongside terrorism. The Russian Federation, Kyrgyzstan, Tajikistan, and Uzbekistan offered their troops to participate in the combined common-and-staff exercise known as Southern Shield 2000 in response to the extremist invasion into Kyrgyzstan in 1999 (ibid.). Additionally, the second exercise's objective was to prevent extremists from Afghanistan from invading the CIS region. Combat training and contact between the military forces, security services, border troops, and interior soldiers were all part of this effort. Established in December 2000, the Anti-Terrorist Centre has its main office in Moscow and a branch office in Bishkek, Kyrgyzstan (Allison 2001). Kyrgyzstan held South-Antiterrorist drills the next year. A signif-icant command staff exercise called "Anti-Terror 2005" was arranged by CIS in western Kazakhstan in August of 2005. Additionally, on April 19, 1995, the Council of Ministries of Defence ratified the CIS Unified Air Defence Agreement, which at the time was the sole defence system in the CIS (Armenia Diaspora 2004). In 1996 and 1997, a number of drills were conducted under the auspices of this Agreement. Within the CIS Anti-Terrorist Centre, a unique database was created in 2004 to compile data on individuals and groups connected to any terrorist activity.

Established in December 2000, the Anti-Terrorist Centre has its main office in Moscow and a branch office in Bishkek, Kyrgyzstan (Allison 2001). Kyrgyzstan held South-Antiterrorist drills the next year. A signif-icant command staff exercise called "Anti-Terror 2005" was arranged by CIS in western Kazakhstan in August of 2005. Additionally, on April 19, 1995, the Council of Ministries of Defence ratified the CIS Unified Air Defence Agreement, which at the time was the sole defence system in the CIS (Armenia Diaspora 2004). In 1996 and 1997, a number of drills were conducted under the auspices of this Agreement. Within the CIS

Anti-Terrorist Centre, a unique database was created in 2004 to compile data on individuals and groups connected to any terrorist activity and counter drug trafficking.

With an emphasis on enhancing the effectiveness of the CSTO partnership's collective security component, 4,000 soldiers from all seven participating nations participated in the largest-ever military exercise, known as Rubezh-2008, which was conducted in Armenia (Rubezh 2011). Also present during Rubezh 2010, which took place in Chorukh-Dayron, Tajikistan, was the battalion of the CRRF. The primary objectives of the exercises were border security, counterterrorism, and illicit drug trafficking (Maksudov 2010).

It is clear from the CIS's formal institutional perspective and structural design that the Commonwealth is merely an intergovernmental body. It "is not a supra-State entity, nor a State." It cannot in any manner be regarded as the legal successor to the old USSR, despite being a loose federation of the former Soviet nations. Nevertheless, in contrast to many other Commonwealths worldwide, the Commonwealth can boast of a meaningful and purposeful charter, intergovernmental organisations with the ability to make decisions collectively, a confederation-like core comprised of the States aiming for closer forms of cooperation, and the principle of sovereign equality of its members. Additionally, the CIS's developing institutional architecture is probably going to develop into a more complex and well-organized framework.

4.8   Conclusion

The chapter has covered the USSR's 1991 collapse and subsequent integration into the CIS under this backdrop. The aforementioned study also makes sense when one considers how Russia's foreign policy changed in the middle of the 1990s, moving closer to its "traditional" area of influence. Recognising the value of the former Soviet battalions, Russia has contacted its erstwhile allies in an effort to fortify the CIS. The CIS quickly evolved into a new kind of regional international organisation to address security completely inside its fold due to Russia's rising engagement in the organisation and the shifting nature of the regional and international balance of power with emerging security concerns.

Since 9/11, there have been several more summit meetings pertaining to security, as a result of this growing concern for member state security. But Georgia's exit from the CIS following its conflict with Russia has raised some concerns about Russia's despotism and the standing of other independent members.

REFERENCES

———. 2011. Official Site of the CIS. Available at: http://www.cis.minsk.by/

———. Charter of the Commonwealth of Independent States. Available at: http://www.cis.minsk.by/main.aspx?uid=180. Accessed on November 17, 2010.

———. CIS. Available at: http://www.cis.minsk.by/webnpa/text.aspx?RN=N90 400111. Accessed on February 2, 2011.

———. Executive Committee of the Commonwealth of Independent States. Available at: http://www.cis.minsk.by/page.php?id=28.

———. Information About the Activities of the Economic Court of the CIS. Available at: http://www.cis.minsk.by/page.php?id=206. Accessed on May 23, 2011.

———. Information About the Institutional Structure of the Commonwealth of Independent States. Available at: http://cis.minsk.by/main.aspx?uid=11216. Accessed on May 23, 2011.

———. Official Site of the CIS. http://cis.minsk.by/main.aspx?uid=192. Accessed on March 22, 2011.

———. SNG (Sectoral Councils—Basis of the CIS Integration). Available at: http://cis.minsk.by/main.aspx?uid=11884. Accessed on March 24, 2011.

———. The Council of Frontier Troops Commanders. Available at: http://www.cis.minsk.by/page.php?id=202. Accessed on March 24, 2011.

———. The Council of Heads of Government of the Commonwealth of Independent States. Available at: http://cis.minsk.by/main.aspx?uid=196. Accessed on March 24, 2011.

Abou, Raymond, and Mansour Pelekanos. 2012. The Commonwealth of Independent States. Transnational Crisis Project, November 27. Available at: http://crisisproject.org/the-commonwealth-of-independent-states-tra nslatio-imperii-or-a-mensa-et-thoro/.

About CIS Inter—Parliamentary Assembly. Available at: http://www.iacis.ru/ html/indexeng.php?id=50. Accessed on March 23, 2011.

Allison, Roy. 2001. Structure and Frameworks for Security Policy Cooperation in Central Asia. In *Central Asian Security: The New International Context*, ed. Roy Alison and Lena Jonson, 221. London: Royal Institute of International Affairs.

Allison, Roy. 2003. Central Asian Military Reform: National, Regional and International Influence. In *Oil, Transition and Security in Central Asia*, ed. Sally Cummings. London, pp. 226–228. New York: Routledge Curzon.

Alma-Ata Declaration. 1991a. 11 Countries Accede to the CIS, December 21.

Alma-Ata Declaration. 1991b. The Preamble, December 21. http://lcweb2.loc.gov/frd/cs/belarus/by_appnc.html.

Armenia Diaspora. 2004. CIS Anti-Terrorist Center Established a New Working Group. Agency WPS. Defense and Security (Russia), November 24. Available at: http://www.armeniandiaspora.com/showthread.php?13522-CIS-anti-terrorist-centerestablished-a-new-working-group. Accessed on March 23, 2011.

Baslar, Kemal. 1998. The Commonwealth of Independent States: Decayed Within a Decade. In *Turkish Yearbook on International Relations*, 91–126. SSRN Scholarly Paper. Rochester, NY. https://doi.org/10.2139/ssrn.272 6478.

Baslar, Kemal. 2001. The Commonwealth of Independent States: Decayed Within a Decade. In *The Turkish Year Book*, Vol. XXXII, 97.

Belarus News. 2005. 14 Years of Belavezha Accords' Signing, December 8. Available at: http://charter97.org/eng/news/2005/12/08/14.

Brzezinski, Z. 1997. *Grand Chessboard: American Primacy And Its Geostrategic Imperatives*. New York: Perseus Books Group.

Brzezinski, Zbigniew, Paige Bryan Sullivan, and Paige Sullivan. 1997. *Russia and the Commonwealth of Independent States: Documents, Data, and Analysis*, 5. Center for Strategic and International Studies. Washington, DC.

Burnashev, Rustam. 2002. *Regional Security in Central Asia: Military Aspects*. In *Central Asia: A Gathering Storm?* ed. Boris Rumer, 134. New York and London: M. E. Sharpe.

CIS Minsk. 2010. Reference About the Documents Accepted During 1991–2010 in the Framework of the CIS (from March 15). Available at: http://cis.minsk.by/main.aspx?uid=8926. Accessed on February 7, 2011.

Commonwealth of Independent States (CIS). Available at: http://cns.miis.edu/inventory/pdfs/cis.pdf. Accessed on December 22, 2010.

Danilenko, G. 1999. Implementation of International Law in CIS States: Theory and Practice. *European Journal of International Law* 10 (1): 51–69. https://doi.org/10.1093/ejil/10.1.51.

Foundation Agreement of EAEC—Agreement on Foundation of Eurasian Economic Community. Available at: http://www.worldtradelaw.net/fta/agreements/eaecfta.pdf. Accessed on June 17, 2011.

Georgia Finalizes Withdrawal from CIS. Available at: http://www.rferl.org/content/Georgia_Finalizes_Withdrawal_From_CIS/1802284.html. Accessed on May 26, 2011.

Georgia Finalizes Withdrawal From CIS. Radio Free Europe Radio Liberty. Available at: http://www.rferl.org/content/Georgia_Finalizes_Withdrawal_From_CIS/1802284.html. Accessed on May 26, 2011.

Goldman, Minton F. 2008. *Russia, the Baltic and Eurasian Republics, and Central/Eastern Europe*. 11th ed., pp. 51, 52. United States: McGraw Hill.

.http://en.rian.ru/opinion/20101229/161977847.html. Accessed on April 8, 2011.

http://www.lcweb2.loc.gov/frd/cs/belarus/by-appnc.html.   Accessed   on November 17, 2010.

Information About the Council of Ministries of Defense of Member-States of the Commonwealth of Independent States. Available at: http://cis.minsk.by/main. aspx?uid=200. Accessed on May 23, 2011.

Jonson, Lena. 2004. *Vladimir Putin and Central Asia: The Shaping of Russian Foreign Policy*, 64. London: I.B. Taurus and Co Ltd.

Kyiv Post. 2009. Ukraine Refuses to Hold CIS Anti-Terrorist Drills on its Territory. Kyiv Post, October 29. Available at: http://www.kyivpost.com/news/ nation/detail/51441/. Accessed on March 27, 2011.

Liberman, Alexander. 2011. Commonwealth of Independent States and Eurasian Economic Community. First International Democracy Report 2011, Centre for Studies on Federalism, p. 4.

Libman, Alexander. 2007. Regionalization and Regionalism in the Post-Soviet Space: Current Status and Implications for Institutional Development. *Europe-Asia Studies* 59 (3): 410.

Maksudov, Maks. 2010. Tajikistan Hosts Rubezh—2010 Counter—Terrorism Exercises. Central Asia Online, April 27. Available at: http://centralasiao nline.com/cocoon/caii/xhtml/en_GB/features/caii/features/main/2010/ 04/27/feature-01.

Markedonov, Sergei. 2010. Post-Soviet Integration: CST, CSTO, CRRF etc. Post-Soviet World, January 20. Available at: http://www.opendemocracy. net/od-russia/sergeimarkedonov/post-soviet-integration-cst-csto-crrf-etc-2. Accessed on November 27, 2010.

Markedonov, Sergey. 2012. The Belavezha Accords Legacy. Russia in Global Affairs, December 27. https://eng.globalaffairs.ru/articles/the-belavezha-acc ords-legacy/.

Meetings of the Leaders of the CIS Member States. Available at: http://www.cis. minsk.by/main.aspx?uid=3358.

Moldova 7 October 2009, Chisinau Hosts CIS Leaders, October 9, 2009. Available at: http://www.newsahead.com/preview/2009/10/09/moldova-9-oct-2009-chisinau-hosts-cisleaders/index.php. Accessed on April 5, 2011.

Mozaffari, M. 1997a. *CIS' Southern Belt: Regional Cooperation and Integration*, 174. London: Macmillan Press LTD.

Mozaffari, Mehdi. 1997b. CIS' Southern Belt: Regional Cooperation and Integration. In *Security in the Commonwealth of Independent Stated*, ed. Mehdi Mozaffari, 172. New York: St. Martin's Press.

Official site of Executive Committee of CIS: Meetings of the Leaders of the CIS Member States. Available at: http://www.cis.minsk.by/main.aspx?uid=3358.

Olcott, Martha Brill. 2005. *Central Asia's Second Chance*, 189. Washington, DC: Carnegie Endowment for International Peace.

Radyuhin, Vladimir. 2003. A New Big Game in Central Asia. CDI Russia Weekly, July 18. Available at: http://www.cdi.org/russia/268-12.cfm. Accessed on May 16, 2011.

Rianovosti. 2010. 2010 a Milestone for CIS" Rianovosti, December 29.

Rubezh 2008: The First Large-Scale CSTO Military Exercise. Available at: http://www.pims.org/news/2008/08/06/rubezh-2008-the-first-large-scale-csto-militaryexercise. Accessed on May 27, 2011.

Russia Ratifies START II, Extension Protocol; ABM—Related Agreements Also Approved. Arms Control Association, Available at: http://www.armscontrol.org/print/671. Accessed on January 18, 2011.

Socor, Vladimir. 2002. *CIS Antiterrorism Center: Making Time in Moscow, Refocusing on Bishkek.* Washington DC: Institute for Advanced Strategic and Political Studies (IASPS) Policy Briefings: Oil in Geostrategic Perspective. November 3. No. 2. Available at: http://www.israeleconomy.org/strategic/socor10.html. Accessed on March 5, 2011.

Spechler, Martin C. 2002. Regional Cooperation in Central Asia. *Problems of Post Communism* 49(6, November/December): 42–47.

Summity SNG. *2000.* Summits of the CIS. "*Kommersant*" newspaper, #10 (1895), January 26. Available at: http://www.kommersant.ru/doc.aspx?DocsID=138369.

The Inter-Parliamentary Assembly of the CIS, Available at: http://www.cis.minsk.by/page.php?id=204. Accessed on March 24, 2011.

Toktogulov, Beishenbek. 2007. NATO's Partnership for Peace (PfP) Program and Regional Security in Central Asia. Ankara. METU, September, p. 33.

Turkish Weekly. 2009. Russia, Belarus and Kazakhstan Agree on Customs Union, December 5. Available at: http://www.turkishweekly.net/news/93507/russia-belarus-and-kazakhstan-agree-oncustoms-union.html. Accessed on June 27, 2011.

Voitovich, Sergei A. 1993. The Commonwealth of Independent States: An Emerging Institutional Model. *European Journal of International Law* 4 (3): 403–417. https://doi.org/10.1093/oxfordjournals.ejil.a035838.

Webber, Mark. 1997. CIS Integration Trends: Russia and the Former Soviet South. The Royal Institute of International Affairs. Russia and Eurasia Programme, London, p. 1.

Xinhuanet. 2009. Russia, Belarus, Kazakhstan to Establish Common Economic Space Before 2012. Available at: http://news.xinhuanet.com/english/2009-12/20/content_12672863.htm. Accessed on June 27, 2011.

CHAPTER 5

Russia's Security Policy in the Post Soviet Space

Abstract This chapter of the dissertation looks onto the patterns of security environment in the post-Soviet space. It further focuses on the themes and patterns that Russia followed while pursuing its security and foreign policy after 1991 in the CIS space. The chapter also explains Russia's attempts in security integration and military cooperation with the post-Soviet states.

Keywords Russia · Post-Soviet Space · CIS · Foreign Policy and Security Policy

5.1 Introduction

I cannot forecast to you the action of Russia. It is a riddle wrapped in a mystery inside an enigma. But there may be a key, and that key is Russian national interest.— **Winston Churchill** (Lo 2002)

This chapter sets out to explain the nature of Russian foreign and security policy in the CIS region, more specifically in the Central Asian region and the Caucasus. It will basically deal with the nature of Russian foreign

© The Author(s), under exclusive license to Springer Nature Singapore Pte Ltd. 2024
R. Pradhan and S. Kakoty, *Security Integration in the Post-Soviet Space and Collective Security Treaty Organization*,
https://doi.org/10.1007/978-981-97-6445-7_5

policy just after the dissolution of the Soviet Union in 1991. Since then there has been spectacular shifts in the contours of Russian foreign policy. Since the collapse of USSR, Russia as a state had to find meanings and answers of its new existence and identity and also its relations with the post-Cold war world system (Mankoff 2009).

Scholars on International Relations have time and again tried to understand the dynamics of Russian foreign policy. CIS has always been a priority area for Russia. The words of Foreign Minister Sergei Lavrov, in the spring of 2007, demonstrate well this Russian positioning. Referring mainly to energy geopolitics, Lavrov stated (2007), *"Russian foreign policy today is such that for the first time in its history, Russia is beginning to protect its national interest by using its competitive advantages."* Russian foreign policy increasingly refocused in Eurasia (Friere and Kanet 2010: 1).

The USSR was a vast territory. Therefore, after its dissolution, its legal successor in the Russian Federation had to look after the new emerging security problems resulting out from the collapse of USSR. Some of the basic security issues were the tackling of the vast nuclear arsenal of USSR spreading out widely throughout Russia and also in Ukraine, Kazakhstan and Belarus. Other problems were handling of border issues since there is long porous borders stretching across the extended territory leading to other grave problems like smuggling of contrabands, drug trafficking, illegal migration etc. Another major issue was the problem of terrorism and Islamic fundamentalism (Ibid.: 2).

It has to be borne in mind here that the post-Soviet space shares its borders with one of the most volatile regions of the world that is Afghanistan. Not to forget the mention of Uzbekistan that houses the IMU and other extremists and radical elements that spread all over the Central Asian region and the Caucasus. Hence the security parameters should be very high. Nikolas Swanstorm opines that religious fundamentalism basically cropped as a very serious threat to all states of the region, Afghanistan is undoubtedly the natural sufferer because of its long-term instability and the practices of organised crime. Much of the problem lies in the social factors like increasing unemployment, lack of welfare state programmes and a constant lack of hope for a better future (Swanstorm 2010).

5.2   Nature of Russian
Foreign Policy: In Theories

Post-Soviet Russian foreign policy has seen a dynamic shift from ideological doctrine to pragmatism. As Ludmilla Selezneva defines, "*Ideology referred to a system of ideas or views describing attitudes to a reality, social issues and to the aspirations of classes, political parties and nations*". And on the other hand, "*Pragmatism is a way of making short term decisions, grasping opportunities to achieve practical results, without considering the long-term consequences and in some cases even the morality of the decisions.*" Ideology was of sole importance to Soviet system and politics. The Marxist-Leninist ideology was seen as an ornament and considered as a central pillar of power. Ideolisation of politics in the Soviet era was intense basically dominated by the theory of 'Class struggle' and 'World revolution' concept. Ideology was the prime concern of Soviet politics. Some elements of pragmatism however were visible during the first half of the Khrushchev's era with his policy of peaceful coexistence with the West. Yet ideology sharply appeared during Khrushchev's era with the famous Khrushchev speech to the UN, during the Cuban missile crisis of 1962 enabling the Cold War concept to be apparently a feature of world revolution ideology. De-ideolisation as a process started with the coming of Gorbachev with his new kind of reforms. First of all, Gorbachev eliminated the 'World revolution' approach and started the epoch of actual cooperation with the West. It seemed that Gorbachev reforms slowly undermined the ideological core of Soviet Union because they changed the rules on which ideological discourse and thus power rested. The doctrine of foreign policy radically changed. The very first years after the collapse of the Soviet Union (1991–1996) can be described as dominated by liberal ideology as Andrey Kozyrev breeder anti-communist aspirations as a foreign minister. There was comprehensive partnership and integration with the Western countries. At that time, Russia's relations with the newly independent states was not set as a Russian foreign policy priority. However, there was a kind of consciousness somewhere and the administration of the CIS was soon established and the devolution of a huge empire took place largely peacefully. It was seen that in the early periods of post-Soviet Russian foreign policy, the degree of pragmatism increased than that of the Soviet times. The policy of openness to the West and similarly cooperation with the West were the most significant pragmatic steps. Primakov's period (1996–1999) brought about the 'policy of alternatives.

Severe anti-Western feelings cropped up especially because of reasons like, firstly, severe economic crisis 'shock therapy' and absence of economic help from the West began in 1992 followed by devaluation of the 'rouble'. Secondly, harsh actions by the West in the form of NATO bombing of Yugoslavia and further NATO expansion etc. lead to relations between Russia and the West became more complicated than the years just after the collapse of the Soviet Union. The concept of alternative foreign policy hence brought about the theory of 'Eurasia'. This period also announced the renewal of relations with the post-Soviet states as a foreign policy priority.

The coming of Putin in the early 2000s set out the foreign policy of Russia in a new direction. It was more Europe-oriented and pragmatism and developing economic relations with other countries not with US as in case of the previous periods. Moreover, this period saw that the Russian foreign policy is based on geographical considerations. As Russia borders Europe, the Middle East, Mediterranean, Central Asia, China and the Far East, Russia has policies towards all these regions. One thing that could be extracted out of this is that Russia's foreign policy towards for example Asia is not the result of pragmatism. Present relations with the CIS countries also appear more pragmatic, CIS being an absolute priority for Russia now. This third period saw inevitable changes from the extremes of the Soviet 'world communist revolution' theory to being an 'ally of the West' to a 'strong Russian state' concept which was ideologically almost neutral and more pragmatic in approach.

The phase after 11 September 2001, Russia took some major steps with cooperation with the West in fighting the 'war on terror'. It also saw the presence of US military bases in the post-Soviet space. However, there was also the demand that the US bases could not stay for long in the 'Russian zone of influence'. Therefore, it could be understood that the Russian foreign policy had three basic priorities; First, the interest of the country being of prime importance; second, integration to the community of democratic states; third, active policy and a balance between West and East. As historian Selezneva suggests, "*There was an essential movement from a doctrinaire to a pragmatic approach. The newly found pragmatism was characterised by the replacement of geopolitics by geo-economics, prioritisation of domestic policy, stress on integration, and multi-directionality in foreign policy*" (Selezneva 2003).

5.2.1   Schools of Thought

Russian geo-strategy and politics differs from that of the Western perspective and others. It is based on many traditions formed both in the period prior to 1917, the Bolshevik Revolution and during the Soviet times. Russian foreign policy is the outcome of several schools of thought. It is imperative to consider and recognise these schools of thought while assessing the influence of geopolitics on current foreign policy decision-making. The schools of thought are: *westernism, eurasianism, neo-eurasianist model*, and the so-called *pragmatic geopolitical model*.

- *Westernism—* The Westernisers promulgated this theory of Westernism. It initially developed during the eighteenth and nineteenth centuries. The dictums of this philosophical approach became dominant among Russian intelligentsia. This school of Westernism showed prominence during the period of Gorbachev's doctrine of 'new political thinking' and the so-called 'Kozyrev doctrine'. It was dominant in the country's foreign policy thinking. The basic principles of Westernism were as follows. Western ways and means were adopted. There prevailed a policy of tolerance towards the West that would mutually benefit both Russia and the West. The Western model of liberal democracy and market economy were accepted or in a way introduced in Russia. The policy of Westernism seemed to guarantee Russia's economic revival by attracting foreign investments also.

- *Eurasianism—* Eurasianism as an ideology became most popular when Russia after the disintegration of the Soviet Union sought to find a unique identity of its own. It was a totally new geopolitical paradigm shift in its foreign policy course. The idea was to be specifically an unmatched a region and of course its geographical stretch and cultural heterogeneity helped Russia to find its own special identity. The concept of Eurasianism contributed Russia to make a political-economic balance between East and the West (Peter 2001).

- *The Neo-Eurasianist Model—* This model made appearance among the Russian emigrants in the 1920s and 1930s. It carries strong anti-American perspectives. This model integrates ideas developed by Russian classical geopolitical authors with elements of traditional Western geopolitics and West-European right wingers. This model delivers a logical basis for the significance of physical spaces, natural resources, military strength and direct control over territory and also to defend national interest when in need by building up of political and military blocs. The trans-Eurasian geopolitical system hence defends the existence of axis like, for example- the Berlin-Moscow-Tokyo-Tehran axis (Legvold 2009).

- *The Pragmatic Geopolitical Model*— This model can be used interchangeably with Putin's vision of administration. This model became quite popular during the first years of the twenty first century. It was a revival and reinterpretation of what was known as "Eurasianism". It gives Russia the unique advantage of economic regeneration, favourable circumstances for engaging itself with the regional institutions and security arrangements and an augmenting its geoeconomic predominance as a regional and world player. The essential elements of this model are identified as follows:

  - economic efficiency
  - competent use of geopolitical resources inherited by Russia from the Soviet Union
  - nuclear weapons as a sign of containment
  - status, role and voting power in the UNSC
  - pragmatism for renewing relations with former allies and friends
  - utilising geopolitical benefits (Isakova 2005)

5.3   TRADITIONAL PRINCIPLES OF RUSSIAN SECURITY THINKING

The traditional principles of Russian security thinking can be judged from its behaviour regarding its external and foreign policies adopted. A certain kind of nature and behaviour has always been the trend. The traditional principles of Russian security thinking are as follows:

- *Fear of external powers*— Russia has been invaded many a times throughout history by neighbouring external powers. Hence Russia always is apprehensive regarding steps taken by any external power having the fear that it might not be against Russia. Instances have been of invasions by Mongols, French and German armies.

- *Desire for security*— Russia has a voracious thirst for security. Therefore, it has many Russian-led military co operations like the Collective Security Treaty Organisation (CSTO), CIS and Shanghai Cooperation Organisation (SCO) together with China. Earlier during the Soviet times there was the Warsaw Pact.
- *Feeling of superiority*— The third traditional principle of Russian security thinking is the feeling of superiority. One reason for this is because of Russia's unique status. Under Putin and Medvedev this thinking comes to the fore in frequent statements on Russia's great power status and that Russia no longer lets itself being ignored or humiliated by the West (Haas 2010: 3).
- *Obedience to state*— The Russians never had any heritage of democratic traditions. It had always had the heritage of state-control. This was also evident in President Putin's policy of returning to a centralised power system. Security thinking has always had a considerable influence on the policy views of the Kremlin of the past and present (Ibid.).
- *Desire for global power status*— Since the reign of Peter the Great Russia has always had the desire for great power status. Putin seems to be continuing this venture. Post dissolution of the Soviet Union, Russia thrives to still influence and spread its wings in the regions surrounding Russia. Since the coming of Putin the re-emergence of Russia as a global power has become a significant political priority for the Russian leadership. From Russian viewpoint, the new international order should be based on multi-polarity not US unipolarity. Russia's great power claims under Putin are based on military strength, energy resources and concentration of power in the presidential hands. Moreover, Russia opposes any kind of US or EU interference in its zone of interest basically comprising the CIS. Motivated by its rapid economic growth, Russia is further developing relations with Latin America and other territories previously under the influence of USSR (Wieclawski 2011: 522).

Hence, Russian security policy always maintains this line of thinking. All these are quite evident from the way Russia formulates its foreign policies towards external powers and the states of the post-Soviet space. In order to analyse Russian foreign policy in general and the in the post-Soviet space in particular, the aforementioned characteristics of Russian security thinking can be very handy.

5.4   Russian Policy Towards CIS

Regarding Russia's policies in the CIS security regional complex, Putin has been successful in establishing Russia's position and stature in the CIS region and Russia does get its deserved respect. This sub region is very much susceptible and crucial to Russian politics, culture and economics. With the coming of Vladimir Putin as the President of Russia there has been a stronger centre and stronger foreign policy discourse.

5.4.1   *Thematic Aspects of Russian Regionalism*

- *Demographic Crisis:*

Russia is a vast country. One of the worst problems facing Russia is the demographic crises. The population of Russia has dropped considerably. Even in December of 1999, this problem was considered to be "*the problem of year 2003*" as a proposed blueprint referred by the Unity Party (Herd 2003). The internal reasons behind this demographic downfall are because during last some fifteen years death rates in Russia have exceeded the birth rate by 800–900 thousand people. During the period of 1992–2004, the natural loss was 10.4 million. This has been a threat because in the near future the requirement for economic manpower will increase. The role of CIS countries and Baltic region is very significant in the case of Russian international migration. The growth of immigrants in Russia from the CIS region and the Baltic States have accounted for more than 900,000 people. Some states of the "Near Abroad" passed citizenship laws excluding dual citizenship. But with the gradual improvement of the economic and social situation in the post-Soviet states restrained the inflow of population into Russia contributing to the issue of demographic problem (Ibid.: 43–46).

- *Transborder Security:*

Russia's security environment has transformed quite seemingly since 1991. Since then security concerns have been top in Russia's priority chart. And, in order to maintain security internally and at home, one of the prior concerns was firstly to strongly secure its long stretching borders and secondly maintain external projection of political-military power and influence (Averre 2003: 63).

Here, we will learn about the main trends in transborder security arrangements, the regions involved and the impact suffered by Russia and the other regions. There has been a changing nature in the concept of security in Russia and the greater CIS region. The changes have basically followed the changes in the security arrangements following the end of cold war. Russia's position with the post-Cold war security arrangements was no more ideological in nature. These new security threats have been not only limited to hard security or traditional threats but newer kind of non-traditional or soft security threats. All these have major impact in policy making of Russia not only domestically but also in foreign relations matters. These non-traditional challenges are transnational in nature which has widespread and hard outcomes like economic dislocation, organised crime, environment degradation, mass migration, the spread of communicable diseases etc. To talk in terms of centre-periphery relations, if Russia remains to be the centre and the Caucasus and Central Asia, the periphery, a stable periphery is utmost necessary. However, establishing a stable periphery has been not very successful yet and the relative openness has made the centre more vulnerable to terrorism, drug trafficking, weapons, illegal migration both as a target and a transit country particularly because the periphery is plagued with these issues. Hence the gravity of this issue can be understood and also the reason as to why the regions of Central Asia and the Caucasus figure prime in the priority list of Russian interest.

Yet Russia's attempt in setting up of political-military security regime in the CIS has not been very systematic partially and successful. Integration of the CIS states with Russia at the centre had been in the very beginning materialised through the Tashkent Treaty on Collective Security. But this treaty formerly attracted only six out of a total of twelve members of the CIS. However, the very name of the treaty became baseless since the withdrawal of Uzbekistan in 1999. Initial parties to the Tashkent treaty were Armenia, Kazakhstan, Kyrgyzstan, Russia, Tajikistan, and Uzbekistan. Later members were Azerbaijan (joined on 24 September, 1993), Belarus (joined on 31 December 1993) and Georgia (joined on 9 December 1993) (Rozanov et al. 2010: 3).

The Collective Security Treaty (later upgraded to Collective Security Treaty Organisation) was set to last for a 5-year period unless extended. On April 2, 1999, only six members of the CST signed a protocol renewing the treaty for another five-year period. The countries that exempted it from signing were Azerbaijan, Georgia and Uzbekistan. In

2005, Uzbekistan withdrew from GUAM and joined the CSTO in 2006 (Ibid.). The other commendable multilateral arrangement including some other countries is the Shanghai Cooperation Organisation. It comprises of China, Russia, Kazakhstan, Kyrgyzstan, Uzbekistan and Tajikistan.

It can be seen however that for Russia's security arrangements, its residual military involvement in the CIS is mandatory. But many other security arrangements have been developing simultaneously because although initially Moscow was ready to take responsibility for security along the external CIS borders, but only a few had let Russia deploy troops on their borders. These states were Belarus, Armenia, Kazakhstan, Kyrgyzstan, Tajikistan and for some short span, Moldova and Georgia (Averre 2003).

Russia's southern borders are real troubled ones. The immediate security challenges differ from that of Russia's European borders. The Southern bordered states are weak, fragmented with ineffective Government actions and security regime in operation. There is considerable chunk of ethnic divisions that account for more than "thirty large ethnic nations as well as a large number of smaller peoples (Ibid.)."

Not only is that, the Southern borders are also plague by the problem of Islamic fundamentalism resulting in armed conflicts and other economic disruption. These porous and unstable borders are a cause of concern and also kicking off the problem of 'soft security threats' paving the way for illicit activities like illegal migration, drug trafficking and terrorism. Regarding the root of the issue of terrorism, Chechnya and neighbouring Afghanistan are posing quite a threat to Russia and the other CIS states. Considering Chechnya as a major immediate threat compromising Russia's national security, Russia took to waging war against Chechnya to prevent secession of part of Russian territory. It was also an indication by Russia that it is very protective about its own territory and territorial claims or interest and does not stop itself from taking the harshest of measures. But it was well spectacled that this action of Russia drew criticism from the international institutions and world over questioning former's commitment in establishing international norms. It also made bitter the Russia-Georgia relations with Russian attempts to seal borders with Georgia via a new visa regime (Averre 2003: 63).

5.5   RUSSIAN FOREIGN AND SECURITY POLICY DOCTRINES DURING PAST TWO DECADES FOLLOWING SOVIET BREAKUP

Right after the breakdown of Soviet Union in 1991, the Russian Federation drafted its own security concept. In May 1992, the Russian Federation described the National Security Concept (NSC) as the highest security document. In fact, the only achievement of Yeltsin in the field of Russian security was the National Security Concept of 1997, though it was not well-formulated yet it paved the way for Putin to formulate the NSC of 2000 (Friere and Kanet 2010: 1). The NSC aimed at safeguarding Russia's national interests against internal and external threats. The first issue of the document appeared at the end of 1997 as this period was plagued with conflicts between the executive and the legislature and the first Chechen War, followed by civil wars in Tajikistan and Moldova and in the Balkans. The NSC of 1997 provided an optimistic view of Russia in international development and gave importance to non-military, socio-economic interests, the problem of terrorism, slow economic growth etc. To improve these circumstances, Yeltsin directed his policy towards cooperation with the West. However, within a few years the situation changed with the change in the policy of NATO and its expansion. It posed a great threat to Russia and hence Russia was forced to change its security policy and a anti-Western inclination was visible. Not only those, the external developments and internal problems were reflected in the NSC draft of 1999 and 2000 that aimed towards reinforcing central authority and vesting power to the President of Russia in guaranteeing national security (Mishra 2007).

When Putin assumed power in March 2000, for the first time the focus on CIS was placed and cooperation with China was seen as balancing the power equation and checking the dominance of the US. In fact, the relation with China was dramatically improved after the Beijing Declaration of July 2000 (Beijing Declaration 2000).

However, post-September 2001 led to a complete policy shift. International politics was completely changed after the terrorist attack of 11 September 2001 in US. During that time, Russia fully supported the US offering cooperation such as passing secret information and air corridors for NATO aircraft and also the establishment of US military bases. Yet, the most notable change regarding the shift in relations between Russia and US led NATO was when in 2001, cooperation was offered by NATO.

In May 2002, NATO-Russia Council (NRC) was created at the Reykjavik summit (Smith 2006).

But since the end of 2004, Russian foreign policy consolidated its influence particularly in the "Near Abroad". The relationship between Russia and US marked a sea change particularly over US policy towards Iran and its interference in Georgia, Central Asia and Ukraine (Mishra 2007).

5.6   RUSSIAN INTERESTS IN THE POST-SOVIET SPACE

It has been an established fact that Moscow has always wanted to maintain a special influence over the post-Soviet space and for this limiting full independence for the Soviet republics was communicated during 1990–91, well before the August coup and subsequent appearance of the CIS (Willerton and Cockerham 2003: 187).

The first step that Russia took towards maintaining a strong foothold as a big brother in the post-Soviet space came about with the establishment of a strong and reliable system of military control and mutually benefiting economic cooperation. Initially the Commonwealth of Independent States (CIS) was to be the foremost organisational set up for fulfilling the aforementioned goals. CIS was to be helping in various ways like prevention of conflicts through peaceful resolution within the former Soviet Union space, help defend the CIS external border by installing troops, help to maintain a common forum for discussing and addressing issues of economic concern as all the states were slowly transforming their economic structures to regulated market economies. Hence these agendas drove multilateral bargaining efforts among the member states. However, slowly the fact came to light that the former Soviet Union states excessive dependence and reliance over Russian resources and markets was a reason behind their deteriorating economic conditions. As Willerton and Cockerham cites Igor Sinyakevich, "During 1992, Russia had a 1.5 trillion rouble trade balance with other CIS states, with its early unilateral moves (e.g., the introduction of non-cash rouble accounting to settle bilateral trade transactions for rouble-zone countries) revealing a continuing proclivity to manipulate its resource and infrastructural advantages to influence other states' commercial and security calculations (Ibid.: 188)."

Therefore, in 1992 a crucial step was taken in order to revive and seek more collective ways for addressing these common policy problems, in the form of the Russian-Ukrainian summit and the Minsk CIS Heads of Government meeting. The former Soviet Union states gradually became more and more involved in regional multilateral forum, collective security and peacekeeping activities (Ibid.: 189).

Meanwhile, most of the post-Soviet states try to balance Russia's power position by creating smaller regional arrangements which essentially include the regional hegemon i.e. Russia. One example of such a regional arrangement is GUAM. GUAM is an alternative grouping as against Russia-led security grouping. GUAM brings out the US factor since military cooperation developed between Ukraine/Moldova, Ukraine/Georgia/Azerbaijan, between GUUAM (GUAM was GUUAM when Uzbekistan was a member) and the US and through NATO's PfP. GUUAM members had always opposed to the participation within the CST since they see it as a part of Russia's attempt and strategic policy to the re-integration of the post-Soviet space. There is a strong link between GUUAM and NATO, it was further solidified in 1999 when GUUAM members attended 50th Anniversary of the NATO summit in Washington DC, it was the same year that NATO's bombardment of Serbia took place. The GUAM states have always given more priority to the trans-Atlantic community than cooperation with Russia. It works in a competitive design along with Russia-led organisations. According to Russian sources, GUUAM members at the Summit discussed military problems and resolution of ethnic conflicts in the former USSR in a similar manner as undertaken by NATO in Kosovo/Serbia. Armenia and Belarus, the two very active members of the CST see GUUAM as a 'pro-NATO' grouping. Moreover, two members of GUUAM, Georgia and Azerbaijan have both expressed interest in joining NATO (Kuzio 2000: 104–106).

The emergence of GUUAM and other regional security arrangements actually show how the CIS has been divided into two equal groups of Pragmatic Russophiles (Russia, Armenia, Kazakhstan, Kyrgyzstan and Tajikistan), the radical Slavophile (Belarus) and the other GUUAM + Turkmenistan group led basically by pro-Western pragmatic elites whose interests are diverging with those of Russia. However, the continued existence of GUUAM is the evidence as how geopolitical pluralism has emerged in the CIS (Ibid.: 110). GUAM is basically now a dead and stagnant organisation.

The CIS member states although are clubbed together, they are not a homogenous group and so have divergent interests. But they have a continuing fear of the re-emergence of a domineering regional hegemon; this has led to nothing but less successful measures taken in terms of multilateral arrangements and Russia in order to maintain its influence in the Eurasian region has to depend largely on bilateral negotiations. From 1993 onwards, an impressive variety of formal economic and security cooperation arrangements were made between Russia and other post-Soviet states. For instance, from November 1993 to 1997, there was the formation of Turmenorosgaz, a Russia-Turkmenistan gas joint stock company, again in 1999 there was reinstalling of Russian military bases in the Tajikistan (Ibid.: 189–190). Hence Russia marks an eventful impact on most of the post-Soviet states. It has been noticed that if Russia is not in very healthy terms bilaterally with each state then it affects their position in a multilateral forum also. For instance, the March 1994 'Group of Four' that was an accord among Russia, Belarus, Kazakhstan and Kyrgyzstan, could be successful only when Russia normalised its bilateral relations with each member (Ibid.: 190–191).

5.7   Motive for Security Integration

Regional security integration in various parts of the world has succeeded. Regional security arrangements have always been better off in dealing with security challenges. Russia being the legal successor to the USSR, regards the post-Soviet space as its own sphere of interest and as such Russia initiated projects like CSTO, EEC, and SCO which have different aims and spheres of operation. Motive behind Russia towards integration in the post-Soviet space has been pure security concerns. To take the case of the CSTO specifically, it can be seen that the reasons behind the establishment of the CSTO were varying circumstances like the Afghan crisis, ethnic and political destabilisation of Central Asia, also the civil war in Tajikistan. Today, the CSTO is regarded as the legal framework for guaranteeing military security throughout the CIS. In 1999 and 2000 when there were serious conflicts rising due to the problem of Islamic fundamentalist in Kyrgyzstan that the signatories to the CST agreed on joint military action and this led to the CST becoming the CSTO. Uzbekistan rejoined CSTO in 2006 leaving GUAM. But the CSTO is still at a growing stage. Russia (with the support of rest of the members) is the main contributor of the CSTO and its military force, both financially and in the composition of future forces (Markedonov 2010).

The political, economic and military prevalence of Russia is indeed one of the prime factors for integration in the post-Soviet space. Taking a lead in all the multilateral agreements and an extensive network of bilateral agreements with its neighbouring states, Russia considers the whole post-Soviet space as its own sphere of influence basically in matters of economics and security. In the context of defence and security the CSTO seems to be developing with a unified staff (Vinokurov 2007).

As cited by Malfliet, Verpoest, Vinokurov, "*The priority of the relations with the CIS states is determined by the following factors; firstly, Russia's main vital interests in the fields of economy, security and defence are concentrated on CIS territory; and effective cooperation with the CIS states counteracts centrifugal tendencies in Russia itself (Ibid.).*"

While the motive of CIS countries regarding integration depends on a traditional set of factors: economic, social, security, political, international. The CIS countries remain Russia's most important trading partners. They import 45 percent of Russian oil and 19 percent of construction equipment. Not only that, almost ten million people from the CIS countries work in Russia and send remittances up to four billion US dollars each year. The development of the CIS has been one of the vital interests of the Russian Federation. Within the CSTO, Russia has begun to supply armaments to the member states at domestic prices. Such steps not only increase Russia's influence in the post-Soviet space but the post-Soviet states also benefit in security considerations (Ibid.).

As the Presidential Decree of 14 September 1995 suggests, "*One of the most important documents laying out the conceptual framework of Russia's official approach to CIS affairs is the Presidential Decree 'On Russia's Strategic Course in its Relations with the CIS States' of 14 September 1995* (Presidential Decree 1995)." Further, the Decree goes on to specify the principal goal in a series of main tasks:

- *Providing for political, military, economic, humanitarian and legal stability.*
- *The CIS states as politically and economically stable entities with friendly bond with Russia*
- *Maximising Russia's role as a leading force in the post-Soviet space*
- *Building a strong integrating entity in the* CIS (Vinokurov 2007: 28).

5.8   Russian General Policies in the CIS Regional Security Complex

Here, are some points that are in favour of Russia's standpoint in taking part as an active core member in the CIS region. These points answer the question as to why do the Russian card works in the CIS region. These are as follows: (Nygren 2008).

Firstly, Russia's viewpoints are taken into consideration and taken seriously by all the CIS states.

Secondly, Russia's economic presence in the CIS sub region has been commendable since its economic recovery in 1998. Russia has been especially strong in energy and hydrocarbon sectors and uses it as a tool for foreign policy. Hence capital investment in the CIS crops up from Russian surplus sources (Herd 2003). Thirdly, Russia on the basis of cultural, political and economic arguments tries to establish an exceeding role in the entire CIS region. Fourthly, another characteristic feature is that although Russia is associated with multilateral forums, it has been observed that most of the foreign policy related matters are dealt in bilaterally. Although, the efforts of newer organisations like the CSTO and SCO in the CIS region is now exemplary (Nygren 2008).

A worth noticing nature of the Former Soviet Union states is that for security concerns and a stable and growing economic activity, they tend to rely on one another and to varying degrees upon Russia (Willerton and Cockerham 2003: 185). It helps the CIS to help identify and coordinate common security arrangements among members, and it has been the primary intergovernmental vessel used by the Russian Federation to consolidate its security relationships with the CIS members. Yet for Russia, a decade long CIS multilateral arrangement have not harboured much practical policy solutions. Russia and other CIS states have relied primarily on bilateral arrangements and agreements (Sakwa 2010).

Yet the former President Vladimir Putin's creditable efforts to consolidate Russia's position in the post-Soviet space have been significant in understanding Russian tutelage in the region (Willerton, John P. and Cockerham 2003).

5.9 Military Cooperation in the Post-Soviet Space

For the development of military-political cooperation in the post-Soviet space in the 1990s, the CIS charter provided that "concrete problems of political-military cooperation among member states shall be governed by specific agreements (Voitovich 1993)."

Many agreements were henceforth adopted by member states. As Kembayev (2009) suggests, some of the agreements concluded were:

- *"On June 26, 1992 eight CIS countries (all except for Azerbaijan and Moldova) signed the Agreement on the Coordination of Export Control over Raw Materials, Materials, Equipment, Technologies, and Services used or capable of being used for the manufacture of weapons of mass destruction and missiles as well as their means of delivery.*
- *On September 9, 1994 all twelve CIS countries signed an Agreement on "Repairing of the Military Equipment and Hardware" which provided that such armament may freely (without customs formalities) go through the borders for the purpose of repairing.*
- *Agreement on "Preferential Deliveries of the Military Equipment to the Border Troops of the CIS States" which provided that the producing states (most importantly Russia) would deliver the military equipment to the other state parties at their domestic prices.*
- *On November 3, 1995 also, all CIS countries adopted two further Agreements on "Standardization of the Armament and Military Equipment" and on "Uniformity of Measurements in the Armed Forces".*
- *On February 10, 1995 an Agreement on "Establishment of the United Air-Raid Defence System" was adopted, it was signed without reservations by eight countries: Armenia, Belarus, Georgia, Kazakhstan, Kyrgyzstan, Russia, Tajikistan and Uzbekistan.*
- *On May 26, 1995 a Treaty on "Cooperation in Protection of Borders with the Non-Commonwealth States" which provided for coordination of protective measures and mutual assistance in safeguarding the inviolability of the CIS borders.*
- *The Collective Security Treaty Organization (CSTO)—One of the significant steps taken under military political cooperation was on May 31, 2001 when under the framework of the Council of Heads of Governments, six countries i.e. Armenia, Belarus, Kazakhstan,*

Kyrgyzstan, Russia and Tajikistan which next year became members of the Collective Security Treaty Organization—CSTO. It endorsed "the Long-Range Plan of Development of the Military Cooperation of the CIS Participant States until the Year of 2005." This document was in anticipation of maintaining peace and security in the post-Soviet space and fight collectively against the thematic threat of terrorism. The military cooperation aspect referred to the various military manoeuvres taken up and air-raid defence systems installed in the region. Moreover, on August 26, 2005 the aforementioned document was replaced by "the CIS Conception of Military Cooperation until the Year of 2010." It was adopted in the framework of the Council of Heads of States of initial six countries and later rejoined by Uzbekistan."The main principles of this military cooperation include a more structured development of single military training and education, joint programmes on technical modernisation and maintenance of armed forces, joint air-raid defence, joint programmes on the production and reparation of military equipment and exchange of information etc. The very name of the document suggests that it caters for widening and deepening military cooperation of CIS member states."(Kembayev 2009)

Hence the CIS Collective Security Treaty Organisation (CSTO) came as a rescue to the poor and inefficient mechanism of the CIS. We will learn more about the security integration process and the CSTO in broad illustration in chapter 3 of this dissertation.

5.10   HAS THE CIS BEEN A SUCCESSFUL COMMON SECURITY SPACE?

After the collapse of the Soviet Union in 1991, Russian Federation became its legal successor state. Initially the Russian Federation was convinced that the collapse of the Soviet Union would not go in vain and a similar kind of organisation in place of it would be instated that is in the form of the Commonwealth of Independent States (CIS). Yet, it did not appear to happen as it was planned since there were different opinions regarding this among different members of the CIS. There was formation of respective armed forces and economic and security policies of the member-states (Haas 2010).

But what happened beyond that and was the CIS a total failure or does it still have any relevance? What was the need for the establishment of the CIS? What was the legal basis for the establishment and development of the CIS?

As Yeltsin puts in CIS was an *"instrument of civilised divorce."*(Libman 2007).

The following piece will lend an analytical discussion on the legal aspects of the establishment and development of the CIS.

- First, after the sudden collapse of the USSR, the CIS was set up in order to manage the process of civilised divorce smoothly and likewise reach to the needs of rearranging the Soviet administrative system and to coordinate the transitions and attune to a market-based economy. Significantly, two major groups developed, one headed by Russia supported by Belarus and Kazakhstan and the other comprised of Azerbaijan, Georgia, Moldova, Turkmenistan and Ukraine.

- Second, the CIS took the form of a loose intergovernmental organisation. It was the result of the indecision on part of both the groups in shaping the legal nature of the CIS. The Russia, Belarus and Kazakhstan group wanted the CIS to become a strong confederation like the European Union but the second group wanted the CIS to be a temporary and consultative forum.

- Third, from the point of view of international law, the CIS has all the attributes of an intergovernmental organisation. Hence, the CIS could have been successful providing the political will and efforts of its member countries.

- Fourth, the CIS could not be a very fruitful structure because although in the very beginning most of the Soviet armed forces were placed under the command of the CIS, and also the CIS countries accepted the Rouble currency as the common currency giving CIS the form of a confederation, yet, the CIS states were reluctant to confer it with anymore powers presuming a threat to their (CIS states') national sovereignty. Not only that, the second group was against signing of any closer political-military agreements and deeply engaging in economic matters. Hence, the loophole lied somewhere here (Kembayev 2009).

- Fifth, CIS attempt to create joint armed forces was a total failure. Moreover, trying to build CIS in the lines of a common geostrategic space also met with limited success. The reason lies behind the limited cooperation of all the CIS member states. It is necessary to mention here that only seven of the CIS countries at present nurture a close relationship in terms of military-political and economic integration. These are Russia, Armenia, Belarus, Tajikistan, Uzbekistan, Kazakhstan and Kyrgyzstan (Ibid.: 91).

• Sixth, although after the decline of the old Rouble zone, the CIS states tried to build up an Economic Union on a new market economy basis, calling for the establishment of trade unions, a customs union, a monetary union and a common market for goods, services, capital and labour keeping the Treaty of 1993 as their basis, yet, all of these remained highly only on paper and very less was actually practically executed. One of the impediments here was Ukraine which despite several attempts by Russia did not sign the CIS charter and become a full member of the would-be Economic Union. Meanwhile, Russia became engrossed in dealing its own problem of state building and economic transition issues.

• Seventh, another reason why the CIS states were not that successful in harbouring a closer integration is that although these states were aware of the need of interdependence among themselves in matters of economy and security, yet these states were apprehensive about a new kind of Russian centralism and hegemony. Not only that, it was also seen that most of the CIS states lacked the respect for 'rule of law'. This was evident from their ignoring of their respective constitutional provisions. Moreover, with the emergence of internal decision-making norms such as the 'dissent norm'—whereby members are free to ignore any collective CIS decision—it has not proven possible to construct a consensus agenda of issues, let alone adopt binding policy responses (Willerton and Beznosov 2007).

• Eight, the failure to establish an effective judicial organ is another reason behind the ineffectiveness of the CIS. It would have been an effective body to ensure that community laws and norms are correctly interpreted and applied. CIS should have taken this example from the European Court of Justice.

• Finally, in terms of strengthening the integration process in CIS, efforts in general were unsatisfactory. The bilateral terms of various CIS states with each other were not satisfactory. As the Russian Foreign Minister Ivanov told in 2001: *"The entire history of the creation of various integration structures shows that without a solid bilateral base of relations, it is difficult to come to multilateral forms of cooperation. For any form of multilateral cooperation presupposes delegation of a part, insignificant perhaps, but still a part of sovereignty to multilateral agencies…We will actively develop bilateral ties, and as these grow stronger, the possibilities will broaden for multilateral cooperation within CIS as well".* (Latawski 2001)

Smaller organisations like GUAM (consisting of Azerbaijan, Georgia, Moldova and Ukraine) were created within groups. It displayed the act of 'group-ism' within groups. Thus, it has been seen that though the CIS had helped in a smooth handling of the breakup of the Soviet Union. Yet, a decade after its formation, it has accomplished little with a minimal mandate, and extremely limited resources. It lacks achievements in matters of external threat.

5.11   Analysis of Russia's Foreign Security Policy in the Post-Soviet Space

This part of the chapter will discuss about Russia's engagements with its closest geographical, political, economic and social neighbours. It will showcase a descriptive analysis of the various foreign policy strategies from the time Putin came to power. It will further deal with different sub-regional security complexes and their relations with Russia. These different sub-regional security complexes are as follows:

- The European security sub-regional complex consisting of Ukraine, Belarus and Moldova.
- The Caucasus security sub-regional complex consisting of Armenia, Azerbaijan and Georgia.
- The Central Asian security sub-regional complex consisting of Kazakhstan, Uzbekistan, Tajikistan, Kyrgyzstan and Turkmenistan.

The Russian vision behind engaging with each and every state of the post-Soviet space is that Russia wants to restore a strong Russian presence in the post-Soviet space and to further restrict the penetration of the so-called external powers especially the US, NATO, EU and the Western Europe on common. In order to learn as to how far Russia has succeeded in its attempt to grab its interest in the post-Soviet space, could be analysed from the following study of its relations with all the different states of the post-Soviet space.

- **The European Security Sub-Regional Complex**
    This European sub-regional complex comprises of three states. These are two Slavic states of Ukraine and Belarus and one small non-Slavic state with special status that is Moldova. Let us examine the relation of Russia with each of these states. This sub-complex has been the special interest of NATO and the US (Nygren 2008: 47).

– *Russia and Ukraine:*

Russia-Ukraine relations have been changing at a sweeping pace since the year 2000, or to say since Putin presidency. Putin tried to resolve economic disputes relating to oil and gas deliveries, pipelines and trade-agreements; and considering the political problems, the issues of border delimitations and demarcations was handled tactfully. In the politico-military arena, the strategic conflict over relations to NATO was defused in the aftermath of the incident of 9/11, and the former conflict over the *Black Sea Fleet* (BSF) and the naval facilities generated some military cooperation. *"Russia and Ukraine's dispute over the Black Sea Fleet needs to be understood as a struggle for control over a historic symbol of national identity, nuclear weapons dispute, as a struggle for sovereignty in relation to the post-Soviet security."* The dispute between Ukraine and Russia over the ownership of the BSF started with the dissolution of the Soviet Union. The dispute centres on Ukraine's claim to the Fleet and the Fleet Command's assertion that, in order for the BSF to be included in the Joint Armed Forces and be considered a strategic component of the Former Soviet Navy, it had to be defined as such under the terms of the CIS agreements. The significance of the Black Sea region as a military theatre decreased after the Cold War, but perceptions of the region's growing economic and geopolitical importance also played a significant role in this conflict. Russian analysts highlighted worries over the growth of Turkish naval presence in the Black Sea and consequent US naval action in the area during the Fleet dispute period. After the Orange Revolution, however, ties between Russia and Ukraine deteriorated, and the newly elected Ukrainian government criticised the Russian BSF's presence there before declaring that it was unlikely that the basing agreement would be extended past 2017. When Ukrainian officials seized control of the Yalta lighthouse, which both Russia and Ukraine claimed was theirs by virtue of the 1997 treaty, the conflict took a sharp turn once more in January 2006 (Deyermond 2008).

But according to CSTO Secretary General Nikolay Bordyuzha, discussions over extending the agreement on the Black Sea Fleet facility in the Crimea after 2017 are required. Security for both Russia and Ukraine is provided by the Black Sea Fleet facility in Sevastopol. It is obvious that stationing the Fleet there is expedient. Bordyuzha stated that it is imperative to talk about extending the current accord. He said that in the event that Ukraine does not renew the agreement, we would take additional actions that will allow us to maintain the Russian Navy's defensive capabilities in the Black Sea region (Bordyuzha 2011).

Moving towards the politico-economic arena, the crucial gas and oil transit issues and the joint production of military and civilian technologies were soon to be taken care of. Yet, the biggest threat to Ukraine was that of energy dependency on Russia. But after the presidential elections in Ukraine in 2004 which brought a new Ukrainian president after the 'orange revolution', this happy reunion of the two largest former Soviet republics was but bound to change. The energy brawl in December 2005 to January 2006 was evidently the display of Russian economic imperialism and Ukraine's energy dependence on Russia and the continuing conflict between the two. However, in the next few years Russia-Ukraine relations would depend upon the clash of interests concerning the interest of the West as well (Ibid.: 64–65).

– *Russia and Belarus:*

Belarus has been the closest of Russia's CIS neighbours (Ibid.: 66). Putin demands for economic integration with Belarus which would mean a privatisation of Belarusian economy; the prime interest of Russia being the energy and pipeline sector. However, since the 2004–2005 "colour revolution" attempts of the democratisation drives of the West, Putin and Lukashenka has kept their personal adverse relationship aside and since then the military-defence cooperation have started to flourish. Russia and Belarus now constitute the closest military ties in the post-Soviet space.

There are still certain unresolved issues between the two, yet the strategic military integration cannot be overlooked which is a very positive aspect of Russia-Belarus relationship (Ibid.: 80–81).

– *Russia and Moldova:*

Since the disintegration of the Soviet Union, Russia and Moldova had a strained relation. The fact that there have been no presidential visits to Moldova until 2000, throws light on their difficult relations. There was a general unwillingness on the part of the Russians especially on the military side to fix onto the 1999 agreement of the Istanbul OSCE summit on the withdrawal of Russian troops and weapons from Transdneister. The major controversy under Putin has been the actual status of Transdneister within Moldova. Apart from that another point of conflict between Russia and Moldova is regarding the latter's relation with the CIS; of Moldova not joining the integration tool of CIS that is the SES and also with respect to Moldova's equations with Romania, EU and NATO. There has also been a talk of NATO membership to Moldova after the 2005 elections. Hence Russia-Moldova relations can be defined as of being complicated and disturbed (Ibid.: 99–100).

• **The Caucasus Security Sub-Complex**

Caucasus could be defined as a sub-region of various other regional security complexes like the greater or the 'super' Middle East regional security complex or other sub-complex like the Caucasus/Caspian Sea/ Black Sea sub-complex, but also it can be regarded as a regional sub-complex in its own right (Buzan 2003). Hence the security of the Caucasus region is strongly interlinked with Russia and the three former Soviet republics of Georgia, Armenia and Azerbaijan. Conflicts in the Caucasus are age-old and frozen in nature and since the demise of the Soviet Union; it has been a constant problem for Russia (Nygren 2008: 101).

During the years of President Yeltsin, this sub-region saw one interstate war between Armenia and Azerbaijan over Nagorno Karabakh region located within the borders of Azerbaijan, two secessionist civil wars - in Abkhazia and in South Ossetia and also a few new ethnicity-based aspects to boost up problems in the greater Caucasus (misplaced peoples in Dagestan and the two Chechen wars and its spill over effects to other parts of the Caucasus). Hence the Yeltsin era of Russia-Caucasus relations were full of developments outside the control of state authorities (Coppieters 1998: 56).

Putin's period had started with all the footprints of Yeltsin's era of negligence especially in case of Chechnya. Putin's attempts in refining the relations between South Caucasian states imply the direct and indirect connection of Russia with Chechnya always. Russia and Chechnya have had always conflicts regarding the approaches of both the countries and the wider international community. While Russia blames Chechnya for breeding international terrorism (since the suggestion of 9/11), the Western criticism of Russia goes against Russian human rights abuses in Chechnya (Nygren 2008: 108). However the September 11, 2001 incidents did pace up Russian-Caucasian relations by trying to forget the unresolved disputes and working together for the call of the hour. In fact, in the CIS Summit in December 2001, Putin met the three Caucasus Presidents separately to discuss regional conflicts and security issues (Ibid.: 103).

– Russia and Azerbaijan:

Russia and Azerbaijan have had tense relations since 1992 due to Russia's partial support to Armenia in the Nagorno-Karabakh conflict by helping Armenia with military assistance (RFE/RL 2001). It was only after January 2001 that Russia's relations with Azerbaijan started improving basically after the high-profile visit of Putin to Azerbaijan. Most importantly Azeri president Heider Aliev remarked, "We have reached mutual agreement on all the questions we have discussed, and this gives me great satisfaction... (Ibid.)" It was the start of what Putin exclaimed "the start of a new phase" (RFE/RL 2001). Another most important example of improving relations between Russia and Azerbaijan was the maturity shown in handling the issues relating to Chechnya. The bilateral relations between these countries were not affected. Slowly military cooperation also followed the general improvement of relations. Hence, Russian-Azeri relations impeccably altered when Putin came to power. The bilateral relations improved not only in the politico-military arena but also in the economic arena as well. It has to be borne in mind that in spite of the fact that Russia improved its relations with Azerbaijan yet it always maintained a balance between all the other Caucasian states, hence no complaints from Armenia also (Nygren 2008: 113).

– *Russia and Georgia:*

From the very onset of Yeltsin's reign in Russia, Georgia became Russia's foreign policy and strategic problem in the Caucasus. In fact, Russia-Georgia relationship is one of the very few bilateral relations that have declined since Putin came to power. Moreover, the relations were affected by a numerous other reason like the ongoing oil and gas race to the Caspian Sea, the new Chechnya war, the general political and economic instability of the region etc. Not only has that, the September 11, 2001 atmosphere furthered aggravated Russia's aggressive attitude towards the problem of Pankisi Gorge (Ibid.: 119). In August 2008, Russia fought and won a five-day war against Georgia. Russia's warfare against Georgia was part and parcel of Moscow's security politics (Haas 2010: 135).

In case of Abkhazia and South Ossetia, Putin's second term was of no easily negotiated solution. The Russian peacekeeping forces installed in Abkhazia and South Ossetia though had a stabilising effect but yet the confusion of relations didn't stop escalating. Russia's relations with Georgia have all the components of old nationalist, ethnic, religious and political conflicts mixed with a dose of hegemonic global and regional great power involvement and international terrorism (Nygren 2008: 152–153).

• The Central Asian Security Sub-Regional Complex

Central Asia as a distinct region is both old and new and has in large parts until quite recently been inhabited mainly with nomadic peoples (Olcott 2001). Today, Central Asia is a distinct sub-regional complex in the Russia-centred sub-regional complex developed at the very beginning of 1992. Central Asia is geographically placed in the part of Asia and the greater Middle East part. Central Asia comprises of five states, these are Kazakhstan, Uzbekistan, Tajikistan, Kyrgyzstan and Turkmenistan. It's a region of weak states and weak powers with weak national and ethnic identities (Buzan and Waever 2003: 23).

The outer borders of Central Asia have been guarded by Russian border troop since 1991. The borders are generally not demarcated and delimited (Nygren 2008: 162).

Initially, in the very early years of the collapse of the Soviet Union, Russia was not very interested in this region. Greater attention to the Central Asian region was placed during the Putin presidency. Anti-terrorism was the new dimension to Russian foreign policy towards Central Asia (Jonson 2004).

Russian interests today in Central Asia are mainly for its security and energy. Central Asia is rich in oil, gas and water resources. Regarding security problems in Central Asia, it displays all the features of a weak state— corruption, drug trafficking, human trafficking, smuggling, terrorism and extremism.

Until September 11, 2001 only Russia and China were the main actors in the Central Asian sub-regional complex but after the 9/11 attacks US made its visible presence in this region. This US engagement further ignited Russia's role and presence in the Central Asian region. There is also harder security issues mostly covered in the veil of anti-terrorism activities. One example of it is the Kant Air base in Kyrgyzstan where a rapid-reaction force has been based since 2001 and here Russia has stationed a smaller contingent of fighter aircraft and helicopters under the CST framework. The Collective Security Treaty (CST) is an important instrument for integration in the region (Nygren 2008: 163–164). Russian integration process in the post-Soviet space can be seen in the form of actions taken under the CSTO, SCO framework.

Hence, post September 11, 2001, the Central Asian region has been both an object and subject of the larger international and world politics.

– *The Caspian Sea Basin:*

Politics rather than economics dominated the interests of great powers in the Caspian Sea region in the Yeltsin era, although geo-economics and geo-politics are interwoven in the Caspian Sea region (Blank 2010). The geopolitics of oil, gas and pipelines is of utmost complexities in the Caspian Sea region. Russia has been taking active part in this game; in fact, oil and gas pipelines in the former Soviet space have been seen as a fabric through which the former Soviet Union is still being preserved (RFE/RL 2001).

Russia's interests in the Caspian Sea are still as much related to strategy as to energy (RFE/RL 2002). The Caspian Sea, the Caucasus and the Black Sea regions are closely interlocked regarding oil, gas production and transportation. Since Putin came to power, he tried to develop good relations with the neighbouring oil and gas exporters that would fasten them to Russian pipelines. Putin made it very clear and sought to strengthen Russia's position in the Caspian Sea and also defend it. Even after '9/11 terrorist attacks', Russia used this terrorist threat as a point to defend the Caspian Sean region and to not demilitarise (Ibid.).

However, in this region, the *Baku–Tbilisi–Ceyhan* oil pipeline (BTC) (Nygren 2008) has been the most controversial which starts from the Azeri oil fields in the Caspian Sea via Tbilisi in Georgia and crossing the Turkish heartland to the south to the Mediterranean port of Ceyhan, all bypassing Russia Ibid.).

– *Russia and Kazakhstan:*

Russia-Kazakhstan relations have been fairly smooth since the demise of the Soviet Union. In October 2002, Russia upgraded its relations with Kazakhstan to the level of being strategic partners and termed Kazakhstan as Russia's 'closest and most consistent ally (RFE/RL 2008).' Russia and Kazakhstan relations actually started accentuating only in the year 2005 when as many as ten summits took place between Kazakh president Nursultan Nazarbayev and former Russian president Putin. In fact, in 2006, Nazarbayev termed the Russia-Kazakhstan relation as the "most effective model for bilateral cooperation in CIS", to which Putin called Kazakhstan "one of the most consistent supporters of the integration process in the post-Soviet space (RFE/RL 2006)." Again in April 2006, Nazarbayev complimented Russia as the "locomotive of all integration processes in the post-Soviet area (RFE/RL 2006)."

In the defence and security sector, Russia and Kazakhstan had undisputed issues in their relationship. Russia has been the most reliable partner in this region (RFE/RL 1997). In fact in May 2006 Kazakh president Nazarbayev exclaimed that Russia and Kazakhstan were "fated by history itself to be eternal friends (RFE/RL 2006)."

– *Russia and Kyrgyzstan:*

Kyrgyzstan has been very much dependent on Russia since the demise of the Soviet Union in economic, security and defence field. Kyrgyzstan has also been in the gambit of direct Islamic fundamentalist aggression. Hence, Russia's support is indispensable for Kyrgyzstan. Against Russia's agreement on taking care of Kyrgyzstan's security, it wants Kyrgyzstan to work towards evicting the US airbase in Manas settled in there for operations in Afghanistan since September 2001 (Nygren 2008). In fact, Kyrgyzstan's president Atambayev told visiting US officials that all foreign troops must be withdrawn from the Manas international airport in 2014. It has been understood that this new statement of Atambayev came ahead of his visit to Moscow. Over the past 18 months from 2012, Kyrgyzstan has received more than $100 million in aid from Russia. Kyrgyzstan is also a member of the Russian-led Collective Security Treaty Organisation (The Hindu 2012).

– *Russia and Tajikistan:*

Regarding relations between Russia and Tajikistan, although Russia was indifferent to almost all the Central Asian states yet Tajikistan was a sole exception (Jackson 2003: 144). Russia and Tajikistan signed a friendship, cooperation and assistance agreement in May 1993 (Ibid.). Russia was a major supporter of Tajik Communist party leader Rakhmonov during the civil war crises. In fact, Rakhmonov came to power with the assistance of Russia. Tajikistan is the only CIS country without an army of its own. Therefore, even during the Tajik civil war, the pilots were Russian and the Russian 201st motorised division fought on behalf of the Tajik central Government (Nygren 2008: 189).

Tajikistan having to share its long and porous border with the volatile Afghanistan has numerous sorts of soft security threats. Tajikistan has been most influenced by developments in Afghanistan since the Taliban came to power in 1996. For all of these reasons Tajikistan has been dependent on Russia for its security (OMRI DD 1996).

– *Russia and Turkmenistan:*

Turkmenistan adopted the neutral status in the year 1993 and subsequently ended the border cooperation with Russia in the year 1999 (Jonson 2004). Turkmenistan keeps itself isolated from the other CIS states. Although it is a member of the CIS but it is not very active and moreover Turkmenistan is not a member of the Collective Security Treaty (CST). Turkmenistan has hence a different attitude towards Russia and other CIS states. It has been almost independent of Russian influence in its economic and security aspects. So, even if in the future some prospects of Russia-Turkmenistan show up it is apprehended to be moderate (Ibid.).

5.12   CONCLUSION

Priority areas of Russian foreign policy have always included the development of bilateral and multilateral cooperation with the CIS Member States, even though the new Russian policy in the post-Soviet space is dependent on five fundamental factors, including: the threat of terrorism and separatism; the building of Putin's vertical structure and concentration of power; economic growth in Russia; and international developments. Russia's top priority has remained strengthening the CIS as a foundation for improving regional interaction among its members, who not only have a shared historical background but also have a considerable capacity for integration in several fields, including security. In order to ensure mutual security, Russia plans to strengthen ties with the CIS Member States. This will involve working together to tackle common issues and threats, chief among them being transnational crime, international terrorism, extremism, drug trafficking, and illegal migration. Here, preventing the destabilisation of the situation in Central Asia and Transcaucasia as well as eliminating the aforementioned dangers emanating from Afghanistan's territory are priorities. Russia views the Collective Security Treaty Organisation (CSTO) as a fundamental component of the contemporary security framework in the post-Soviet era. The mission of turning the CSTO into an all-encompassing international organisation that can combat contemporary threats and problems in the region under its purview and the mounting pressure of various global and regional elements remains top most priority of Russia with regard to CSTO.

As a result, Russia consistently works to advance the CSTO as a vital tool for upholding security and stability in the Organization's sphere of influence, with a particular emphasis on strengthening the organization's capacity for peacekeeping, its quick response mechanisms, and the coordination of foreign policy among CSTO member states.

REFERENCES

Averre, Derek L. 2003. Transborder Security and Regionalism. In *Russian Regions and Regionalism: Strength through weakness*, ed. Graeme P. Herd and A. Aldis, 63. USA and Canada: Routledge Curzon.

Beijing Declaration by the Peoples Republic of China and the Russian Federation of 18 July 2000 [Online Web]. Accessed September10, 2013. http://www.discerningtoday.org/members/beijing_declaration.html.

Blank, S. 2010. International Rivalries in Eurasia. In *Key Players and Regional Dynamics in Eurasia: The Return of the Great Game*, ed. Maria Raquel Friere and Roger E. Kanet, 136–138. UK and US: Palgrave Macmillan.

Bordyuzha, Nikolay. 2011. Transnational Threats and Challenges: Strengthening the Coherence of the OSCE Response and Interaction with Other International Actors. Speech Delivered on 30th June, 2011 at the 2011 Annual Security Review Conference: Vienna.

Buzan, Berry, and Ole Waever. 2003. *Regions and Powers: The Structure of International Security*. Cambridge University Press.

Coppieters, B. 1998. Introduction, in Coppieters, B., Nodia, G., & Anchabadze, Y. (Eds.). Georgians and Abkhazians: the search for a peace settlement (Sonderveröffentlichung / BIOst, Okt. 1998). Köln: Bundesinstitut für ostwissenschaftliche und internationale Studien. https://nbn-resolving.org/urn:nbn:de:0168-ssoar-4438.

Deyermond, R. 2008. *Security and Sovereignty in the Former Soviet Union*, 102–110. Colorado and London: Lynne Rienner Publishers. Inc.

Friere, Maria R. and Roger E. Kanet. 2010. Russia in Eurasia: External Players and Regional Dynamics. In *Key Players and Regional Dynamics in Eurasia: The Return of the Great Game*, ed. Maria Raquel Friere and Roger E. Kanet. London: Palgrave Macmillan UK. https://doi.org/10.1057/978023 0290754.

Haas, Marcel De. 2010. *Russia's Foreign Security Policy in the 21st Century: Putin, Medvedev and Beyond*, 3. USA and Canada: Routledge. https://www.routledge.com/Russias-Foreign-Security-Policy-in-the-21st-Century-Putin-Medvedev-and-Beyond/DeHaas/p/book/9780415681933.

Herd, Graeme P. 2003. Russia's Demographic Crisis and Federal Instability. In *Russian Regions and Regionalism: Strength Through Weakness*, ed. Graeme P. Herd and A. Aldis. USA and Canada: Routledge Curzon.

Isakova, Irina. 2005. *Russian Governance in the Twenty-first Century: Geo-Strategy, Geopolitics and Governance*, 15–16. New York: Frank Cass.

Jackson, N.J. 2003. *Russian Foreign Policy and the CIS. Theories, Debates and Actions*, 144. London: Routledge.

Jonson, Leena. 2004. *Vladimir Putin and Central Asia. The Shaping of Russian Foreign Policy*, 63–67. London, New York: I.B. Taurus.

Kembayev, Zhenis. 2009. *Legal Aspects of the Regional Integration Processes in the Post-Soviet Area*, 72–74. Verlag Berlin Heidelberg: Springer.

Kuzio, T. 2000. Geopolitical Pluralism in the CIS: The Emergence of GUUAM. *European Security* 9 (2): 104–106.

Latawski, P.C. 2001. The Limits of Diversity in the Post-Soviet Space: CIS and GUUAM. Accessed March 21, 2012. http://www.google.co.in/url?sa=t&rct=j&q=&esrc=s&source=web&cd=1&ved=0CCkQFjAA&url=http%3A%2F%2Fwww.da.mod.uk%2Fcolleges%2Farag%2Fdocumentlistings%2Fcee%2Fg93%2FG93.chap18%2F&ei=T7Ur76HIiSrgerz4CoDw&usg=AFQjCNGjwIJI-ubbeV8NCPPaZlg99FtgYg&bvm=bv.51773540d.bmk.

Lavrov, Sergey. 2007. Speech by Russian Minister of Foreign Affairs Sergey Lavrov at SCO Council of Foreign Ministers Meeting, Bishkek, July 9, 2007, available at: http://www.mid.ru/brp_4.nsf/0/6348382D9C12B077C3257314001B98B8.

Legvold, R. 2009. The Role of Multilateralism in Russian Foreign Policy. In *The Multilateral Dimension in Russian Foreign Policy*, ed. Elana Wilson Rowe and Stina Torjesen. USA and Canada: Routledge.

Libman, Alexander. 2007. Regionalization and Regionalism in the Post-Soviet Space: Current Status and Implications for Institutional Development. *Europe-Asia Studies* 59 (3): 401–430.

Lo, Bobo. 2002. *Russian Foreign Policy in the Post-Soviet Era: Reality, Illusion and Mythmaking*. New York: Palgrave Macmillan.

Mankoff, Jeffrey. 2009. *Russian Foreign Policy: Return of the Great Power Politics*. New York: Rowman & Littlefield Publishers, Inc. https://rowman.com/ISBN/9781442208254/Russian-Foreign-Policy-The-Return-of-Great-Power-Politics-Second-Edition.

Markedonov, Sergei. 2010. Post-Soviet Integration: CST, CSTO, CRRF etc [Online Web]. Accessed March 25, 2012. http://www.opendemocracy.net/od-russia/sergei-markedonov/post-soviet-integration-cst-csto-crrf-etc-2.

Mishra, A. 2007. *Security in New Russia*, 215–216. Delhi: Kalpaz Publications.

Nygren, Bertil. 2008. *The Rebuilding of Greater Russia: Putin's Foreign Policy Towards the CIS Countries*. Routledge & CRC Press. https://www.routledge.com/The-Rebuilding-of-Greater-Russia-Putins-Foreign-Policy-Towards-the-CIS-Countries/Nygren/p/book/9780415590457.

Olcott, Martha Brill. 2001. Revisiting the Twelve Myths of Central Asia. Working Paper. Russian and Eurasian Program. Carnegie Endowment for International Peace. Sep. 1, 2001. Available at: https://www.jstor.org/stable/resrep1273.

OMRI DD. 1996. *OMRI DD*. January 31.

Peter J.S. Duncan. 2001. Westernism, Eurasianism and Pragmatism: Foreign Policies of the Post-Soviet States, 1991–2001. Working Paper Prepared for the Conference 'Ten Years Since the Soviet Union', SSEES, University College London, November 9–10.

Presidential Decree. 1995. *Russia's Strategic Course in its Relations with the States-Participants of the Commonwealth of Independent States*. September 14.

RFE/RL. 1997. *Newsline*. October 31.

RFE/RL. 2001. *Caucasus Report*. January 11.

RFE/RL. 2006. *Newsline*. January 13.

RFE/RL. 2006. *Newsline*, April 5.

RFE/RL. 2006. *Newsline*. May 9.

RFE/RL. 2008. *Newsline*.

Rozanov, Anatolij Arkad′evič, Elena F. Dovgan', and Anatolij Arkad′evič Rozanov. 2010. *Collective Security Treaty Organisation: 2002–2009*. DCAF Regional Programmes Series 6. Geneva: Geneva Centre for the Democratic Control of Armed Forces (DCAF).

Sakwa, R. 2010. Senseless Dreams and Small Steps: The CIS and CSTO Between Integration and Cooperation. In *Key Players and Regional Dynamics in Eurasia: The Return of the Great Game*, ed. Maria Raquel Friere and Roger E. Kanet, 379–415. UK and US: Palgrave Macmillan.

Selezneva, L. 2003. Post-Soviet Russian Foreign Policy: Between Doctrine and Pragmatism. In *Realignments in Russian Foreign Policy*, ed. Rick Fawn, 10–27. London and Portland: Frank Cass & Co. Ltd.

Smith, Martin A. 2006. *Russia and NATO Since 1991: From Cold War Through Cold Peace to Partnership?* New York: Routledge. https://www.routledge.com/Russia-and-NATO-since-1991-From-Cold-War-Through-Cold-Peace-to-Partnership/Smith/p/book/9780415498937.

Swanström, Niklas. 2010. Traditional and Non-traditional Security Threats in Central Asia: Connecting the New and the Old. *The China and Eurasia Forum Quarterly*. August 8.

The Hindu. 2012. *The Hindu*. February 21.

Vinokurov, Evgeny. 2007. Russian Approaches to Integration in the Post-Soviet Space in the 2000s. In *The CIS, the EU and Russia: Challenges of Integration*, ed. Katlijn Malfiet, Lien Verspoest, and Evgeny Vinokurov, 3–4. New York: Palgrave Macmillan.

Voitovich, Sergei A. 1993. The Commonwealth of Independent States: An Emerging Institutional Model [Online: Web]. Accessed May 14, 2012. https://ejil.org/pdfs/4/1/1211.pdf.

Wieclawski, J. 2011. Russian Foreign Policy: Sources and Implications. *International Journal*. 66 (2): 522.

Willerton, John p. and Mikhail A. Beznosov. 2007. Russia's Pursuit of its Eurasian Security Interests: Weighing the CIS and Alternative Bilateral-Multilateral Arrangements. In *The CIS, the EU and Russia: Challenges of Integration*, ed. Katlijn Malfiet, Lien Verspoest, and Evgeny Vinokurov, 54–56. New York: Palgrave Macmillan.

Willerton, John P. and Cockerham G. 2003. Russia, the CIS and Eurasian Interconnections. In *Limiting Institutions? The Challenge of Eurasian Security Governance*, ed. James Sperling, Sean Kay, and S. Victor Papascoma, 187. Manchester and New York: Manchester University Press. https://doi.org/10.7228/manchester/9780719066047.

CHAPTER 6

CSTO: Structures, Activities and Role in Maintaining Collective Security in the Post-Soviet Space

Abstract This chapter will focus on the security integration process of the post-Soviet space in general and that of the role of CSTO in particular. The chapter will be a descriptive analysis of the creation and evolution of the CSTO and the legal basis of its foundation. It will also lay down an analysis of the successes and failures of this Russian-led organisation in countering the soft and hard security threats of the post-Soviet space.

Keywords CSTO · Security integration · Post-Soviet space · Structures and activities

6.1 INTRODUCTION

One of the traditional principles of Russian security policy is its insufficient want and desire for security. This thing gets expressed itself in expansion and buffer zones since the days of the Soviet Union. Collective security arrangement at that time existed in the form of the Warsaw Pact. Nowadays this feature of Russia is seen in its collective security integration in the shape of the Russian-led military cooperation in the CSTO as well as with China in the Shanghai Cooperation Organisation (SCO) (Haas 2010: 3).

The pursuit of integration process in the post-Soviet space is not just about institutions but also about ideas and vision that the region is some sort of political community. Though the Commonwealth of Independent states (CIS) lacks the internal drive for development, the CSTO does show some coherent qualities with continued development. The only disadvantage with the CSTO is that it has a relatively restricted command with only seven members till very recently. The members are Russia, Armenia, Belarus, Kazakhstan, Kyrgyzstan, Uzbekistan and Tajikistan. Whatsoever, the CSTO indicates a small step towards the genuine way for the development of a strong and dynamic integration process in the post-Soviet space (Sakwa 2010: 195). In fact, on May 2008, Russian president Dmitri Medvedev stated that strengthening Russia's ties with other former Soviet Republics would be the leading concern for his presidency and in fact his first foreign visit was to Kazakhstan (Moscow Times 2008).

6.2   Russia's Aims Towards Integration Process in the Post-Soviet Space

Russia always had the drive to create something in consonant with the Russia Empire or the Soviet Union. It was a drive to maintaining stability in the region as a vital element to its national interest and the draft 'Basic Provisions of the Concept of the Foreign Policy of the Russian Federation' in December 1992 insisted that the creation of a "*belt of good-neighbourliness*" was Russia's primary goal. Putin's presidency saw two main concerns:

- Focus on strengthening internal hierarchy within Russia.
- Attempt to make Russia the system forming power or *Ordnungsmatch* in the CIS.

Earlier, relations with CIS member states were complex. Hence Putin came about with the development of sub-regional organisations like the CSTO whereby Russia could take the lead and bind its allies to itself. As Buzan and Waever explain, "*the aim here was to give an institutional form to the creation of a regional security complex* (Sakwa 2010)." This would also help Russia pursue its broader goals of notable opposition to the North Atlantic Treaty Organisation (NATO) to prevent the latter's extension into the post-Soviet space. New forms of potential integration in the post-Soviet Eurasia remain possible though in certain respects, the existing level of association might be difficult to maintain. Therefore, the question of concern remains whether Russia while going on for a collective integration would be able to count on the support of its neighbours and which of the countries could be used against Russia and which of them could be the potential strategic partners.

In the post-Soviet era, regional integration has been limited. It has been sensed that economic integration has not become very effective while security integration has been rather more effective and productive. Security integration has aimed to boost up the power of leaderships in the region and hence have developed in a more profound manner (Collins 2009).

A very important key feature of Russian foreign policy is the aspect of multilateralism. Both Boris Yeltsin and Vladimir Putin sincerely professed deep connection to the principle of multilateralism in foreign policy of Russia. Moreover, another feature of Putin presidency that is energy politics also shapes Russia's engagement in multilateral institutions. Regional multilateral initiatives like CSTO and SCO can be treated as exhibitions of the concept of multilateralism (Torjesen 2009).

Russia's engagements with the former Soviet countries reap reciprocal benefits in these relationships between equals. Though Russia does have a dominant role in the region yet beneficial outcomes have yielded both for Russia and the other post-Soviet states. The Russian leadership credits international importance to the idea of Russia being "*one of the largest Eurasian powers...... [which] predetermines Russia's responsibility for maintaining security in the world on both global and regional levels* (ibid.: 76)."

- **The key characteristics of Russia's multilateral engagement in the post-Soviet space includes:**

    - The significance of Russian influence/dominance in the former Soviet space as an instrument for enhancing great power status globally.
    - An increasingly ambitious and pragmatic engagement in the 'near abroad'.

- Efforts to balance the introduction of market principles with the perceived imperative to establish Russian leadership.
- A reactive and competitive regional multilateralism against 'Western' multilateral arrangements.
- Limits to Russian institutional power that result in multilateral efforts supported by bilateralism and informal relationships between heads of state in the region (ibid.: 14–15).

Basically, three multilateral institutions largely serve towards legitimising Russia's foothold in the post-Soviet region. These institutions are the CIS, the Eurasian Economic Community (EEC) and the CSTO. While the EEC institutionalises the economic alliance of Russia with Central Asian states, the CSTO institutionalises security alliance of Russia in the post-Soviet space (Legvold 2009: 55). The Collective Security Treaty and its successor the CSTO has been a concrete step by Russia towards a mutual security arrangement. It may be defined as a collective action agency intended to deal with thematic threat like terrorism, but being a military organisation, it points outward and addresses to threats originating beyond the borders of its members. It is often treated as a counterpart to NATO (ibid.).

6.3   THE COLLECTIVE SECURITY
TREATY ORGANISATION (CSTO)

Security relation is an arena where Russia has been relatively powerful and successful. Russia's military might have been profound worldwide and alliances and multilateral security cooperation constitute Russia's military genius. The development of Russia-led security organisation, CSTO was set up in the 1990s to address the emerging regional security needs. A key intention of Russia's efforts towards security integration through CSTO was its desire to secure the military dependability of the states of post-Soviet space. The aim was to create a 'security belt' around the Russian Federation and in this way, maintain Moscow's hegemonic presence on the Eurasian continent. Russian analyst A. Hramchihin states that, "*Russia sees in it one of the rudiments of USSR, which are highly valued in Kremlin on considerations of a purely psychological nature* (Rozanov and Dovgan 2010)."

As a matter of fact, among the various efforts to create a collective security system in the post-Soviet space, the CSTO has been the most successful attempt. It is because CSTO has a clear military dimension. The participating countries of the CSTO have a very different perspective regarding its goals and objectives. The member-states of the Russia-led CSTO are from the three most important strategic routes—the European (Belarus), the Caucasian (Armenia) and the Central Asian (Kazakhstan, Kyrgyzstan, Uzbekistan and Tajikistan). These allies of Russia often perceive Russia as a country that will provide a 'security umbrella' and assist modernisation of arms and weapons on a preferential basis. Basically, these countries like to think of Russia as their security guardian (ibid.).

But it seems that the CSTO would have been a mere 'paper tiger' if not for the CSTO Common Military Force. The military force of CSTO has been increasingly active in the Central Asian region. About 10,000 personnel have been tasked with the responsibility of responding to external threats of the region (Tsygankov 2010). Currently, the CSTO's military component consists of Collective Rapid Deployment Forces, to further include ten battalions (4,000). Russian military experts while commenting on these plans consider that, *"it likely that higher readiness formations contributing to this new structure would remain in the host country on combat readiness status to react to any potential threat from the south* (Gazeta 2012)."

6.4 From CST to CSTO

It was on May 15, 1992 during the Tashkent meeting of the Council of the Heads of States of six CIS countries namely Armenia, Kazakhstan, Kyrgyzstan, Russia, Tajikistan and Uzbekistan, *"taking into account the formation by the states parties of their own armed forces* (CIS 1992)", signed the Treaty on Collective Security also known as the Tashkent treaty.

The prime essence of it constituted the following provisions---
In the case one of the state parties is subjected to an aggression by any state or a group of states, this shall be considered as an aggression against all the state parties of the present Treaty. In the case an act of aggression is directed against any of the state parties, all other state parties shall provide it necessary assistance, including military assistance, and shall also support it by all means available in exercise of the right of collective defence under Article 51 of the Charter of the United Nations. The state parties shall immediately report to the Security Council of the United Nations about the

measures taken in conformity with the present Article. While implementing these measures the state parties shall abide by the relevant provisions of the United Nations Charter. (CIS 1992)

6.4.1   The Specifics of the Collective Security Treaty

Following the disintegration of the Soviet Union when new kind of security threats had to be dealt by the newly independent states along with their own troubles of state-building, the demand of the hour was the finding of a model that could successfully guarantee security to these states. Regarding the military cooperation of the CIS, Anatoily Rozanov cites three developments, "*Multilateral military and military-technical cooperation in the framework of the council of Defence ministers of the CIS member states, Multilateral military, political-military and military-technical cooperation in the framework of the Treaty of Collective Security and Bilateral cooperation in the military field based on bilateral treaties and agreements* (Rozanov and Dovgan 2010: 3)."

The Treaty of Collective Security (TCS) was signed on 15 May, 1992 in Tashkent. Previously it was referred to as the Tashkent Treaty but the name inapt once Uzbekistan in 1999 quit from the Treaty. The initial parties to the Collective Security Treaty were Armenia, Kazakhstan, Kyrgyzstan, Russia, Tajikistan and Uzbekistan. Later members were Azerbaijan (joined on 24 September, 1993), Belarus (joined on 31 December 1993) and Georgia (joined on 9 December 1993) (ibid.). The Collective Security Treaty later renamed the Collective Security Treaty Organisation (CSTO) was set to remain for a 5-year period unless further extended. On April 2, 1999, only six members of the CST signed a protocol renewing the treaty for another five year period except Azerbaijan, Georgia and Uzbekistan. However, in 2005, Uzbekistan withdrew from GUAM and re-joined the CSTO in 2006. However, Uzbekistan very recently withdrew its membership from CSTO for a second time on 28th June 2012. Conceptually, the TCS is of a strictly defensive nature. It gives priority on political basis for dealing with military conflicts. The states, party to the Treaty call for mutual cooperation with each other in the area of international security (ibid.: 5).

- **According to the concept of the TCS, the collective security of the participating states is based on the following main principles:**

- Indivisibility of Security: an aggression against one participating state is aggression against all.
- Parallel and similar responsibility of the participating states in providing security.
- Maintenance of territorial integrity, respect for sovereignty and non-interference in internal affairs.
- Collective nature of the defence, provided on a regional basis.
- Consensus-based decision making on the key issues of providing collective security.
- Correspondence of force organisation and readiness to the scale of military threat. (ibid.)

- **Three main stages of the Collective security system:**

  - Completing the establishment of armed forces of the participating states, developing a programme of military and military cooperation among participating states and starting its implementation, developing and adopting legal acts regulating the functioning of the collective security system.
  - Creating coalition group of forces to repel a possible aggression, introducing related operational planning creating a joint air defence system.
  - Completing the creation of the collective security system (ibid.).

The political and security scenario since the 1990s had started changing drastically. By the end of 1994, the situation in the Caucasus became extremely disturbed. The problem in Chechnya extended and Islamic fundamentalism in Dagestan, victory of Taliban regime in Afghanistan had direct effects in the neighbouring Central Asia. This entire situation demanded an effective action of a collective security system. By 2000–2001, in order to increase the efficiency of the TCS system, reform attempts came about in the form of summits of the TCS Heads of the States.

These summits were as follows:

a. **The Minsk session of the Collective Security Council, 24 May 2000:**
    The important decisions and documents adopted during this session were—

- Memorandum on the efficiency of the TCS of 15 May 1992 and its adaptation to the contemporary geopolitical situation.
- Provision on the procedure for taking and implementing collective decisions for the uses of forces and means of the collective security system.
- On the main principles of the coalition strategy of the states participating in the Treaty on Collective Security of 15 May 1992.
- Model of the regional system of collective security.

It accomplished the task to undertake practical steps in the creation of regional structures in the collective security system and mechanisms for use of multinational forces and means in providing the necessary support to TCS participating states in crisis situation.

b. **The Bishkek session of the Collective Security Council, October 2000:**

It adopted a set of interrelated decisions defining the process of practical creation of components of the collective security system, and the system as a whole. An initiation for the creation of the Central Asian regional forces with the formation of its nucleus limited in scale Collective Rapid Reaction Forces (CRRF) was made. Not only that, it was also decided that a creation of the Central staff body will be made for the interaction among the regional security systems. The parties also signed an 'Agreement on the Status of the Forces of the Collective Security System' and adopted a Plan for the main activities in the creation of the collective security system 2001–2005.

c. **The Yerevan session of the Collective Security Council, May 2001**

The most essential step taken in this session was the signing by the Heads of States of the Protocol on the procedures for creating and functioning of the forces of the collective security system of the participating states of the TCS. The Council's decision was to create an intergovernmental body for military command of the collective security system of the TCS parties. In the year 2001, the TCS parties took practical steps towards the establishment of rapid reaction forces of the Central Asian region of the collective security with 1300 personnel. These forces were adapted to conduct mobile operations and swift occupation for eradication of limited groups of terrorists (ibid.: 10–13).

6.4.2   Creation of the CSTO

By the mid of 2001, there occurred a balance of power shift in the Caspian and the Central Asian region. The US apart from focusing on economic consolidation, became more available as a military-political power by building military bases. Russia's military-political presence was till then in this region mainly through the instruments of TCS and the 201st infantry division stationed in Tajikistan. However, the TCS states did not have the military-technical and financial capacity. Therefore, just after ten years later at the anniversary session of the Collective Security Council on 14 May 2002 in Moscow, TCS was transformed into an international regional organisation namely the Collective Security Treaty Organisation (CSTO). CSTO creation led to not only the strengthening of internal integration of the states but it also gave it an international significance. The CSTO Charter and Agreement on the CSTO legal status entered into force on 18 September 2003. By December 2003 the personnel strength of the CRRF in the Central Asian region increased 2.5 times. The multinational HQ of the armed forces of the member states tasked with operational command and control of the Collective Rapid Reaction Forces began working on January 1, 2004. The CSTO member states also introduced the preferential regime of military technical cooperation. Russia at that time contributed 50% of the financing of all activities in the framework of CSTO, while other five members were to contribute 10% each (ibid.: 13–16). In the CSC session of Minsk on 23 June 2006, the decision to reinstitute Uzbekistan in CSTO was signed (Tyshchenko 2009).

As put by Weinstein, "*if anti-terrorism and suspicion of NATO brought the CSTO powers together, the American invasion of Iraq firmly cemented the CSTO relations on the basis of fear of American power… [and] democracy enforcement*" (Weinstein 2007).

Hence, as Anatoly A. Rozanov cites, "*The CSTO was established on the basis of an international treaty towards the achievement of specific objectives (strengthening peace, international and regional security and stability, collective protection of the independence, territorial integrity and sovereignty of member state), acts in accordance with the principles of international law, has an independent system of bodies and autonomous will, independent of the will of the member states, expressed in the rights to make decisions, including mandatory ones, and to conduct international cooperation activities* (Rozanov and Dovgan 2010: 22)."

- **The documents adopted after the creation of CSTO are:**
  - The decision of the CSTO Collective Security Council *"On the Concept for creating and functioning of the mechanism for the CSTO peacekeeping activity"* of 18 June 2004.
  - Priority directions for the activity of the CSTO in the second half of 2006, approved by a CSC decision of June 2005.
  - Plan for the collective actions of the member states of the CSTO for the application of the UN Global Counter Terrorism Strategy 2008–2012, approved by a CSC decision of 5 September 2009 (ibid.: 25).

6.5   STRUCTURE OF THE CSTO

The following structures function presently in the CSTO—

- Collective Security Council (CSC)
- Council of Foreign Ministers (CFM)
- Council of Defence Ministers (CDM)
- Committee of the Secretaries of the Security Council (CSSC)
- Permanent Council
- CSTO Parliamentary Assembly
- Secretariat
- Supporting bodies of CSTO

6.6   MILITARY-TECHNICAL COMPONENTS OF THE CSTO

The CSTO is in a process to increase its military-technical component. CSTO Secretary-General Nikolai Bordyuzha, revealed plans on the characteristics of the organization stressing on two main objectives: transforming the CSTO into a multi-functional international arrangement which will be better equipped in responding to broader issues that will further contribute in enhancing its military component. The decision was followed by the CSTO summit in Moscow on September 5, 2008 as a result of the 2008 conflict in Georgia. Technically, the CSTO's military component clearly envisages enhancing of the affinity of both management and weaponry with the help of timely joint operations (Bugajski 2010).

The significant step in the military field of the CSTO was the signing of the agreement on the status of the force formations of the collective security system on the main principles of military-technical cooperation, the protocol on the procedures for creating and functioning of the forces of the collective security system of the states participating in TCS, the model of a regional collective security system and the provisions on the procedures for taking and implementing decisions for the use of forces of the collective security system.

The creation of the **Collective Rapid Reaction Forces (CRRF)** in August 2001 was a fundamental step taken towards developing the military component of the CSTO. The CRRF works as a nucleus of the CSTO in the post-Soviet Central Asia and Belarus and Armenia. Military exercises of the CRRF are taking place since 2004 and also include the practising of anti-terrorist task. An anti-drug operation is conducted annually by the name of "Channel" since 2003. Operations for countering illegal migration have been going on since 2006 under "Nelegal CSTO" (Dovgan 2010: 61). Russia's plans for the ten-battalion stronger CSTO Rapid Deployment Force to provide security in the Central Asian region against "threats to sovereignty" will aim to provide for the greater degree of military control in this region, enabling the accumulation of forces during emergency situations. Moreover, Russia also plans to establish an anti-aircraft defence system to sustain the vigour of the forces.

An agreement on the peacekeeping activity of the CSTO was signed on 6 October 2007 at the Dushanbe Session of the Collective Security Council (CSC). It foresees the creation of the CSTO peacekeeping forces (PF) in a permanent basis. According to this agreement, the CSTO member states will act collectively employing military, police and civilian personnel in order to prevent, deter and terminate military activities between states or within a state in the case of intervention by a third country. The decision for conducting a peacekeeping operation on the territory of a CSTO member state will be taken by the Collective Security Council with account for the national legislation and on the basis of an official request. The composition, organisation and personnel strength of the CSTO peacekeeping forces will be determined by an individual decision of the CSC for each operation. The peacekeeping forces are made up of peacekeeping contingents of the CSTO member states. The contingents are trained on the basis of common programmes equipped with common and weapons and communications. They take part in regular joint exercises. Again, on 4 February, 2009 at a session of CSC in Moscow, the heads of states—the members of CSTO decided to create CSTO Collective Operational Reaction Forces (CORF). The signed framework agreement on the CSTO Collective Operational Reaction Forces determines the status, the functioning and the procedure for employing CORF defined in Article 2 of the Agreement. CORF has the main tasks like support in preventing and repealing armed aggression and localising military conflicts, participation in countering international terrorism and transnational organised crime, illegal trafficking of narcotics, strengthening the protection of state borders and sites of key importance on the territories of member states, emergency management and humanitarian assistance. The quantitative parameters of CORF as determined on 14 June 2009 of the CSC Moscow session are as follows— it consists of military contingents of approximately 18,000 total personnel strength and special purpose forces including 1500 officers and staff of the respective structures. Russia assigns to CORF the 98th Guards Airborne Division and the 31st Guards Assault Brigade. Armenia, Belarus, Kazakhstan and Tajikistan contribute one assault brigade each and Kyrgyzstan contributes a reconnaissance company. The special purpose police detachments "Zubr" and "Ryis" from Russia, the special rapid reaction unit from Kyrgyzstan have already been assigned to CORF special purpose forces.

Russia aims that the CSTO has the potential grow into a united military-economic long-term program covering the period until 2015. As Nurshat Ababakirov cites Dmitriy Medvedev, "*the CSTO has a "special mission", and to support it in its early years of operation, it is crucial to develop the organization's military potential.*" Russia is expected to support it with weapons, whereas other member states may provide with fuel, foodstuffs for the force (Nurshat).

6.7   CSTO's Role and Action in various spheres

Secretary General of the CSTO Nikolai Bordyuzha states, "*The Collective Security Treaty Organization (CSTO) is operating in a complex geopolitical environment. In addition to existing challenges and threats, new negative trends have arisen in recent years* (Bordyuzha 2011)."

Lately, the foreign policy component has also come to the forefront. The member states have been closely cooperating on the international arena and on key regional and global issues like countering various challenges already mentioned earlier (Rozanov and Dovgan 2010).

The member states achieved practical coordination and definition of common approaches to issues such as strategic and long-term stability form non-proliferation of weapons of mass destruction and missile technologies, reform of OSCE, post-conflict settlement in Afghanistan, enhancing the efficiency of United Nations etc. (Bordyuzha 2005).

Regarding the case of Afghanistan, the Russian led CSTO is assertively expanding its strategic influence in the region of Central Asia as it is the one which is most affected by the activities that take place in Afghanistan. CSTO has successfully established security relationship with Afghanistan for maintaining a regional air defence system. In 2007, a CSTO working group visited Kabul which led to talks that marked the beginning of 'direct contacts' between CSTO and the Afghan Government. More focus was put on the revival of Islamic radicalism and drug trafficking. The CSTO strongly feels that these security issues need to be resolved. Not only is the CSTO interested to resolve these issues but the Afghan side also is interested and hence look forward train military and law enforcement officers in Russia and purchasing Russian artillery. All these assistances needed for improving the border security of Afghanistan in terms of both personnel and technical training. Regarding the implementation of such security terms, the CSTO created a working group on Afghanistan in 2005 under the auspices of the organisation's Foreign Ministers' Council to strengthen Afghan security institutions and improve anti-trafficking measures. Thereafter, on 14 March, a CSTO statement revealed that the group intends to transform the Channel 2006 anti-drug initiative to check the practice of trafficking out of Afghanistan (Weitz 2008).

As per the foreign policy component of the CSTO, it strengthened since the meeting of ministers of foreign affairs of the CSTO member states on 5 November 2002 that dedicated to discuss about the situation around Iraq. Not only that, implementing CSC decisions, the CSTO member states cooperated and established contacts with the UN, OSCE, SCO and others. Regarding the political dimension of the CSTO, one vital accomplishment is that since 2 December 2004, CSTO has an observer status in the United Nations General Assembly. The Agreement on the CSTO peacekeeping activity came into force on 16 January 2009. CSTO has been repeatedly helping the UN peacekeeping forces through operations in the required area of disturbance, for instance—the participation of CSTO in Afghanistan in the fight against drugs and terrorist activities. On 2 March 2010, the UN General Assembly adopted by consensus a resolution on the "Cooperation between the United Nations Organisation and the Collective Security Treaty Organisation" through which it laid the necessary legal foundation for practical cooperation between the United Nations Organisation and the CSTO (Rozanov and Dovgan 2010).

The challenges in the post-Soviet space are varied and require adequate political response from the CSTO. CSTO hence has developed a well-oiled system of political coordination. For this, it has equipped itself with the necessary military power and the Collective Rapid Reaction Force (CRRF) and its peacekeeping contingent, the East European and Caucasus regional groups of forces and the Central Asian Collective Rapid Deployment Force, amount the organization's military component. The CRRF is a universal tool capable of resolving conflicts of varying degrees of intensity, conducting special operations to crash terrorist attacks and violent extremist action and preventing and responding to emergency situations. The CSTO is making joint efforts to counter new kind of situations to collective security. Instances of some joint operations code named are Kanal, Nalagal and Proxy. Since the 2010 unrest in Kyrgyzstan, the CSTO has improved its crises management capabilities a lot including political monitoring infrastructure to prevent conflicts. If a crisis breaks out in the territory of CSTO, the CSTO has developed and tested a sequence of actions to provide timely logistic and humanitarian aid and information support. The CSTO Head of States informal meeting on 12 August 2011 was held in Astana where Agreements were reached to promote CSTO's solidarity, mutual support and capabilities to protect the constitutional systems, sovereignty and territorial integrity of its members and to use the organisation as an intermediary in resolving bilateral disputes. Proposals are being developed for joint efforts against drug trafficking, terrorism, extremism and other organised crimes. It includes a program to militarise the CRRF by providing military-technical assistance to armed forces, border troops and law enforcement agencies of some CSTO members. Measures are also being developed to improve CSTO's collective response to natural and man-made disasters, and there are proposals for adapting the decision-making process to deal with emergency situations. Hence it has been seen that reforms are continuously being made for the improvement of the collective security system under the CSTO (Bordyuzha 2011).

The CSTO has a minuscule membership of just six members. And each member has unlimited trust in this mechanism, instances of feedback from different member states on the CSTO mechanism speaks so. Bilateral cooperation under the CSTO mechanism has been seen all over. For instance—we can take the examples of cooperation between CSTO and individual members. On December 20, 2011, members of the Collective Security Treaty Organization (CSTO) reached an agreement which deters any member of CSTO to let a foreign country install its military base on the territory of CSTO without unanimous consent of all the members of the CSTO. It also gives Russia the power to veto any foreign country with plans to establish bases in the territory of member countries. Hence, this move empowers Russia's efforts to counter balance the US military presence and influence in its neighbourhood.

CSTO's momentum has been increasing over the past few years. Apart from collective drills, CSTO started conducting sportive competitions among military and non-military personnel. The motive behind was to raise the prestige of military service, nurture patriotism, and promotion of healthy lifestyle. The Russian military defence majorly funds these activities and therefore dominates it thus recalling the Soviet style of supra-national integration.

6.8 Cooperation between CSTO and Individual Member states

We can make case studies of various co operations under the CSTO mechanism, most relations being bilateral.

- **CSTO and Belarus**

Nikolai Bordyuzha on 21 February 2012 at a press conference stated that, *"Belarus has always been traditionally a very active member of the CSTO."* Belarus has forwarded a good number of "very creative proposals" aiming at the improvement of CSTO activity. These proposals include implementation of CSTO collective protection and crisis response mechanisms (Westerlund 2013).

It has been observed that President of Belarus, Alexander Lukashenko is in favour of stepping up military and political cooperation of Belarus and Russia in the CSTO. As Lukashenko told Nikolai Patrushev, the secretary of the Security Council of Russia, *"Positive and negative aspects of our military and political union CSTO are prominent more than ever. Yet we can state that all CSTO members agree the organisation is developing in the right direction. It has acquired more dynamics recently* (Tvr 2012)." Nikolai Patrushev in fact welcomes a closer cooperation of Russia and Belarus within the framework of CSTO for the mutual benefit of the two countries (ibid.).

Very recently bilateral relations among Belarus and Kazakhstan have shown prospect all around like in trade and economic relations, implementation of the agreements and cooperation between the two states in the CIS, CSTO and SES (ibid.).

- **CSTO and Armenia**

Armenia is a full member of the CSTO. Nikolai Bordyuzha is in full support for Armenia, and regarding CSTO'S position on the Karabakh conflict, he says that the organisation is not interfering but monitoring the situation. As Bordyuzha recalling Russia's efforts into CSTO of the Armenian-Azerbaijani summits says, "There is an OSCE Minsk Group acting as a mediator in negotiations." Regarding CSTO's position in case of the Karabakh conflict, the Secretary General of CSTO claimed that the CSTO is not only a military organisation but also has political and peacekeeping potential, thus justifying CSTO's position in the conflict. Armenia further has the full support of CSTO in the conflict and will get the required assistance as full member of the CSTO (Westerlund

2013). There would be possible deployment of the CSTO peacekeepers in Karabakh as a support to Armenia to which Armenia will applaud and welcome to the CSTO decision (Hayrumyan 2012). However such cooperative attempts of the CSTO and Armenia has been seen by Azerbaijan as an anti-Azerbaijani policy. The statements of the Secretary General have somehow provoked the situation. However, a spokesman of the organisation clarified that the CSTO is not a side in the Nagorno-Karabakh conflict. The OSCE MINSK group co-chaired by Russia is just working on settling the conflict (Westerlund 2013).

Another illustration of Armenia and CSTO cooperation is the "Cooperation 2012", which is a CSTO military exercise to be held in Armenia on 3–8 September 2012. The theme of the cooperation is named as *"the application of the CSTO joint forces and measures in Caucasus with the CSTO forces of quick reaction"*. Armenian Minister of Defense accomplishes the general leading of the preparation and holding of the military exercises. Representatives of the Ministries of Defense of the CSTO member-countries, interested Ministries and the representatives of every Force of the CSTO member countries may be included in the staff of the leadership of the exercises. The first staff negotiations of the CSTO member-countries' delegates and Armenian interested Ministries will take place on February 28-March 1 during which these the preparation issues of the military exercise will be discussed (Times 2012).

- ## CSTO and Kazakhstan

Kazakhstan is one of the greatest Central Asian countries with a long border with Russia. It has very tight economic and trade relations with Russia and Russian minority resides in Kazakhstan. It is in all probability the closest ally of Russia and a very loyal member of the Russia-led CIS organizations and the CSTO (Lurer 2012). During Kazakhstan's presidency of the CSTO, the protection of information and further strengthening of Collective Rapid Reaction Force (CRRF) were to be amongst the priorities of CSTO member states. As Nursultan Nazarbayev stated, *"Kazakhstan considers the Collective Security Treaty Organization (CSTO) as an important institute for mutual cooperation in the sphere of military construction, protection of territorial integrity and sovereignty of the member states, as well as a tool providing national security"* (Weitz 2010). Kazakhstan has been a very loyal member of the CSTO. For instance, it was in August 2006, that CSTO held its largest military exercises in Aktau in Kazakhstan, named *Rubezh 2006*. The 2500 defence personnel as well as many armoured vehicles and war planes were from CSTO member states Kazakhstan, Kyrgyzstan, Tajikistan and Russia participated in the exercise. All the CSTO's major command components comprising of its standing joint headquarters, permanent joint staff and secretariat participated in the exercise (ibid.).

- *CSTO and Russia*

The CSTO may be conceived as a Russian instrument of uniting its member states on ideological grounds with Russia being the leader of the organization. Through the CSTO, Russia continues to diffuse its political interest and influence and reaching out for leadership in military cooperation (Moscow Declaration 2008). Moscow regards the CSTO as a key organization to respond to regional challenges and other hard security threats (Mowchan 2009). Russia wants a strong CSTO so that it could be used as a mechanism to shape the geo-strategic designs in the post-Soviet space in Russian lines (ibid.).

- *CSTO and Kyrgyzstan*

Kyrgyzstan is located in Central Asia. It is located at a very crucial zone for drug trafficking and potential terrorism. It also has its closeness to Afghanistan and its territory thrives with U.S. activity. For this reason, Russia has its full military presence in Kyrgyzstan. The Kant Air base of Russia have been in fact expanding and upgrading. Highly designed Soviet style Su-25 ground attack aircraft and Su-27 fighter aircraft has been developed. The number of fighter aircrafts has also been increased with the increase in the number of personnel. The Kant airbase is of great significance as it majorly carries out its tasks during the operations of CSTO (Habibe Ozdal 2010). While analyzing CSTO's role in the recent events that took place in Kyrgyzstan where the CSTO did not took effective steps, the significance of the CSTO was questioned. As some analyst pointed out, "*But when CSTO member Kyrgyzstan erupted in violence earlier this year, the CSTO did nothing, exposing the organization to criticism that it is a paper tiger* (Kucera 2013)."

During the crisis of Kyrgyzstan, the provisional government of Kyrgyzstan has requested the help of Russian troops. This Kyrgyz crisis was then referred to CSTO by Russia. But what came into the light of facts was that CSTO proved inefficient in responding to the Kyrgyzstan crises. The valid on reasons such that as supported Article 2 of the CSTO charter, the organisation could help in such a situation only in the event it threatens the security, sovereignty and territorial integrity of one or several members and that the crisis further threatens international peace and security. Moreover, Article 4 of the CSTO charter states that *"in case an act of aggression is committed against any of the Member States, all [other] Member States will provide ... necessary assistance, including military ..., as well as provide support with the means at their disposal in exercise of the right to collective defence in accordance with Article 51 of the UN Charter"*. Hence, the official reason given regarding CSTO's very less role in this crisis was that the situation called for internal political turmoil and domestic concern rather than an external threat, so the CSTO was not in a situation to respond in a concrete way (ibid.).

- **CSTO and Uzbekistan**

The relations between the CSTO and Uzbekistan have not been very steady. Uzbekistan had been one of the founding members of the Collective Security Treaty, which was once known as the Tashkent Treaty but the name became void once Uzbekistan withdrew from the treaty in 1998 and went to join GUAM. But it later rejoined CSTO again. However, things were not still very stable with Uzbekistan recently until it finally for a second time withdrew from the CSTO on 28th June 2012.

But during the CSTO summits the ambiguity regarding the membership of Uzbekistan was indeed raised. In October, 2011, Belarusian President Alexander Lukashenko made a highly critical statement towards Uzbekistan for the "triple game" the country plays in its foreign policy (Tolipov 2012). Such a game is incompatible with Uzbekistan's membership in the CSTO, Lukashenko said. Moreover, the Belarusian President warned that without the CSTO, it will be difficult for Uzbekistan to safeguard its independence; "we shouldn't joke here; the world today is very unstable." Lukashenko pointed out two things; firstly, all other members except for Russia and Belarus as sources of divergences and disunity among the member countries. The second statement singled out Uzbekistan as a member causing problems for the CSTO. Thus, Lukashenko implied that only Russia and Belarus have the right positions within the CSTO, while Uzbekistan is especially problematic. Lukashenko's statements revealed the persistence of geopolitics and ambiguity concerning integration processes in the post-Soviet space. These circumstances are especially challenging for Uzbekistan. In this complicated context, Kasimov's participation in the CIS and CSTO summits on one hand, acknowledged the "historical role" the CIS has played throughout the post-Soviet period acknowledging that it was difficult to imagine what would have happened if the CIS had not existed. On the other hand, his attendance at the CSTO summit was more reserved. His seeming optimism about the CIS and moderate "no-veto approach" to the CSTO's decision regarding the deployment of foreign military bases, once again reflected Tashkent's "one-step forward, one step back" strategic posture within these two post-Soviet structures (ibid.).

At the CIS summit, Uzbekistan's position was expressed in terms of its long-term national interest connected to Uzbekistan's need for modernization and for cooperation to correspond with its national legislation and international obligations. Karimov confirmed that Uzbekistan remains in the organization but failed to demonstrate any clear desire to reduce its cooperation with the US. A strategic partnership agreement between the U.S. and Uzbekistan is in force since 2002. Uzbekistan together with all CSTO members is part of the NDN which, among other things, requires mutual trust and cooperation not only between the CSTO members but also between them and the U.S./NATO. The CIS and CSTO summits in Moscow seem to have been preceded by an ultimate warning from Belarus and Russia towards Uzbekistan to make a choice regarding the direction of its foreign policy. The summits coincided in time with the new strategic turn in Afghanistan and expectations to coordinate policies ahead of the Russian presidential elections. The new stage of post-Soviet regional integration will depend on Russia's attitude towards other former Soviet states (ibid.).

However, recent news suggests that Uzbekistan has finally suspended its membership in the CSTO. The consequences however could be disastrous as its departure from this defence bloc would lead to new security risks in the region and it seems that US might have an extra advantage due to this step of Uzbekistan. Uzbekistan's decision favours the position of US by building a cavity in the otherwise security arrangement made by Russia in its area of influence. But a silver lining could also be seen amidst this decision, as from the very beginning Uzbekistan has not proved to be a very stable and loyal member of the CSTO and been creating problems within the organisation. By its departure at least Russia can now consolidate the CSTO and increase cooperation among the remaining active members. It is believed that nevertheless, CSTO's importance will accelerate once the US-led forces withdraw finally from Afghanistan (Radyuhin 2012).

- **CSTO and Tajikistan**

Tajikistan is a small, mountainous and landlocked Central Asian country. It is also a very active member of the CSTO. Tajikistan is most affected by developments in Afghanistan as it shares a very long and porous border with it. Tajikistan participates in all Russian-led integration and regional security schemes, including the Russian-led CSTO. Tajikistan contributes an infantry battalion to the group's Collective Rapid Reaction Force (CRRF). In April 2010, Tajikistan hosted the CRRF's military exercises Boundary 2010 that aimed at preventing possible incursions of "terrorists from Afghanistan (Nieuws 2011)." In September 2011, the CSTO conducted exercises in Tajikistan as part of Tsentr 2011, which also trained the group's militaries in preventing possible popular uprisings (ibid.).

However, the CSTO Agreement on Foreign Bases limits Tajikistan's options to establish relations with non-CSTO countries and let those countries set up bases and hence reaffirms Russia's hold on the country, confirming how vulnerable the Tajik state has become to Russian political pressure. Tajikistan is excessively dependent on remittances from its migrant workers in Russia, and the Kremlin has repeatedly indicated that the presence of these workers in the country is conditional on Dushanbe's willingness to follow Moscow-dictated foreign policy directives (ibid.).

Regarding Tajik cooperation with the CSTO, an anti-terror drill for the Collective Security Treaty Organization's (CSTO) Central Asian group, dubbed Rubezh-2010 (Frontier-2001) has opened in northern Tajikistan (Tajikembassy 2012). Moreover as an active CSTO member, Tajikistan has also provided humanitarian aid under the framework of implementation of collective response actions to Kyrgyzstan when the south of Kyrgyzstan had suffered from outcome of rioting and ethnic crises in June 2010 (Khushqadamov 2012). Also, in a news report, Tajikistan foreign minister, Zarifi urged members of the CSTO to intensify the struggle with the threats emerging from cyberspace (Nieuws 2011).

6.9   Weaknesses of CSTO

The CSTO is still evolving; hence it has not overcome all its difficulties. There are still some shortcomings in the structure and the working of the organization. Below is the analysis of the CSTO considering its loopholes and areas to improve:

- The CSTO is fairly new, created very recently. Among twelve CIS member states only seven are members of the CSTO. This **limited membership** might be contributing to fewer results in working as a vital element in the post-Soviet space.
- Second, the **case of Uzbekistan** could be taken which sets an example of being a highly unstable member of the CSTO. It quit the organization for the first time in 1999 and then re-joined it in 2006 after the criticism by the West regarding the Andijan crisis and very recently withdrew officially for a second time in 2012. This implies how the members of the organisation lack seriousness about the organisation. They join and leave at their own will.
- Third is the **case of conflict among members of the CSTO**. There have been bilateral and regional tensions among member states on issues related to borders, water issues, and transportation blockades, payments due of rent from military bases etc. Russia being the stronger member, most of the member states sometimes faces uneasy situations with Russia but of course they need inevitable economic and security relations with Russia. If these minor and some major conflicts are taken care of within the members of the CSTO, it is likely to yield fruitful results in the working of the CSTO.
- Fourth, **the functioning of the organization is flawed**. Appeasement of Russia is sometimes a driving force in cooperation within the "alliance". Much more resources are utilised in making the organisation capable of countering the NATO forces rather than committing to work for the benefit of the member-states and trying to work for collective security issues of the region.
- Fifth, the CSTO was put to test during the very recent **Kyrgyzstan crisis**. No action on the part of CSTO was taken in order to prevent the crisis or calm down the situation. Referring to the CSTO charter

calling for collective defence against an external attack, the organization did not intervene in Kyrgyzstan, its role was utterly limited and as a result thousands of civilians had to suffer (Bektour 2011).

- Lastly, another shortcoming on the path of the CSTO is the **duplicity of issues**. The presence of other regional organizations such as the SCO and the GUAM etc. in the post-Soviet space, there is repetition of tasks relating to issues of security like terrorism, drug-trafficking.

6.10   Conclusion

Due to the Organization's impact on the national and regional security of those nations, this chapter covered the creation, composition, and operations of the Collective Security Organisation as well as the member states' involvement in those activities. To further the conversation, the chapter also concentrated on the organization's current shortcomings and offered some solutions to overcome them.

References

Bektour, Iskender. 2011. Kyrgyzstan Flirts with Democracy. *Al Jazeera*, October 13.

Bordyuzha, Nikolai. 2005. Collective Security Treaty Organisation. *Mezhdunarodnaya Zhizn* 2: 72.

Bordyuzha, Nikolay. 2011. Transnational Threats and Challenges: Strengthening the Coherence of the OSCE Response and Interaction with Other International Actors. Speech delivered on 30th June at the 2011 *Annual Security Review Conference*. Vienna.

Bugajski, Janusz. 2010. Georgian Lessons, Georgian Lessons—Conflicting Russian and Western Interests in Wider Europe. *Centre for Strategic and International Studies*.

CIS. 1992. CIS Treaty on Collective Security. May 15. At Preamble.

Collins, Kathleen. 2009. Economic and Security Regionalism among Patrimonial Authoritarian Regimes: The Case of Central Asia. *Europe-Asia Studies* 61 (2): 249–281.

Dovgan, Elan F. 2010. *Fifteen Years of the Economic Court of the Commonwealth of Independent States*, p. 61. Minsk.

Gazeta. 2012. www.gazeta.ru. *Moscow*, September 12.

Haas, Marcel De. 2010. *Russia's Foreign Security Policy in the 21st Century Putin, Medvedev and Beyond*, 3. USA and Canada: Routledge.

Habibe, Ozdal. 2010. Putting the CSTO to the Test in Kyrgyzstan, 4th October. *The Journal of Turkish Weekly*. Available at http://www.turkishweekly.net/col umnist/3383/.

Hayrumyan, Naira. 2012. CSTO to Armenia-I Am Declaring War [Online Web]. Accessed on March 29, 2012. http://www.lragir.am/engsrc/commen ts25210.html.

Khushqadamov, Halima. 2012. *Tajikistan as the CSTO Member to Provide Humanitarian Aid to Kyrgyzstan* [Online Web]. Accessed on March 6, 2012. http://khovar.tj/eng/archive/1072-tajikistan-asthe-csto-member-state-to-provide-humanitarian-aid-to-kyrgyzstan.html.

Kucera, Joshua. 2013. CSTO, Humbled (or not) by Kyrgyzstan, Vows to Improve Intervention Force. *The Bug Pit—The Military and Security in Eurasia*, December 10.

Legvold, R. 2009. The Role of Multilateralism in Russian Foreign Policy. In *The Multilateral Dimension in Russian Foreign Policy*, ed. Elana Wilson Rowe and Stina Torjesen, 55. USA and Canada: Routledge.

Lurer. 2012. Lurer.co., Armenia to Get Necessary Assistance as CSTO Full Member-Nikolai Bordyuzha [Online Web]. Accessed on March 13, 2012. http://lurer.com/?p=13017&l=en.

Moscow Declaration. 2008. Declaration of the Moscow Session of the Collective Security. *Council of the Collective Security Treaty Organization*. September 5.

Moscow Times. 2008. Medvedev Plugging CIS on First Trip, May 23. Issue. 3908. Available at http://www.themoscowtimes.com/news/article/medvedev-plugging-cis-on-first-trip/367645.html.

Mowchan, John A. 2009. The Militarisation of the Collective Security Treaty Organisation. *Centre for Strategic Leadership* 6 (9): 1–6.

Nieuws. 2011. Tajikistan Calls for CSTO to Strengthen Fight Against Cyber-crime [Online Web]. Accessed on February 16, 2012. https://www.cpni.nl/index.php/nieuws/tajikistan-calls-for-csto-to-strengthen-fight-against-cyberc rime/.

Nurshat, Ababakirov. The CSTO Plans to Increase its Military Potential. *CACI Analyst Bi.*

Radyuhin, Vladmir. 2012. And Then There Were Five. *The Hindu*, p. 11.

Rozanov, Anatoliy A., and Elena F. Dovgan. 2010. *Collective Security Treaty Organisation 2002–2009*, 1. Geneva/Minsk: Procon Ltd.

Sakwa, Richard. 2010. Senseless Dreams and Small Steps: The CIS and CSTO between Integration and Cooperation. In *Key Players and Regional Dynamics in Eurasia: The Return of the Great Game*, ed. Maria Raquel Friere and Roger E. Kanet, 195. UK and US: Palgrave Macmillan.

Tajikembassy. 2012. *Embassy of Tajikistan to Pakistan*. Tajikistan Holds CSTO Anti-terror Drills. [Online Web]. Accessed on April 14, 2012. http://www.tajikembassy.pk/m-news21.aspx.

Times. 2012. Times.am. CSTO 'Cooperation 2012' Military Exercises Will Be Held in Armenia [Online Web], February 28. Accessed on February 30, 2012. http://times.am/?l=en&p=5199.

Tolipov, Farkhod. 2012. CSTO Summit Raises Ambiguity Regarding Uzbekistan's Membership. *CACI Analyst* [Online Web]. Accessed on March 14, 2012. http://cacianalyst.org/?q=node/5694.

Torjesen, Stina. 2009. Russia as a Military Great Power: The Uses of CSTO and SCO in Central Asia. In *The Multilateral Dimension in Russian Foreign Policy*, ed. Elana Wilson Rowe and Stina Torjesen, 1–7. USA and Canada: Routledge.

Tsygankov, Andrei. 2010. Mastering Space in Eurasia: Russia's Geopolitical Thinking after the Soviet Break-Up. *Communist and Post-Communist Studies No. 36*: 101–127.

Tvr. 2012. President of Belarus Stands for Activation of Politico-Military Cooperation of Belarus and Russia within Framework of CSTO. http://www.tvr.by/eng/president.asp?id=63519.

Tyshchenko, M. 2009. A Threat to the Yield of Milk. *Lenta.ru*, August 22, p. 16.

Weinstein, Adam. 2007. Russian Phoenix: The Collective Security Treaty Organization. *The Whitehead Journal of Diplomacy and International Relations* VIII (1): 167–178.

Weitz, Richard. 2008. *China-Russian Security Relations: Strategic Parlellism without Partnership or Passion*, 59. Strategic Studies Institute, U.S. Army War College.

Weitz, Richard. 2010. Why Is the CSTO Absent in the Kyrgyz Crisis? *Central Asia-Caucasus Analyst* 12 (11): 6–8.

Westerlund, Fredrik. 2013. The CSTO Framinfog Security—A Constructive Perspective Analysis. *Division for Defence Analysis*. Report No. FOI-D-0502-SE.

CHAPTER 7

Increasing Diversity in the Threat Perception of the CSTO Member States

Abstract This chapter mainly focuses on the security scenario in the post-Soviet space after the demise of the Soviet Union. The cardinal points of discussion would be regarding the backdrop of the post-Soviet space, the relation between the newly independent states and the role that radical Islam plays in the wider regional security context. It is here that the chapter will focus on the symbiotic reply by the post-Soviet states against the threats posed and the founding of the Tashkent treaty as a consequence.

Keywords Security · Threat Perception · CSTO · Post-Soviet space · Traditional and Non-traditional security threats

7.1 Introduction

The sudden disintegration of the Soviet Union brought severe repercussions to its former republics. New security related problems such as ethnic clashes, drug trafficking, organized crime, terrorism, extremism etc. cropped up. Other challenges to the newly independent states were its incapacity in the nation building process and further more terrorist infiltration into the republics through the instable Afghanistan with which the

R. Pradhan and S. Kakoty, *Security Integration in the Post-Soviet Space and Collective Security Treaty Organization*, https://doi.org/10.1007/978-981-97-6445-7_7

post-Soviet states shares a very long and porous border. Another issue of concern is the illicit drug trafficking that took place due to poor border security. Along with drug trafficking, many other crimes are related like organized crime, terrorism and insurgency in the region which posed traditional security threats. The border was porous and not tightly secured due to an unreal division in the 1920th and 1930th by the Soviet authorities and the mountainous terrain made it further difficult to secure in a solid way (Jackson 2005). But this wasn't all. The border problem was not only with Afghanistan but also evident within the former Soviet states. There was never a concrete border demarcation during the Soviet times within the Soviet republics and hence ethnic clashes and other border related problems remained.

7.2   TRANSNATIONAL SECURITY CHALLENGES AFTERMATH OF SOVIET UNION'S DISINTEGRATION

According to the estimation of the Interfax 75% of all Afghan narcotics pass through Central Asian region, and European Commission estimates it as 65% (Marat 2006). Four out of six main routes of drug trafficking that passes through Central Asia are:

(a) Kandahar-Balkh-Jaujan-Uzbekistan-CIS-Europe
(b) Kadahar-Herat-Turmenistan-CIS-Europe
(c) Peshawar-Chitral (Northern Pakistan)—Afghan Badakshan-the Gorna-Badakshan Autonomous Oblast (Tajikistan)-Kyrgyzstan-CIS-Europe
(d) Konduz-Khatlonskaia Oblast of Tajikistan-Russia-Europe (Akimbekov 2002).

The four major routes prove the nature of high penetration of the illegal drug trafficking and illicit crimes into the Central Asian region. It is assumed that Islamic Movement of Uzbekistan (IMU) has a base located in Tajikistan to control this menace. However, there is no confirmation about explicit connections between IMU and drug traffickers.

Newly independent post-Soviet states have problems that range from poverty, economic instability to unemployment. This had resulted as a consequence of mass privatization of state property, closing of factories creating unemployment situations whish had further resulted in migration of workers both legally and illegally and utterly poor conditions have forced many to engage in crimes like human trafficking knowingly or unknowingly.

The Civil War of Tajikistan from 1992 to 1997 had gruesome consequences. Socio-economic conditions of people declined to a new low, more than 50,000 people were dead and about 800,000 displaced (Nourzhanov 2005). An Agreement on Peace was though concluded in the year 1997 between the fighting sides yet the real stress still remain with the masses that are in the receiving end. The Tajik civil war displayed how in the Central Asian culture the division into tribes, clans, regions and kinship play a significant role in the politics of the countries. The region is divided into *zhuz* for Kazakhstan, north and south in Kyrgyzstan, *mahalla* in Uzbekistan and regionalism in the event of Tajikistan (*mahalgaroi*) and Turkmenistan. The feeling of belonging to a tribe or clan is so intrinsic that people feel more faithful towards their tribe or clan than the national government; like that of *Turkmenbashi* in case of Turkmenistan.

However, even in the present day the evils of poverty have not subsided in the post-Soviet states and in fact the gap between the rich and the poor has been ever increasing. The socio-economic conditions have further weakened due to the problems of increasing corruption. As defined by Orozbek Moldaliev, "*Corruption is a dangerous phenomenon and a serious destabilizing factor for the reform efforts...It breeds a sense of distrust among the population toward the authorities, lower political activity, and creates mass pessimism and low morale* (Moldaliev 2000)."

Another factor that leads to the declining socio-economic condition of the people of Central Asian states is attached closely to the multi-ethnic nature of Central Asian states. Due to Soviet policy, sizable amount of people became forced migrants and as a result there still exists a substantial number of minorities in these countries. Sizable number of minorities has also been a factor for further minority problems and conflicts in various Central Asian regions. Key conflicts in the region has been one between the Meskhetian Turks and Uzbeks in the Ferghana valley in June 1989 and another major conflict was between Kyrgyz and Uzbeks in the city of Osh in June 1990 (Akcali 2005). Another and a very recent clash took place between ethnic minorities in June 2010 again in the city of Osh (Bertelsmann 2012). This in fact gives a picture that inter-ethnic differences are very much prevalent even today.

While calculating the demographic element of the Central Asian states it is seen that a majority population of ethnic minorities live in Kazakhstan and Kyrgyzstan. In fact, in Kazakhstan, there are only 46% Kazakhs and others belong to other national minorities like Russian constituting of 35%. Taking the case of Kyrgyzstan, there are 53% Kyrgyz, 18% Russians and 13% Uzbeks. Rest of the Central Asian states i.e. Uzbekistan, Turkmenistan and Tajikistan have less minorities. Almost 70% of their population constitute of ethnic majorities (Akcali 2005).

There have been changes in the population percentage of ethnic constituents since two decades of independence yet ethnic tensions though in smaller scale do exist. Petty clashes throughout different times between different ethnic groups have been noted. Some of the petite clashes recorded are clashes between Kyrgyz-Uzbek in 1990 and 2010, Kyrgyz-Dungan in 2007, Russian-Kazakh in 1986, clashes between Uzbek-Tajik, Kyrgyz-Tazik etc. These clashes might be petite in nature yet they do pose danger and instability in the whole of Central Asian region as ethnic clashes have a disposition to spread in a wild way (Akiner 2005).

These ethnic tensions create larger discontent among the Central Asian population. Huge protests have taken place from time to time and again against the ruling elites. Colour revolutions are seen to be a part of such protests. Tulip Revolution of 2005 confirms the dissatisfaction of people in Kyrgyzstan against the corrupted rule of Askar Akaev and the fraudulent means adopted during the parliamentary elections (ibid.). Another uprising happened in Kyrgyzstan in 2010 which again ended with a power change (Nichol 2010).

Another worth mentioning event in this context is the Andijan massacre which was initially a fair endeavor of mass protest which however ended tragically killing almost 300 to 500 people as an estimation made by the Office for Democratic Institutions and Human Rights. Another estimation claimed is that more than 1000 people were killed and secretly buried (OSCE and ODIHR 2005).

Although in contrast to Central Asian republics, Armenia and Belarus have a comparatively homogenous population. In 2009 Belarus constituted of 83.7% Belarusians, 8.3% of Russians and remaining percentage of the others (Population Census 2009). In 2010, Armenia constituted of 97.9% of Armenians making it the only country with mono-ethnic population (*Nagorno–Karabakh*). In spite of this, issue of Nagorno-Karabakh still remains even if it is ongoing since the beginning of demonstration in

1988. This conflict still remains a bone of contention between Armenia and Azerbaijan.

7.3 Terrorism and Instability in Afghanistan

The disintegration of the Soviet Union led to religious freedom in the post-Soviet space. Yet, there were always apprehensions towards Islam radical groups by Russia. By 1960s–1970s, 'extremist' Muslims marked themselves as "anti-Soviet" and "anti-social" and hindered its believers to join the Soviet military (Roi 2001).

It was only in the 1980s that Islam found its importance in the region more than ever because of the efforts of some Muslim movements that surfaced during that period. Since, majority of the Islam supporters centered in rural areas of Uzbekistan and Tajikistan, hence these movements originated from these areas. One of the very initial indications of such movements was observed in Uzbekistan where an active role was played by Tohir Yuldashev of Adolat Party (later the head of IMU) to foster the role of Islam in politics. Adolat Party was banned in 1992 by the Tajik government; however, its followers later on actively participated in the Tajik civil war supporting Islamic side. Yuldashev alongwith his followers and Jumaboi Ahmadzhanovich Khojaev (IMU military strategist) after the end of civil war joined Al-Qaeda forces in Afghanistan (Weitz 2004).

Socio-economic and security problems were always prevalent in the Central Asian states. But it was after the 9/11 catastrophe that the Central Asian region got international attention. Elements like geographical location, economic instability, unemployment, poverty, porous borders etc. made the Central Asian region more vulnerable to the activities of Taliban in Afghanistan be it spread of terrorism, religious extremism, drug trafficking, human trafficking and through the Central Asian region it passes on to Russia, Europe and the US. Events like the Tashkent car bombing and terrorist attacks of 1999 in the southern part of Kyrgyzstan-Batken brought the issue of international terrorism on the CIS agenda. And such threats have been further increasing because of Afghanistan as it houses more extremist groups like IMU, Hizb-ut-Tahrir etc. The most important area of concern is the poorly guarded porous border of Afghanistan that borders three of the Central Asian states and hence it is a big threat for maintaining the stability and regional security of the Central Asian region (Akimbekov 2002).

The Afghan issue however has its origin much before the Taliban came into power in 1996 and dates back to the first "Great Game" between the great powers of the nineteenth century. When the British Empire marked the Durand Line, it left a huge number of Pashtuns in British India. Moreover, agreements were settled between Russian and British empires of 1873 and 1887 that included provinces with large Uzbek, Tajik and Hazaras population within Afghanistan. It had impact on the Afghan civil war of 1978 where the President Muhammad Daud was toppled by the popular Democratic Party of Afghanistan (PDPA). Soviet Union in the year 1979 engaged itself in the Afghan civil war and withdrew its forces finally in 1989 (ibid.).

The Afghan skirmish ultimately came to an end in early 1992 and in April the communist regime led by President Najibullah collapsed. Attempts were made by Gulbuddin Hekmtyar, the leader of Islamic Party of Afghanistan to come into power but with vain. The Taliban established authority in 1994. The situation in Afghanistan deteriorated (Hyman 1998). The cold war came to an end, Russia and the US also gradually showed little interest in the Afghan problem and further conflicts ripped the country from inside. As consequence of the Tajik civil war of 1992, about 60,000 Tajik refugees crossed the Afghan border seeking refuge and in contrast thousands of Afghan refugees escaped seeking refuge in the other side of the border i.e. Central Asia. Hence, issues and problems of Afghanistan and Central Asian region are very close-knit and inter-twined (ibid.).

The Central Asian states also realized the inter-connectedness of Afghanistan with them hence realized the gravity of the situation when in 1996 the radical Islamic Taliban came to power in Afghanistan, the leaders of Kazakhstan, Uzbekistan, Tajikistan and Kyrgyzstan were highly alarmed. They sought Russia's help and met with Russian Prime Minister Viktor Chernomyrdin in Almaty on October 4, 1994. Russia actively responded to the problem and considering Central Asia to be its "near-abroad" and "backyard" came up with a unified anti-Taliban coalition. Northern Afghanistan, where this coalition was established became the buffer zone between Taliban Afghanistan and the CIS south. The Taliban had by the year 2000 controlled almost all the territories of Afghanistan leaving just the Panshir valley. Taliban was also alleged to have connections with the Al-Qaeda and its lead during that time Osama Bin Laden (Cornell and Spector 2002).

IMU in the year 1999 and 2000 intended to build Islamic Caliphate in Fergana Valley. Juma Namangani, a military leader of the IMU with his followers joined the Islamic Tajik opposition after parting from Uzbekistan in 1992–1993. However, the IMU still continues to be in Tajikistan even after the end of the Tajik civil war. In the meantime, IMU built relations with Afghan advances and Taliban which makes Afghanistan an immediate threat to the security of the Central Asian region. Although the threat of IMU may have been subsided during US-led war against terror in Afghanistan in the year 2001 when IMU bases have believed to be targeted and attacked by the US army, yet new threats have emerged in the form of new extremist movement of Hizb-ut-Tahrir al-Islami (The Party of Islamic Liberation). Hizb-ut-Tahrir appeared in the Central Asian region since late 1990s and prominently operates in Uzbekistan, Tajikistan and south of Kyrgyzstan. It shares similar goals as the IMU of building Islamic Caliphate in the Fergana Valley however it is less radical than the IMU.

Several loopholes such as regional instability, corruption, poverty, weak economy, large scale unemployment, low standard of living, misinformation about traditional Islamic values, decreasing health conditions, lack of social welfare schemes etc. are all incentives for cultivating extremist movements in the Central Asian region.

7.4   Efforts for Promoting Regional Security in Central Asia

The threats and challenges in the Central Asian region be it the "Afghan" issue or border issues that have already been discussed above have in a vital way developed the urge among Central Asian states to be interdependent on each other for maintaining regional security.

As a result of cooperative efforts of the Central Asian states, Kazakhstan, Kyrgyzstan and Uzbekistan in 1994 established Central Asian Union (CAU) (Moldaliev 2000). CAU was established in order to boost cooperation amongst the Central Asian states. CAU was later in July 1998 joined by Tajikistan and it was renamed as Central Asian Economic Community (CAEC). Additional functions were taken up by CAEC varying from intra-regional trade to security and military cooperation between states. In 1995 a Joint Council of Defense Ministers was formed to deal with regional security and defense coordination comprising of air defense, military exercises and cooperation with NATO PfP Programme.

Again in 1995, a peacekeeping battalion by the name Centrasbat was founded by Kazakhstan, Kyrgyzstan and Uzbekistan (Toktogulov 2007). In the year 1999, the incursion of IMU to southern Kyrgyzstan posed security threats. During this time CAEC's foreign Ministers and Heads of National Security joined on military activity and figured terrorism to be a global and international threat (Toktogulov 2007: 30).

As a result of it, in April 2000 an agreement on fighting terrorism, extremism and trans-border crimes was signed by the presidents of the member states. The members of CAEC however realized how significant and beneficial it was for them if Russia could become a part of this anti-terrorist programme and therefore asked Russia to sign this agreement. From then onwards CAEC started closely working with CIS's Collective Security Council. In a way it could then be protected behind the Russia shield. Another issue discussed strongly by the members of CAEC was the issue of drug trafficking. To address this issue the CAEC was renamed to Central Asian Cooperation Organisation (CACO) in 2001 (Swanstrom 2004). However it was not a whopping success. Another gigantic step was initiated by Uzbekistan in the area of disarmament and arms-control. Negotiations took place among the Central Asian leaders on Central Asian Nuclear Weapons Free Zone (CANWFZ). CANWFZ got full support from Kazakhstan and Kyrgyzstan in the Almaty Declaration on February 28, 1997 (Dastan 2000).

Again, to address the Afghan issue which is considered to be a direct threat to the peace and regional stability of Central Asia; Uzbekistan initiated a '6 + 2' group of 'neighbours and friends' (Diamont 2000). The group comprised of six countries bordering Afghanistan with US and Russia. The group signed the basic principles of peaceful settlement of disputes in Afghanistan during a meeting in Tashkent in 1999 and also appealed the United Nations Drug Control Programme (UNDCP) to contribute in minimizing illegal drug trafficked from Afghanistan. In the year 2000, the '6 + 2' group in an attempt to tackle the problem of narcotics trade approved a Regional Action Plan (Swanstrom 2004). The effort of this group was a fair attempt at focusing on such grave issues, yet it cannot be pronounced as a total success.

The Central Asian states highly intend to bring about regional stability and hence have always been actively cooperating with each other. Kazakhstan, Kyrgyzstan and Uzbekistan have always been committed in any common task needed in the hour to fight the posing threats and challenges. However, it has been Tajikistan which was unable to fully contribute itself in such tasks mainly due to its larger internal problems such as the extensive Tajik civil war from 1992 to 1997 (Diamont 2000). It failed to be a part of the agreements explained above.

7.5   Conclusion

The chapter very elaborately analysed the security challenges and threat perception prevalent in the post-Soviet space. It has given a layout about the issue of Afghanistan and how its geographical nearness to the Central Asian region plays such an important role in detonating the problem of terrorism, illicit narcotics trade and drug trafficking and other related organized crimes. Emphasis was put on the very picture of threat in challenging the peace and stability of the post-Soviet states. The chapter further discussed the security dilemma of the Central Asian states and the efforts taken by the states to preserve and promote safety, security, stability and peace in the region.

References

Akcali, Pınar. 2005. *Nation-State Building in Central Asia: A Lost Case?* In *Central Eurasia in Global Politics: Conflict, Security and Development*, ed. Mehdi Parvizi Amineh and Henk Houweling, 109. Brill, Leiden, Boston.

Akimbekov, Sultan. 2002. The Conflict in Afghanistan: Conditions, Problems, and Prospects. In *Central Asia: Gathering Storm*, ed. Boris Rumer, 69–113, p. 70. New York: M.E. Sharpe Inc.

Akiner, Shirin. 2005. *Violence in Andijan 13 May, 2005: An Independent Assessment*, July, p. 20. Silk Road Paper. Sweden.

Cornell, Svante E., and Regine A. Spector. 2002. *Central Asia: More than Islamic Extremists. Washington Quarterly* 1 (Winter): 193–206. p. 196.

Dastan, Eleukenov. 2000. *Perspectives on Security in Kazakhstan.* In *Crossroads and Conflict: Security and Foreign Policy in the Caucasus and Central Asia*, ed. Gary K. Bertsh, Cassady Craft, Scott A. Jones, and Michael Bek, 246. Routledge. New York and London.

Diamont, Todd. 2000. *The Six-Plus-Two Group Unveils Anti-trafficking Action Plan for Afghanistan.* Eurasia Insight. September 15. Available at http://www.eurasianet.org/departments/insight/articles/eav091500.shtml. Accessed on June 15, 2011.

Hyman, A. 1998. *Afghanistan and Central Asia.* In *Regional Security and the Future of Central Asia: The Competition of Iran, Turkey, and Russia*, ed. Hooman Peimani, 129. London: Praeger.

Jackson, Nicole J. 2005. The Trafficking of Narcotics, Arms and Human in Post-Soviet Central Asia: (Mis)Perceptions, Policies and Realities. *Central Asian Survey* 24 (1) (March): 39–52, p. 40.

Marat, Erica. 2006. Impact of Drug Trade and Organized Crime on State Functioning in Kyrgyzstan and Tajikistan. *China and Eurasia Forum Quarterly* 4 (1): 96.

———. 2009. *Ethnic Composition of the Population of the Republic of Belarus*. Population Census 2009. Vol. III, National Statistical Committee of the Republic of Belarus. Available at http://belstat.gov.by/homep/ru/perepic/2009/itogi1.php. Accessed on July 20, 2011.

Moldaliev, Orozbek. 2000. Secutiry Challenges for Kyrgyzstan. In *Crossroads and Conflict: Security and Foreign Policy in the Caucasus and Central Asia*, ed. Gary K. Bertsh, Cassady Craft, Scott A. Jones, and Michael Bek, 267, Routledge, New York and London.

———. 2005. OSCE and ODIHR. *Preliminary Findings on the Events in Andijan, Uzbekistan*, p. 8, 23. Warsaw.

Nichol, Jim. 2010. The April 2010 Coup in Kyrgyzstan and its Aftermath: Context and Implications for U.S. Interests. *Congressional Research Service*. 7-5700, R41178, June 15. Available at http://www.fas.org/sgp/crs/row/R41178.pdf.

Nourzhanov, Kirill. 2005. Saviours of the Nation or Robber Barons? Warlord Politics in Tajikistan. *Central Asian Survey* 24 (2): 112.

———. *Nagorno–Karabakh*. Global Security. Available at http://www.globalsecurity.org/military/world/war/nagorno-karabakh.html. Accessed on August 2, 2011.

Roi, Yaacov. 2001. *Islam in the CIS: A Threat to Stability?* p. 2. London: The Royal Institute of International Affairs: Russia and Eurasia Programme.

Swanstrom, Niklas. 2004. The Prospects for Multilateral Conflict Prevention and Regional Cooperation in Central Asia. *Central Asian Survey* 23 (1) (March): 41–53. p. 44.

Toktogulov, Beishenbek. 2007. *NATO's Partnership for Peace (PfP) Program and Regional Security in Central Asia*, September 30. Ankara, METU.

———. 2012. Bertelsmann Stiftung's Transformation Index (BTI). *Kyrgyzstan Country Report*. BTI 2012. Gütersloh: Bertelsmann Stiftung.

Weitz, Richard. 2004. *Storm Clouds over Central Asia: Revival of the Islamic Movement of Uzbekistan (IMU)*, p. 466. Studies and Conflict and Terrorism.

CHAPTER 8

Competitive Security Cooperation in the Post-Soviet Space: A Comparative Study of CSTO With SCO and NATO

Abstract The disintegration of the Soviet Union in 1991 led to increased penetration of regional security organizations like SCO, OSCE, and NATO in post-Soviet space. Russia and China have normalized ties since the 1980s, but the new international world order suggests peaceful cooperation. Russian foreign policy emphasizes multilateral security cooperation, leveraging military might for great power status. The CSTO maintains stability in post-Soviet space, while NATO and SCO play significant roles in the region, influencing Russian interest in its 'near-abroad'.

Keywords CSTO · SCO · NATO · Competitive security cooperation · Post-Soviet space

8.1   INTRODUCTION

The sudden disintegration of the Soviet Union in 1991 created a power vacuum in the post-Soviet space resulting of penetration of outside powers into the region. This Chapter is such an attempt to examine the enhanced penetration of other regional security organizations, such as Shanghai Cooperation Organization (SCO), Organization for Security

© The Author(s), under exclusive license to Springer Nature   163
Singapore Pte Ltd. 2024
R. Pradhan and S. Kakoty, *Security Integration in the Post-Soviet Space and Collective Security Treaty Organization*,
https://doi.org/10.1007/978-981-97-6445-7_8

and Cooperation in Europe (OSCE), and North Atlantic Treaty Organization (NATO) in post-Soviet space. The Chapter will also discuss the cooperation of these organizations with former Soviet states and Russia's attitude towards this cooperation.

Russia and China have continued normalisation and improvement of their ties since the 1980s. As both being great powers in a world dominated by the US, Russia and China finds themselves to be in the same side of the coin of critical issues in international politics (Mankoff 2009).

As far the relations between Russia and US-led NATO, the vital question is as to how the two organisations would put aside their fifty years of confrontational relation and go ahead in a cooperative manner working in a specific region together? Is cooperation between US and Russia really a possibility? It however seems that the new international world order suggests that both these former blocs work together peacefully in a more troubled space as the post-Soviet (Ponsard 2007).

8.2   SHANGHAI COOPERATION ORGANISATION (SCO) AND SECURITY INTEGRATION IN THE POST-SOVIET SPACE

The SCO is a regional organisation which was founded in 2001 in Shanghai by the leaders of China, Kazakhstan, Kyrgyzstan, Russia, Tajikistan and Uzbekistan. Earlier it was known as Shanghai Five (Gill 2001). Shanghai Five was renamed Shanghai Cooperation Organisation (SCO) after the inclusion of Uzbekistan. On the other hand, NATO is an intergovernmental military alliance since the time of cold war. It was founded on the basis of the North Atlantic Treaty signed on 4 April, 1949. Presently the NATO has an extended membership of 28 countries (NATO 2013).

The SCO was created very recently only in 2001 on the basis of a treaty signed in 1996 by leaders of countries—Russia, China, Kazakhstan, Kyrgyzstan and Tajikistan. The prime objective behind the initial agreements was the concern for the Islamic extremism. Afghanistan after falling into the hands of the Taliban, posed security threats to Central Asia and the Caucasus. Hence, then known as the so-called Shanghai Five along with Uzbekistan signed the Declaration of the Shanghai Cooperation Organisation in June 2001.

Russia's outlook towards China has been characterised as s a preference for bilateral interactions and co operations and compromises rather than useless conflicts that would result in fruitless endeavours (Ivanov 2005).

Sino-Russian cooperation has been considerably growing and visible in the recent years. There has been growth in trade and investment and economic cooperation. Russia and China had also opposed US action in Iraq and wants US to withdraw NATO forces from Central Asia eventually. The Shanghai Cooperation Organisation has been an apparent institutionalising factor of cooperation between Russia and China. Through the SCO both these countries along with the other smaller members have been in an ongoing relationship of regular summits and working level meetings. It is necessary to mention here that in order to expand economic opportunities and promotion of person-to-person and cultural exchanges between these two countries, 'Year of Russia in China' in 2005 was held and 'Year of China in Russia' in 2006 was held that helped (Mankoff 2009) (Map 8.1).

The SCO is a sprouting regional organisation with the post-Soviet Central Asia being an important hub for both Russia and China's regional strategy and economic policies in the region except Turkmenistan. The SCO is not just an important regional organisation but its significance lies in it being of wider attention to global politics, security and economics. SCO is of global significance also because two of its larger members, China and Russia. These two larger members are huge in territory, economic strengths; military might and as an addition also occupies positions as permanent members of the UN Security Council. More over Russia and China often consider themselves as alternative power centres in relation to the West. Hence a regional organisation like the SCO has quite a weight consisting of two great giants of the international world order. The SCO provides a significant study in Eurasian regionalism and international relations because it depicts the coming together of two non-Western powers for regional cooperation yet setting implications for Western powers (Aris 2011).

As the SCO specifically deals in with China, Russia and the post-Soviet Central Asia, hence it is imperative to understand the backdrop of that region, its geography, history, politics, the cultural affinities, and last but not the least the impact from its neighbouring areas, its geopolitics etc. The SCO is a basic component of China and its emerging regional strategy. The adoption of the 'good neighbour' policy in the 1990s placed strong and favourable relations with bordering countries at the heart of Chinese foreign policy. Against this background, the SCO is very significant as the first fully fledged regional organisation, of which China is a forever and significant member. In this way, it represents a crucial test case

Map 8.1 Shanghai cooperation organization (*Source* Bailes et al. 2007)

of China's regional strategy, especially given that there is already evidence of the Chinese leadership seeking to replicate its approach to the SCO in other regions of the world (Ibid).

Not only that, the SCO is also a notable development in case of Russian foreign policy dimensions. Russia is another big member of the SCO and the SCO 'area of action' is considered by Russia as its "near-abroad".

However, in the recent years, Russia has pursued a renewed multilateral strategy aimed at developing closer relations with those former Soviet states which are most likely to cooperate with Russia (Ibid: 2). Moreover, while estimating the importance of SCO for Russia, the establishment in September 2004 of an inter-agency commission on Russian participation is significant as it confirms how SCO is also important to Russia (Troitskiy et al. 2007).

One important observation on part of both Russia and China is that if in any case Russia's is somehow considered to be a secondary member of SCO, then the organisation will account to losing its gravity, legitimacy and aspirations and the other members of SCO are smaller and newly formed governments and less experience in handling issues. Hence both Russia and China have interest in preserving and promoting Russia's position in the organisation. In fact, Russia along with China in the year 2004 was one of the prime initiators of SCO Regional Anti-terrorist Structure (RATS) (Ibid: 31). In 2006 SCO Shanghai Summit stating Russia's official position, the then President Putin mentioning the SCO called it *'a new model of successful international cooperation' (President of the RF 2006)*. What seems is that by strengthening SCO, Russia and China leave will not hesitate to oppose and grant US and other Western designs in the region of Central Asia.

Not only has the SCO benefited Russia, it has also been of great help to China by institutionalising its presence in Central Asia both economically and in security terms. It is through SCO only that China can mark its valid presence in the post-Soviet space. To Russia, the SCO provides an additional means of maintaining Russian influence in the post-Soviet space and for acting as a watchdog to Chinese activities in its area of interest. China prefers using of SCO to combat militant Islamic organisations threatening the Central Asian republics as well as Chinese Xinjiang (Bogaturov 2004).

The SCO is also the result of a thought of deepening bilateral ties between Russia and China in considerable extent for a desire to balance against the dominant power of the West, specifically the US. The most apparent and vital aspect of the SCO is however been in the sphere of security although the organisation tries to play a prominent role in establishing economic and cultural role among its member-states. At the 2006 summit, Russian president Putin announced that the organisation has become a powerful factor in ensuring stability and security in Eurasia (President of Russia 2006).

- Aims and strengths of the SCO

The first and foremost aim of the SCO is mutual security avoiding conflicts among the members.

> The main aim of the SCO as proclaimed in its charter of 2002 is, "*to strengthen mutual trust, friendship, and good-neighbourliness between the member states. They are to adhere to the principles of mutual respect to sovereignty, independence, territorial integrity, non-aggression, and non-interference in internal affairs, non-use of force or threat thereof and no seeking of unilateral military advantage (SCO Charter 2001).*"

The second most important aim of the SCO members is to promote regional security and internal stability by fighting terrorism, separatism and extremism. In fact, in 2001 itself a special 'Convention against Terrorism, Separatism and Extremism' was adopted. Countering these threats became the primary goal of the SCO Charter (Troitskiy et al. 2007). Therefore as already mentioned earlier, the Regional Anti-Terrorist Structure (RATS) was created to avert attempted terrorist attacks and hundreds of them were actually averted as a Russian spokesperson claimed (Weitz 2006).

To fight terrorism, the SCO member states have had several military exercises, both multilateral and bilateral (Oldberg 2005). First large scale military exercise that took place was *Mirnaia misiia*-2005 (Peace Mission) (Weitz 2006), the second large scale SCO exercise was held in Chelyabinsk, Russia in July 2007 and in the year 2010, a Peace Mission was held on September 9–25 at Matybulak training area in Kazakhstan. Here more than 5,000 personnel from China, Russia, Kazakhstan, Kyrgyzstan and Tajikistan participated (Boland 2010).

After the phenomenal 9/11 incident, SCO became a part of a larger international anti-terrorist mechanism. There had been SCO's anti-terror military exercises since then. The SCO RATS emphasise the maintenance and strengthening of peace, security and stability in the region and works towards countering security threats. It also extends collaboration and discusses on regulatory enactments on cooperation with the Regional Representation of the UN Office for Drugs and Crime in Central Asia, UN Counter-Terrorism Committee, UN Al Qaida and Taliban Sanctions Committee, Committee—1267 (Samarkhan 2011). At a RATS meeting

in Tashkent in April 2006, fourteen terrorist organisations were identified directly threatening the security of the region including the Taliban,
the Islamic party of Turkestan and Hizb-ut Tahrir. At the same time the
RATS regime has been praised for preventing over 250 terrorist attacks
in member states since its establishment (Lanteigne 2006).

Another interest among SCO members as already analysed before-
hand is withstanding the West and Western type of democracy. Especially
after the so-called 'Colour Revolutions' in 2003–2004, the SCO member
states were more apprehensive about such a situation in the post-Soviet
Central Asia (Spirova 2008). Moreover a very visible aspect of SCO's attitude towards the West is that United States has repeatedly been denied
observer status in the organisation.

8.3   SCO and CSTO: A Comparative Study

It seems that much of the concern about the SCO is blown out of propor-
tion because it has been observed that though SCO talks about taking
steps towards military cooperation and integration, but it has no armed
force of its own and a much fewer general staff or any of the other
attributes of a unified command structure. There are no common military
forces, no joint command and a combined planning staff (Weitz 2006).
SCO members are free to make their own decisions on security matters,
have the right to join other blocs and alliances without prior consultation
with other member states (Mankoff 2011). Not only those, the Central
Asian members of the SCO also belong to NATO's PfP program, and
most have strong bilateral ties with the United States. It provides Kazakhstan, Kyrgyzstan, and Tajikistan large amounts of military assistance
(Weitz 2009).

It has been also seen that in the aftermath of the 9/11 crisis, the SCO
was in the same side with the US and the West in the fight of 'War on
terror'. SCO members Kyrgyzstan and Uzbekistan accepted US' presence
in their territory by signing bilateral agreements with US permitting the
stationing of U.S. bases on their territory (Mankoff 2011). Also in the
2008 War in Georgia, SCO summit refused to give Moscow more than
equivocal support for its military intervention.

While the SCO backed Russia's active role in resolving the Georgian
conflict but the SCO member states hesitated to recognise South Ossetia
and Abkhazia's independence. One of the prime reasons in not recognising their independence by the SCO giant, China, is that it would

create a same problem and example for its own separatist regions as China combats separatism in Taiwan, Tibet and Xinjiang. While Russia without any doubt expected much stronger support from the members of the organisation, did not receive enough support (Swanstorm 2008). Hence in comparison with the CSTO or for that matter other regional organisations like the CIS or the Eurasian Economic Association, the influence of SCO is relatively limited.

In political-military terms also, the SCO is somewhat a loose partnership and it also does not obligate members to spend a fixed amount of budget on its operations like the NATO or the CSTO. The SCO does not have a mutual defence clause or any standing army of its own. The potential of SCO to become a mighty tool of foreign policy also varies over time because the degree of attention paid by the SCO to geopolitics varies over time. For instance, on one hand, the SCO following the 2003–2005 Colour Revolutions in Georgia, Ukraine, the SCO member Kyrgyzstan, appeared to provide a device for overturning the status quo throughout the post-Soviet space. And as a result, the SCO increasingly set itself up in opposition to the U.S.-led campaign for democratisation. As Russian foreign minister, Lavrov remarked following the 2007 SCO ministers' meeting in Kyrgyzstan: "*It is clear to everyone that one-sided approaches to solving regional and international problems, [those] not relying on international law, are out of place, and that ideological approaches to international affairs, including any kind of "democratization" schemes are ineffective because they do not account for the historical, cultural, and civilization peculiarities of the countries involved (MFA Russian Federation 2007)."*

On the other hand, it remains a fact that the SCO did not oppose the establishment of NATO bases in Uzbekistan, Kyrgyzstan and Tajikistan in 2001 which were set up in order to fight terrorism in Afghanistan and stabilise the situation in the Ferghana Valley (Oldberg 2009).

Another problem with the SCO has been that there have been gaps between declarations and actual actions. It is because the SCO lacks a parliamentary body like in case of NATO which has the NATO's North Atlantic Assembly (Weitz 2006). It shows that the democratic basis of the SCO is also weak (Baylis 2007).

Researchers point out that China respects Russia's strategic role in the Central Asia and the CSTO (Portyakov 2007). Although there are instances of closer cooperation of SCO with CSTO yet some Russian analyst are apprehensive of such cooperation because of growing Chinese influence in the SCO and others in favour of developing the CSTO have complained of parallel military structures, which sometimes may put members before contradictory obligations (Evan 2007). In the military sphere Russia stakes on CSTO which is a real defence alliance where the members are committed to defend each other against external aggression. Moreover, as the CSTO is built on the former Soviet structure, it seems to have a tighter military cooperation than the SCO. The CSTO performs more frequent military exercises, a 4000 personnel strong rapid deployment and an emergent collective peacekeeping force (Henry 2007).

Russia moreover has much stronger bilateral ties with four Central Asian states than China. And after Uzbekistan rejoined the CSTO in 2005, formerly evicting American base, Russia and Uzbekistan intensified military cooperation in the form of a 'Treaty on Allied Relations'. Russia had similar treaties with Kazakhstan and Tajikistan. Russia has a permanent base in Tajikistan having 7000 service personnel since 2004 and also there is hope for the deployment of a new air base there (Oldberg 2005).

As Zarifi told a news conference in Dushanbe in 21 July 2011, *"Negotiations on the military base and the use of the Aini airport by Russia have been under way since 2008. These questions are not simple or easy. So far, the positions of the sides haven't reached a necessary degree of rapprochement that would make it possible to sign an agreement. But work is going ahead at the level of experts. I think that this vital document is going to be signed during the CIS jubilee summit this September in which Russian President Dmitry Medvedev will also take part* (ITAR TASS News Agency 2011)."

Meanwhile, even if China does recognise Russia's military security in the post-Soviet Central Asia yet there are limits in contact between the CSTO and the SCO. This was well evident when in the year 2007 when China refused a Russian proposal of arranging the planned SCO exercise concurrently with the CSTO as CSTO is Russian-led. Hence, it seems that somehow China will always be apprehensive of Russia and certainly does not want to play a second fiddle to Russia at least in the SCO dimension (Evan 2007). And, Russia's uncertainty about Chinese designs led many Russian officials to view the CSTO, of which China is not a member as a superior alternative (Socor 2007).

Mikhail Troitsky talks about a dilemma that Russia suffers through while comparing the SCO and the CSTO on which would have a comparative advantage, *"Russia faces a dilemma: should it work for the SCO to become more militarised, or rather seek to focus it on a 'soft' security and economic agenda? In the former case, the SCO might overshadow the CSTO or at least create confusing choices for Central Asia states. In the latter case, China may gain additional leverage within the SCO and the relative importance of EurAsEC might decline (Ibid.)."*

It has been observed that if there is immediate security threat within post-Soviet Central Asia that requires a military response, the CSTO is most likely to be the one to act quickly by sending troops to hold the border because it has Collective Rapid Deployment Forces and the Russian military would be leading the effort and contributing the greatest number of troops. It also helps in taking quick actions in times of emergency. As cited by Matveeva, Anna and Giustozzi, *"It was applied to peacekeeping in Tajikistan when contingents from Kazakhstan, Kyrgyzstan and Uzbekistan were used alongside Russian forces under an overall CIS mandate to maintain security in the border areas* (Giustozzi and Matveeva 2008)."

Hence, analysing these facts it can be concluded that the SCO is still a organisation which is growing. Since it is more of a Chinese effort hence the economic aspect of the SCO sounds more than the aspect of security. Drawing all the facts such as SCO having a lack of tool and mechanism for the security purpose in the post-Soviet Central Asia, the CSTO seems to be at an advantageous position than it. Moreover, another fact is that the CSTO apart from the four Central Asian states has its membership in the European and the Caucasus region also while the SCO sums up only the Central Asian region with Russia and China. Hence SCO is fairly a new organisation and is yet to grow improving both in structure and in handling tasks.

It seems Russia's concern about Chinese economic presence through SCO into Central Asia is a general fear of gradually becoming a junior and less important partner in the organisation and the region. It definitely does not want to become a second fiddle to China. It is an established fact that Russia is the predominant power in the CSTO and the Eurasian Economic Community. Comparing SCO and CSTO, in the security sphere the CSTO is undoubtedly more equipped and powerful because it has been designed as a traditional defence arrangement, security and collective defence being the priority and the SCO has renounced any form of military integration with only some amount of small joint military exercises (Troitskiy et al. 2007).

The SCO still lacks a lot of important elements to become a mature military security organisation and it does not have any integrated military-political structure, permanent operational headquarters, a rapid reaction force, as well as continuous political deliberations. Therefore, it could not be truly labelled as the 'NATO of the East' (Haas 2007).

8.4   NORTH ATLANTIC TREATY ORGANISATION (NATO) IN THE POST-SOVIET SPACE

The North Atlantic Treaty Organisation (NATO) has been a collective defence effort of the West and the US. NATO was a military alliance that was designed to protect members from the non-members.

The relationship between NATO and Russia is a complex one, sometimes the highs and sometimes the lows. Both of them have a difficult history and the framing of future depends on that relation. From 1949 until the 1990s NATO and Russia (then the Former Soviet Union) have been having conflicting interests only. The primary obstacles that seemed to be fulfilling in case of building a fruitful relation between NATO and Russia was the identity gap between them and the inability to cooperate in a true sense. The whole ideological mindset of these two organisations was contradictory. Yet the international security environment has been changing and these two entities have been evolving since then. Since the Soviet days NATO, an alliance strongly led by the US has been seen as a rival. The NATO enlargement and democratic transformation is an element of generating problems in relations with Russia. From a realist perspective, the expansion policy of NATO weakens Russia's position in the European space, a space that Russia considers a part of itself, its own backyard. And the potential for such conflict is not ideational. One of Russia's main concerns is that the contagion effects of the "Colour Revolutions" in Georgia and Ukraine have largely dissipated (Aurel 2008: 41).

As Russian reformer Anatoly Chubais explained in 1997, "*Frankly, the politicians who support this decision [to enlarge NATO] believe that Russia is a country that should be put aside, a country that should not be included in the civilized world—ever. That is a major mistake*" (Aslund 2007).

In the year 1999, Russia severed its official relations with NATO when NATO under the leadership of USA undertook a so-defined 'humanitarian intervention' against Yugoslavia on account of Kosovo. This was viewed by Russia as a violation of the UN Charter and the principle of territorial integrity. NATO's adoption of a Strategic Concept that widened its responsibility to areas beyond the North Atlantic was perceived by Russia as legitimising NATO interventions in the former Soviet space. The relations between NATO and Russia were restored in 2000. Yet Putin's military and foreign policy doctrines of 2000 still mentioned NATO as a problem for Russia (Neumann 2005).

Though relations between Russia and NATO started to move away from the deadlock when in the 'War against Terrorism' after September 2001 and specifically in May 2002, a common council in the name of the NATO-Russia Council (NRC) was formed. The major goals of this council were to promote cooperation in the fight against terrorism, crisis management, non-proliferation, arms control, regional air defence, rescue operations and emergency situations. During this phase Putin concluded, "*NATO was turning into a more political and less military organisation and that its relations with Russia had reached a new level and quality*" (Adomeit 2007).

Yet what Putin was strongly concerned was to stop NATO's enlargement eastwards since 2001. Not only that, Russia is against any NATO troops and nuclear weapons stationed in these countries. Although Russia accepted the fact that these countries accepted NATO membership yet further NATO expansion eastwards is not welcomed by Russia. More difficult to tolerate for Russia was the NATO membership of the three Baltic countries (formerly part of the Soviet Union) which also recently became members of NATO. Moreover, Ukraine, Georgia and Azerbaijan have talked openly of NATO membership to which Russia totally oppose. Russia's relations with NATO came at a low point during the war with Iraq where Ukraine, Georgia and Azerbaijan participated in NATO exercises and supported US operations in Iraq (Ibid.).

Russia is in competitive terms with NATO. It maintains the military element of the CIS, namely the CSTO in order to sustain the post-Soviet space in a more protected frame and away from the influence of the NATO and the US. Russia puts military pressure on some CIS states that are not in the CSTO. It also maintains a naval base at Sevastopol in Ukraine. In Moldova it maintains forces (although reduced) in the Transnistria region (Andreev 2012). It supports Armenia and retains a strategic radar station in Azerbaijan. On 11 September 2002 Putin issued an ultimatum demanding that Georgia take measures against the Chechen 'terrorists' seeking refuge there and pressed it to agree to cooperation against them (Nygren 2008). The CSTO is totally dependent on Russian forces, since the other partners cannot afford to contribute, and the maintenance of these forces has become a heavy responsibility of the Russian armed forces.

During the war in Afghanistan in 2001, NATO bases were set up in the Central Asian states of Uzbekistan, Kyrgyzstan and Tajikistan that strengthened their bargaining position alongside Russia, so that they could demand and in fact got the fee for the Russian bases (Wall Street Journal Europe 2003). Yet there was no loss of Russia's influence in Central Asia. The Islamist guerrilla activities around the Fergana Valley currently seem to have ceased. The Russian leadership now wants that the US presence in Central Asia will be temporary. In order to show that Russia retains interests in the region, it established a new airbase in Kyrgyzstan near the US one in November 2002, and Putin himself inaugurated it (Ibid).

8.5   NATO Expansion and the Response of Russia/CSTO

As the Wall Street Journal cites, "*NATO enlargement moves the military responsibility of Germany and the US closer to Russia's borders.*"*(Wall Street Journal Europe 2003)* NATO's eastward expansion perceives a threat to Russia. The prospect of having NATO at the doorstep of Russia is unacceptable to Russia. Sections of the Russian military are looking towards the anticipation of upgrading the role of Russian weaponry to counter threat from NATO. NATO yet still determines to remain as the most important security organisation on the continent (SIPRI Yearbook 2007).

Taking the case of Georgia which was previously a member of the CSTO, a colour revolution in the name of Rose Revolution evidently sponsored by US-based NGOs occurred in Georgia in 2003, Georgia slowly going off into the grip of the US as the new Government installed was US friendly. Hence, Georgia has been an instance of NATO expansion as it wants to be a member of NATO. This further fuels the tension in the region leading to a tense diplomatic crisis in Russia-Georgia relations. Between the years 2005 and 2007, Putin often emphasised issues of the need of restoring Russia on the same level as the developed countries, believing in a multipolar world order, the rejection of the idea of "exporting democracy," the development of the CSTO, and Russia's privileged position in the CIS and criticism against the US policies in this regard (Pop 2009).

In fact, after the Russo-Georgian war of 2008, the strengthening of the CSTO increased further, it being one of the prime reasons. It was one of the causes of the speedy militarisation of the CSTO. The Moscow Declaration of the Collective Security Council of the CSTO on September 5, 2008 was considered "*the first real consolidated position of the alliance, a view on international politics and the place of CSTO in it.*" (David 2008)

> These document refers to, "*Georgia's attempt to resolve the conflict in South Ossetia by force.......the growing military capabilities and escalating tensions in the Caucasus region;*" "*the situation in Europe, the proliferation of medium- and short- range ground-based missiles; strengthening the role of the United Nations as well as the situation in several conflict zones; the situation in Afghanistan; the situation around Iran; the prospects of establishing relations between the CSTO and NATO on a number of issues; and support for the initiatives of the Russian Federation relating to a treaty on European security*" (Medvedev 2008).

> The Russia's Foreign Policy Concept announced on July 17, 2008, stated, "*Russia will promote in every possible way the Collective Security Treaty Organization (CSTO) as a key instrument to maintain stability and ensure security in the CIS area, focusing on adapting the CSTO as a multifunctional integration body to the changing environment, as well as on ensuring capability of the CSTO Member States to take prompt and effective joint actions, and on transforming the CSTO into a central institution ensuring security in its area of responsibility*" (The Foreign policy Concept of the Russian federation 2008).

However, the main concern of CSTO regarding NATO's expansion policy is latter's growth of its military infrastructure and information campaign. As Nikolai Bordyuzha remarked, "*On the Western European direction, against the existing power balance, NATO's military structures keep approaching the CSTO's zone of responsibility* (Bordyuzha 2011). *This disrupts the current balance of forces and cannot help but concern us.*" Also, in the 8th CSTO Information Conference, Bordyuzha said, "*Real threat of arms race has existed as well as rising level of tension and distrust.... The CSTO needs a joint tool to counter joint information superiority*" of the Western countries (Ibid.)."

Russia has in fact built CSTO as a force to being able to counter NATO forces in Europe and further Russia wants to make CSTO a better equipped military structure and a pro-Russian military bloc to successfully handle security problems in the post-Soviet region (Marlène 2008).

As President Medvedev expressed:

> The Russian Federation and other member states of the Collective Security Treaty Organization, Central Asian states, are ready for full and comprehensive cooperation with the United States and other coalition nations in combating terrorism in the region. This fight should be comprehensive and modern, and based on military and political components – only in this case will it have a chance of success. (Medvedev 2009)

Considering the presence of Colour Revolutions in the post-Soviet space, it can be seen in two ways: it can be considered as a 'single phenomenon', a sequence of non-violent protests that succeeded in overthrowing authoritarian regimes during the first decade of the twenty first century. Or can be understood as a process of regime transformation in the CIS by minimising Russian influence in the region since the newly established regimes are pro-Western in orientation. Colour revolutions mostly took place across the post-Soviet space in 2003–2005 in the name of Rose Revolution in Georgia in 2003, (Tatum2009) Orange revolution in Ukraine in 2004 (Karatnycky 2001) and Tulip Revolution in Kyrgyzstan in 2005 (Olcott 2005). Russia was disturbed by their occurrence basically for its causes and implications. It is the role of the West that bothers apart from the role of the social factors like poverty, corruption, income inequality etc. As an article in 2005 in the *Renmin Ribao* cited, *"If we do not speak about the internal political situation, the ability of the Colour Revolutions to succeed cannot be separated from the behind the scenes manipulation by the United States* (Jeanne 2009)." However, much active steps have not been taken by the CSTO yet in terms of responding strictly towards colour revolution crises till now. Therefore, in the unlikely event of a colour revolution in the CIS complex in future, the Heads of the CSTO member states have agreed to establish a joint rapid reaction force that can legally intervene in case of an internal conflict (Ibid).

8.6   NATO AND CSTO IN A COMPETITIVE FRAMEWORK

According to Allison, the CSTO-NATO competition can be identified in a way whereby CSTO is still evolving from a military-political organisation to one that is more capable of taking huge responsibilities not only within the region but also in the extended part covering Afghanistan as problems in Afghanistan impacts its surrounding post-Soviet Central Asia as well (Allison 2008) (Map 8.2).

Russia for the first time played a leading role in forming a military alliance in the post-Soviet space by the name of Collective Security Treaty Organisation by the amalgamation of originally seven post-Soviet states basically in a military framework. Yet the feeling of threat still prevailed in the form the US-led NATO's eastward expansion in the CIS borders and the US further planned the deployment of the national missile shield in the East Europe. As analyst Dadan Upadhyay observed, these kinds of threats altogether prompted the CSTO to uplift itself and thus created a Collective Rapid Reaction Force (CRRF) for deployment in the Central Asian region. Since then the CSTO has been emerging as an effective security bloc, an alternative to counter the threats from the US and NATO in the post-Soviet space.

During a press conference, following the Moscow CSTO summit on February 4, 2009, President Medvedev stated that,

> The Collective Rapid Reaction Force should be an effective, all-purpose instrument that can be counted on to realize security objectives throughout the CSTO. And these would include resisting military aggression, conducting special operations to eliminate terrorists and extremists, the

Map 8.2   NATO and CSTO in their areas of operation (*Source* http://en.wik ipedia.org/wiki/File:NATO_CSTO.PNG)

fight against organized crime and drug trafficking, as well as dealing with the consequences of natural and industrial disasters..... The Collective Rapid Reaction Force will have the same sort of training as the troops of the North Atlantic Alliance. (Medvedev 2009)

The US and NATO have been constantly present in the part that borders Russia and its 'sphere of influence' that is the regions of Afghanistan, Iran and the Middle East on the guise of democracy promotion and upholding the values of freedom. This has made the CSTO all the more important to become a stronger military-political regional security bloc. This in fact is not a new thing, the presence of US and NATO forces though have been more visible especially since the "9/11 catastrophe" following the "War against Terror", yet the US forces have been there near the borders of the Soviet space since cold war times. After the disintegration of the Soviet Union, Russia did play a leading role by always considering the post-Soviet Central Asia as it's 'sphere of influence' and hence does not approve of the region's much exposure to external powers especially the West. The CRRF signed an agreement on June 14, 2009 that was designed to repel aggression, carry out special operations and fight terrorism. The CRRF under the command of CSTO consists of special military units as a result of contributions from its member states. Russia's 98th Airborne Division and the Russian airborne troop, 31st Airborne Assault Brigade are the founding pillars of the CRRF. Additional responsibilities of the CRRF is responding to emergencies, dealing with humanitarian crises, strengthening armed forces in the borders and safeguarding the public and military facilities of the member states, and meeting the challenges recognised by the Collective Security Council. Russian President Dmitry Medvedev cited, *"The Collective Rapid Reaction Force will be well-equipped and will operate just as well as that of NATO and.... It will be a mobile force designed to respond to any critical developments and not only of military nature. It will be promptly used in case of any urgent necessity upon the authorisation of the Collective Security Council of the CSTO,"* he said (Upadhyay 2011).

In the course of actions, the CSTO have also signed an agreement in 2009 with the UN for developing and maintaining its own peacekeeping force. This step helps the CSTO in coming up as a substitute to NATO. For operations both on the CSTO territory and outside of their borders on the UN mandate strength, the member states are in the course of forming a peacekeeping contingent. Another significant development of the CSTO is that on December 20, 2011 all the CSTO members unanimously agreed on that a foreign base will only be established in the territory of the member states only with the full consent of all the CSTO members. Hence, the new agreement lets Russia get an edge over the US and the West and can successfully avoid the deployment of the US airbases in Central Asian states. On the event of the 20th anniversary of the Collective Security Agreement and the 10th anniversary of the CSTO, to quote Kazakh President Nursultan Nazarbayev, *"In order to deploy military bases of a third country in the territory of the CSTO member-states, it is necessary to obtain the official consent of all its members* (Radyuhin 2012).*"*

Russian president Medvedev said, *"The decision we have made with regard to military bases of a third country is very important for the consolidation of positions within the CSTO".* Moreover, at the Moscow summit, much of the agenda were for the higher rate of orderliness of CSTO functioning (Upadhyay 2011).

Russian ambassador Igor Lyakin-Frolov further emphasized the main goal of CSTO is to contribute better in strengthening regional security and make the CSTO a more responsible zone. And leading Russian business daily Kommersant said, *"This is one of the key measures worked out by Moscow for turning the CSTO from a 'decorative structure' into a 'fully fledged military-political bloc,' whose members take into account not only their own financial benefit, but also the interests of the partners." (Ibid.)*

Regarding the US military airbase at Manas in Kyrgyzstan, Kyrgyzstan's President Atambayev has over and over again demanded for its closure in 2014 with the expiry of the prevailing agreement. Moreover, the CSTO members showed their agreement with Russia by disapproving the unilateral deployment of strategic missile defence systems in Eastern Europe. As a statement by CSTO read, *"The unilateral deployment of strategic missile defence systems by one state or a group of states without due account for the lawful interests of other countries and without extending legally-binding guarantees to the latter may damage international security and strategic stability in Europe and the world as a whole"* (Bridge 2011).

Russia has opposed NATO's plan of deploying the missile defence system in East Europe as it sees this step as a pretext for the US to build up a shield surrounding Russia.US however, refuse these accusations and also reject to share the missile shield control. It further refuses to sign a written assurance appealed by Russia that will assure that their system does not intend to target Russia in any way. Though the CSTO's main objective is collectively assuring and working towards military security yet recently there has been an inclination to transform itself into a multifunctional organisation aimed at countering hard and soft security threats. CSTO has been evolving slowly by engaging in more positive cooperation with the UN, CIS, SCO, EurAsEC. It has designed its own peacekeeping forces and CRRF and hence is emerging as an important player in the new global security set up. As Medvedev said in 2009, because of CSTO's positive engagement with the UN it is making itself *"worthy competitor to NATO"*. Before one of the CSTO summit in Moscow in December, a new radar station which is capable of monitoring missile launches from the North Atlantic, and the future European missile defence system, was put into operation in Russia's Baltic region of Kaliningrad. On December 1, it became part of the national missile early warning system which strives to serve Russia's promptness to counter threats posed by NATO and the West, which Medvedev told the station command, *"I hope this station will operate well and fulfil the tasks at hand"* (Upadhyay 2011).

Also considering the case of Iran, Russia's interest over Iran fundamentally diverges from those of the US. The US and the West blame Iran of making nuclear weapons under the pretext of peaceful nuclear programme and threatening military intervention. Iran however denies the charges and affirms that the nuclear programme is purely for meeting the country's electricity needs. But for Russia, for over a decade, Iran has been a significant element of Russian foreign policy. The US administration here wants the assistance of Russia in stopping Iran's nuclear programme. The position of CSTO in the context is in total support for Iran and it strongly opposes the use of force and military strike against Iran. On actions if taken by US against Russian ally Iran, the CSTO head makes its position clear by saying, *"The position of the CSTO member countries concerning the possible attack of the USA on Iran is united and consists of the idea that no strikes should be made. If this happens, this will shake many and from all points of view"* (Kudenko 2012).

Also, in the words of Nikolai Bordyuzha, the Secretary General of CSTO, *"Our position is clear, that is we firmly oppose military actions against Tehran and support the continuation of negotiations between Iran and six international mediators......, We hope the situation in Iran will be settled by political and diplomatic means. It's the peaceful resolution of the conflict that can improve the situation"* (Xuequan 2012).

All that CSTO insists is that Iran should cooperate with the IAEA (International Atomic Energy Agency). And pointing towards the international community, the CSTO urges the non-use of force and the settlement of problems with Iran in a peaceful way. Russia's support for Iran's nuclear policy is driven by both economic and geopolitical factors. Russia considers Iran as a partner and de facto ally towards adjusting the power balance in the Middle East region and limiting US influence in this region (Cohen 2013).

8.7   NATO and the CSTO: Issues of Cooperation

The issue of cooperation between the CSTO and NATO seems to be rising at times though there is more of a competitive nature of relations among these two organisations. Even back in the cold war days, NATO did not have relations with another such organization like the CSTO and even though CENTO and SEATO (the Southeast Asian and Central Treaty Organizations) existed, NATO didn't really interact with them in organisational basis. There are certain inherent structural limitations on NATO working in full cooperation with the CSTO. The factors responsible for limitations of NATO-CSTO cooperation -

- *Firstly*, it is more likely that individual member countries of NATO work with the CSTO like in CSTO exercises rather than NATO participating with the CSTO. Many events that take place in Russia as NATO events are events of individual countries of NATO exercises.
- *Secondly*, the limitation that could be seen in NATO-CSTO close cooperation is that presently NATO is more focussed on its internal problems. Apart from its role in humanitarian intervention like the one in Kosovo in 1999 and more recently in Libya, and some counter-terrorism missions in Afghanistan, NATO still has internal debates regarding its long-term focus and hence rather than focussing on other similar organisations like CSTO.
- *Thirdly*, the NATO could not establish formal ties with the CSTO because of the consensus principle of NATO where US does not become a part of such a consensus. Some parts of the US security establishments still see CSTO as a potential way for Russia to stretch its dominance over the post-Soviet space. NATO actually pretty much does not want to recognise CSTO (Gorenburg 2011).

8.8   Conclusion

Both the Shanghai Cooperation Organisation (SCO) and the North Atlantic Treaty Organisation (NATO) have geopolitical interests in the Gulf and Central Asia. The US military is present in Afghanistan, Djibouti, Iraq, Kuwait, Qatar, Saudi Arabia, the UAE, Bahrain, and Oman; the British and French militaries are present in Afghanistan and Bahrain; and the former is a military alliance whose members have established significant presences throughout the Greater Middle East. By contrast, the SCO is a political bloc with a low degree of military integration among its members. China has a logistics station in Djibouti, similar to Russia's military presence in Kyrgyzstan and Tajikistan, while India has a military presence in Tajikistan.

While the three NATO countries are stronger in terms of military deployments and power projection capabilities, the three SCO members benefit from superior geographic proximity. While NATO countries have acquired both land power in Afghanistan and sea power in the Gulf, the major SCO nations have concentrated their respective land might in Central Asia. While the military might of the SCO and NATO have grown, interstate conflict as well as major economic, political, and social issues plague Central Asia and the Gulf. Given this, the military presence of nations outside of NATO and the SCO may have a shaky base and encounter numerous obstacles in the future.

References

Adomeit, Hannes. 2007. *Inside or Outside? Russia's Policy Towards NATO*. FG 5 2007/01. January.

Allison, R. 2008. Russia Resurgent? Moscow's Campaign to Coerce Georgia to Peace. *International Affairs* 84 (6): 1145–1171.

Andreev, Yuri. 2012. Former Soviet Space: Ukraine's NATO Membership Could Provoke Global Catastrophe. *Strategic Culture Foundation*. January 19.

Aris, Stephan. 2011. *Eurasian Regionalism: The Shanghai Cooperation Organisation*, 1. UK and US: Palgrave Macmillan.

Aslund, Anders. 2007. *How Capitalism Was Built: The Transformation of Central and Eastern Europe, Russia, and Central Asia*. Cambridge University Press.

Aurel, Braun. 2008. *Russia's Backyard: The Place of the Near Abroad in Russian Foreign Policy*, 41. Amazon Publishers.

Bailes, Alyson J. K., Pál Dunay., Pan Guang and Mikhail Troitskiy. 2007. *The Shanghai Cooperation Organization SIPRI Policy Paper No. 17*. Stockholm: Stockholm International Peace Research Institute.

Baylis, John. 2007. International and Global Security in the Post-Cold War era. In *The Globalisation of World Politics: An Introduction to International Relations*, ed. John Baylis, Steve Smith, and Patricia Owens, 1–9. USA: Oxford University Press.

Bogaturov, Alexei. 2004. *International Relations in Central-Eastern Asia: Geopolitical Challenges and Prospects for Political Cooperation*, 9. The Brookings Institution. http://www.brookings.edu/fp/cnaps/papers/bogatu rov2004.pdf, June.

Boland, Julie. 2010. *Learning from the Shanghai Cooperation Organization's 'Peace Mission-2010' Exercise*. October 29. Brookings. Available at: http://www.brookings.edu/research/opinions/2010/10/29-asia-war-games-boland.

———. 2011. Transnational Threats and Challenges: Strengthening the Coherence of the OSCE Response and Interaction with Other International Actors. Speech delivered on 30th June. At the 2011 *Annual Security Review Conference: Vienna*, 2011.

Bridge, Robert. 2011. Russia Talks Tough on CSTO. *Russian Times*.

Cohen, Ariel. 2013. *Russia's Eurasian Union Could Endanger the Neighborhood and U.S. Interests*, 1. BackGrounder. The Heritage Foundation. June 14.

David, Erkomaishvilli. 2008. Collective Security and Unilateral Decisions— Security Prospects for the Post-Soviet Space. *CEJISS* 2 (2) (November): 33.

Evan, Feigenbaum. 2007. The Shanghai Cooperation Organization and the Future of Central Asia, *Delivered to the Nixon Center*. 6 November. http://dushanbe.usembassy.gov/sp_09062007.html, Accessed on December 21, 2010.

Gill, Bates. 2001. Shanghai Five: An Attempt to Counter U.S. Influence in Asia? Opinion. May 4, *Brookings*. Available at: http://www.brookings.edu/research/opinions/2001/05/04china-gill.

Giustozzi, Antonio and Anna Matveeva. 2008. The SCO: A Regional Organisation in the Making. Crisis states Working Papers Series 2, 39. *Crisis States Research Centre*. London School of Economics and Political Science, London. UK.

Gorenburg, Dmitry. 2011. Why NATO Won't Recognise the CSTO. 2011 [Online Web], http://valdaiclub.com/near_abroad/27800.html, Accessed on April 24, 2012.

Haas, Marcel de. 2007. The Shanghai Cooperation Organization and the OSCE: Two of a Kind?. *Helsinki Monitor: Security and Human*

Rights. No. http://www.clingendael.nl/publications/2007/20071100_cscp_ art_haas.pdf, Accessed on February 11, 2011, p. 7.

Henry, Plater-Zyberk. 2007. Who is Afraid of the SCO? *Conflict Studies Research Centre*. Sandhurst, p. 3.

Ivanov, Igor. 2005. On the New Version of the National Security Conception of the Russian Federation. In *Russian Foreign Policy in Transition: Concepts and Reality*, ed. Andrei Melvill and Tatiana Shakleina, 122. Budapest: Central European University Press.

Jeanne, Wilson. 2009. Rethinking Colour Revolution. *Journal of Communist Studies and Transition, Politics* 25 (2–3): 369–395.

Karatnycky, Adrian. 2001. Ukraine's Orange Revolution. *Foreign Affairs*. April.

Kudenko, Aleksey. US Attack on Iran will Shake Everyone—CSTO Chief. [Online Web]. http://rt.com/politics/us-attack-iran-csto-835/, Accessed on March 21, 2012.

Lanteigne, M. 2006–2007. In Medias Res: The Development of the Shanghai Cooperation Organisation as a Security Community. *Pacific Affairs* 79 (4): 605–622.

Mankoff, Jeffrey. 2009. *Russian Foreign Policy: Return of the Great Power Politics*, 206. New York: Rowman & Littlefield Publishers. Inc.

———. 2011. *Russian Foreign Policy: The Return of the Great Power Politics*, 2nd ed., 352. Lanham, MD: Rowman & Littlefield.

Marlène, Laruelle. 2008. Russia's Central Asia Policy and the Role of Russian Nationalism. *Central Asia-Caucasus Institute and Silk Road Studies Program*. April. p. 17.

Medvedev, Dmitry. 2007. MFA Russian Federation, Speech by Russian Minister of Foreign Affairs Sergey Lavrov at SCO Council of Foreign Ministers Meeting. Bishkek. July 9. Available at: http://www.mid.ru/brp_4.nsf/0/634 8382D9C12B077C3257314001B98B8.

———. 2008. Press Conference Following the Collective Security Treaty Organisation Summit. Moscow. 5 September 2008. President of Russia Website. [Online Web], http://archive.kremlin.ru/eng/speeches/2008/09/05/2125_type82912type82914type82915_206180.shtml, Accessed on March 13, 2012.

———. 2009. Press Conference Following CSTO and EurAsEC Summits. Moscow. 4 February. President of Russia Website, [Online Web], http://www.kremlin.ru/eng/speeches/2009/02/04/1956_type82914type82915_ 212504.shtml, Accessed on 13 March 2012.

Neumann, Iver B. 2005. Russia as a Great Power. In *Russia as a Great Power: Dimensions of Security Under Putin*, ed. Jacob Hedenskog, Vilhelm Konnander, Bertil Nygren, Ingmar Oldberg, and Christer Pursiainen, 33. Oxon, USA and Canada: Routledge.

North Atlantic Treaty Organisation. 2013. What is NATO? August. Available at: http://www.nato.int/nato-welcome/index.html.

Nygren, B. 2008. *The Rebuilding of Greater Russia—Putin's Foreign Policy towards the CIS Countries*, 119. New York: Routledge.

Olcott, Marha Brill. 2005. Kryzstan's Tulip Revolution, *Carnegie Endowment for International Peace*. March 28.

Oldberg, Ingmar. 2005. "Foreign Policy Priorities Under Putin: *A Tour d'horizon*. In *Russia as a Great Power: Dimensions of Security Under Putin*, eds. Jacob Hedenskog, Vilhelm Konnander, Bertil Nygren, Ingmar Oldberg and Christer Pursiainen, p. 14. Oxon. USA and Canada: Routledge.

———. 2009. Russia's Great Power Strategy Under Putin and Medvedev. *Eurasia Daily Monitor (EDM)* 6 (108): 2–23.

Ponsard, Lionel. 2007. *Russia, NATO and Cooperative Security: Bridging the Gap*. Oxon, USA and Canada: Routledge.

Pop, Irina Ionela. 2009. Russia, EU, NATO and the Strengthening of the CSTO in Central Asia. *Caucasian Review of International Affairs* 3 (3): 278–290.

Portyakov, Vladimir. 2007. The Shanghai Cooperation Organisation: Achievements, Problems and Prospects. Paper Presented at an International Forum of the Centre for East and South East Asian Studies. *Lund University*, pp. 1–12.

———. 2006. President of Russia Website "Press Statements Following the Shanghai Cooperation Organisation Council of Heads of States Session".

Radyuhin, Vladimir. 2012. "And Then There Were Five", in *The Hindu*, 11 July.

Samarkhan, Kurmat. 2011. SCO RATS to Improve Anti-terror Work Through Joint Efforts of Its Member States, Dzhumanbekov. *Kazinform*. 9 February. http://www.inform.kz/eng/article/2349905, Accessed on February 9, 2011.

Socor, V. 2007. Organizational Setbacks at OSCE's Year-end Ministerial Conference. Jamestown Foundation. vol.4, no. 225.

———. 2006. Speech of the President of RF Vladimir Putin SCO—A New Model of Successful International CooperationJune 14. Available at official web-site of the President of the RF.

———. 2008. Corruption and Democracy The "Color Revolutions" in Georgia and Ukraine. *Taiwan Journal of Democracy* 4 (2): 75–90.

Swanstorm, Niklas. 2008. Georgia: The Split that Split the SCO. *Central Asia-Caucasus Institute Analyst*. March 9.

Tatum, David Jesse. 2008. The Foreign Policy Concept of the Russian federation.

———. 2009. Democratic Transition in Georgia: Post-Rose Revolution Internal Pressure on Leadership. *Caucasian Review of International Affairs* 2 (3), Spring: 156–171.

Troitskiy, Mikhail, Pan Guang, et al. 2003. Wall Street Journal Europe.

———. 2007. The Shanghai Cooperation Organization. SIPRI Policy Paper No. 17. *Stockholm International Peace Research Institute*. May, p. 208.

———. 2009. Growing Pains. *The Journal of International Security Affairs* (17), Fall 2009.

Upadhyay, Dadan. 2011. *Global Research, Russia and India Report*.

Vivid Maps. 2018. Current military alliances in the world. available at: Current military alliances in the world - Vivid Maps

Weitz, Richard. 2006. Terrorism in Eurasia: Enhancing the Multilateral Response. *China and Eurasia Forum Quarterly* 4 (2): 40.

Xuequan, Mu. 2012. CSTO Opposes Using Force Against Iran. English.xinhuanet.com, April 13. [Online Web], http://news.xinhua net.com/english/world/2012-04/13/c_122970617.html, Accessed on April 27, 2012.

Zarifi. 2011. ITAR TASS News Agency.

CHAPTER 9

Russia's Eurasian Strategy: A Way Forward

Abstract China competes with Russia, the leading player in the post-Soviet arena, through regional alliances such as the EAEU. Russia wants to establish a coordinated strategy with other states and limit Chinese dominance in Central Asia. Political unrest has negatively impacted economic ties between Europe and Russia, although commerce between the EAEU and Asia has expanded dramatically. Russia now prioritises forging closer links with the West and expanding its trade and economic connections with Europe, marking a shift in the country's approach to its immediate neighbours. In 2014, the EAEU was formally founded.

Keywords Russia · Eurasia · EAEU · Central Asia · China · Security strategy

9.1 Introduction

Given its breach with Ukraine and tensions with the West, Moscow is looking to redirect its policy towards Asia and increase its influence in the post-Soviet area. Instead of splitting apart from the West, Russia wants to reinvent itself as a significant Eurasian great power. In an attempt to gain influence in "Greater Eurasia" and amass more international leverage,

© The Author(s), under exclusive license to Springer Nature Singapore Pte Ltd. 2024
R. Pradhan and S. Kakoty, *Security Integration in the Post-Soviet Space and Collective Security Treaty Organization*,
https://doi.org/10.1007/978-981-97-6445-7_9

Russia has taken the lead in constructing the Eurasian Economic Union, a very strong multilateral organisation that is transforming the geopolitical and economic landscape of the region. Asia is changing, though, and Europe needs to realise this right away. How Russia adapts its Eurasian strategy in the context of rising Asia to oppose Europe's unparalleled influence in the region with the goal of restricting Russia within its own sphere of influence remains the crux of this chapter.

9.2   Russia's Eurasian Identity and Vladimir Putin

President Vladimir Putin of Russia is an advocate for deeper ties amongst the former Soviet republics and sees the fall of the Soviet Union as a significant geopolitical calamity. In order to maintain its influence in the post-Soviet sphere, Russia has stepped up its efforts, especially by fortifying the Eurasian Economic Union (EAEU), which is composed of Kyrgyzstan, Belarus, Kazakhstan, Armenia, and Russia (Pant 2022). Moscow's ultimate objective is not to recreate a powerful supranational state like the Soviet Union, but rather to retain influence over developments in the post-Soviet surroundings, even if the EAEU has been the most successful regional integration initiative since the Soviet Union's breakup in 1991 (Perovic 2019).

Russia is fortifying its position in a cutthroat international arena by utilising multilateral institutions such as the EAEU. It seeks to play the role of Eurasia's doorkeeper, keeping the governments in the region under its control and preventing them from assimilating into Western organisations. Moscow also aims to strengthen its position through regional alliances at international fairs. Russia's place in post-Soviet Eurasia is precarious and dependent on the actions of foreign powers as well as the interests of the governments in the area (Gotz 2022). Despite being members of the EAEU, several post-Soviet countries are averse to giving up their political autonomy and instead want to benefit financially from their ties to Russia. Understanding that using force could backfire, the Kremlin wants to make sure the EAEU, which is dominated by Russia, is prosperous and appealing to all of its members, not just those who share its objectives.

9.3   GREAT POWER GAME IN THE POST-SOVIET SPACE

Russia is still the most significant player in the post-Soviet arena, but through regional alliances like the EAEU, it is up against challenge from other nations, most notably China. Russia wants to establish a coordinated strategy with other states and limit Chinese dominance in Central Asia. Russia's international standing and relations with the West and Asia will be affected by the country's move towards Asia and Moscow's attempts to fortify relationships with its neighbours (Wani 2023). Political unrest has negatively impacted economic ties between Europe and Russia, although commerce between the EAEU and Asia has expanded dramatically.

Trade and economic cooperation are likely to continue expanding in the Asia–Pacific and Eurasian regions as a result of the US-China trade war. In order to prevent missing out on economic possibilities and moving eastward, Europe needs to reevaluate its policies (Cerutti et al. 2019). Russia has always viewed the post-Soviet area as a key interest zone and has only accepted surrounding sovereignty when it does not jeopardise its regional dominance and national interests.

Russia, Kazakhstan, and Belarus founded the Eurasian Economic Union in Astana, with the presidents of those countries asserting their immense influence because of shared historical, cultural, ethnic, political, and economic links, as well as wider security concerns. Because Moscow continued to maintain its hegemonic position and its neighbours were still weaker, Russia did not actively pursue an integrationist agenda during the 1990s and 2000s (Pieper 2020). Russia prioritised deepening its commercial and trade connections with Europe as well as rapprochement with the West.

Russia started to take a more assertive stance towards its close neighbours in the early 2000s. This was linked to three significant developments: the establishment of reform-minded elite groups in the post-Soviet sphere, enhanced resources from oil and gas sales abroad, and political and economic stability during Vladimir Putin's presidency (Perovic 2019).

With the Baltic states joining NATO in 2004 and the European Union and NATO signing partnership agreements with other post-Soviet states, Western nations and organisations began to establish a foothold in the post-Soviet sphere. China increased its economic involvement, particularly in Central Asia, while Russia's influence in the energy transportation sector decreased. While oil and gas pipelines connect Central Asia directly with China, Azerbaijan's gas and oil currently reach Western markets through Georgia and Turkey (Perovic 2019; Stafford 2015; Hunter 2016).

Six former Soviet nations—Belarus, Kyrgyzstan, Kazakhstan, Tajikistan, and Russia—reformed the Collective Security Treaty (CSTO) into a military alliance in 2002. The CSTO members have agreed to cooperate, conduct joint military drills, and retain the authority to veto the construction of new foreign military sites within CSTO member states, although not yet being a fully fledged alliance like NATO (Weinstein 2007).

The organisation and the Shanghai Cooperation Organisation (SCO) signed an agreement in 2007. The SCO has grown to be a significant platform for discussion on political, economic, and security matters amongst the countries of the Asia–Pacific region (Xue 2021). This action was in line with Russia's new foreign policy, which aimed to fortify its influence over regional organisations while fostering ties with other governments and institutions. Even though a number of economic coalitions were established in the 1990s, these institutions lacked much effectiveness. Beginning in the early 2000s, Russia used state-run energy corporations to bolster its economy and fend off the influence of other countries. Nonetheless, Moscow stepped up its efforts to integrate inside a global framework in 2008–2009.

With the addition of Armenia to the 2010 customs union, the Eurasian Economic Community—which was founded in 2000 by Russia, Belarus, Kazakhstan, Kyrgyzstan, and Tajikistan—was further reinforced. A free trade area was agreed upon by the Commonwealth of Independent States (CIS) in 2011, and the Common Economic Space was established by Russia, Belarus, and Kazakhstan in 2014. Armenia and Kyrgyzstan become members of the organisation in 2015, deepening their commercial ties. 2014 saw the official founding of the EAEU (Stronski 2020).

9.4   Putin's Reconceptualization of Eurasia

Vladimir Putin brought back to life the idea of Eurasia, which was first introduced by Russian experts on foreign policy while he served as prime minister. In his presentation of a new conceptual framework for Eurasia, Putin dismissed the notion of a post-Soviet union as a "revival of the Soviet Union" (Legucka 2023). He proposed that a strong international organisation might emerge as a "pole in the modern world." Putin tried to dissipate the notion that a potential Eurasian Union would be interpreted as an effort to isolate them or oppose them.

Putin suggested creating a free trade zone between the European Union and the newly formed Eurasian union, which is headed by Russia. However, Russia's Eurasian strategy changed as a result of the Ukraine crisis and President Viktor Yanukovich's removal in February 2014.

In its foreign and economic policies, the Kremlin gave greater weight to the Asian vector and stepped up its efforts to expand its influence in the post-Soviet region. China's economic growth hastened Russia's eastward shift, which started prior to the Ukraine crisis. A \$400 billion USD 30-year agreement was signed in May 2014 between Beijing and Moscow to supply China with gas via a new pipeline. This is consistent with China's pursuit of a "sovereign" road in its foreign policy and Russia's internal discourse on the right to pursue its own "sovereign" path to democracy (Perovic 2019).

9.5   Russia-China Cooperation in Eurasian Space

According to Russian foreign policy experts, expanding collaboration with China is a moral move as well as politically and economically beneficial. The objectives of both nations are to safeguard their national sovereignty, expand their influence, and advance a non-Western model of global development. Putin emphasised the economic significance of Asia by announcing that Russia is now open to China. But Russia cannot afford to split from Europe since doing so would be detrimental to its economy and cultural character. Although Russia is still a modest element for the majority of Asian countries, Asia has grown in importance to Moscow as an economic partner. Perovic (2019) highlights the persistent discrepancy between the political objectives of enhanced Sino-Russian relations and the real Chinese investment, especially in Russia's undeveloped Far Eastern regions.

As part of Beijing's Belt and Road Initiative, Russia is constructing infrastructure to connect China with markets throughout Europe and beyond. The majority of projects, though, are located in Kazakhstan and other Central Asian nations. Russia's move to Asia is viewed as a narrative strategy towards Europe and an acknowledgement of geoeconomic realities. Russia views Asia as a potential route back to Europe given the tensions with the West and Brussels' unwillingness to interact with Moscow or the EAEU. Many think that Moscow will have more clout in dealing with Brussels if it forms coalitions with other strong powers. Russia is attempting to establish more equitable relations with Europe and increase international clout by turning its attention to the east. By creating Greater Eurasia, Russia will continue to be at the centre of both its immediate neighbourhood and the broader "Russian World." Russia needs control over regional developments in order to prevent its neighbours from establishing independent trade and political ties. Russia is binding its neighbours together in a complex web of military, security, political, and economic ties in order to accomplish this goal of increasing mutual dependence. In order to maintain Russian supremacy and promote regional partnerships, the EAEU is essential.

9.6   EAEU & EU

Western commentators see the European Economic Area (EAEU) as a Russian-managed coalition of states that would support Brussels, rather than as an efficient regional organisation similar to the European Union. The EAEU's ability to function as an effective multilateral organisation is questioned because none of its members—including Russia—are prepared to give up significant authority to an international organisation. Furthermore, others question the organization's capacity to accomplish meaningful integration given the elimination of trade barriers within the organisation and the necessity of openness, the rule of law, and economic liberalization—all of which are antagonistic to the interests of authoritarian governments. Furthermore, national political leaderships are frequently loyal to authoritarian nations, and EAEU bureaucrats might rather avoid taking chances. No other post-Soviet international organisation has attained a greater level of integration, notwithstanding possible challenges.

A technical agreement, the EAEU treaty seeks to increase economic integration and eliminate obstacles to the free flow of labour, capital, products, and services. Its institutional structure and decision-making procedure are broadly similar to those of the European Union. The heads of member states form the Supreme Eurasian Economic Council, which is responsible for most decision-making. Daily work is overseen by the permanent Eurasian Economic Commission (EEC), which has its headquarters in Moscow. The EAEU Court of Justice and the Interstate Council are two additional governing organisations. Eliminating trade barriers within a country is a violation of its sovereignty. External customs tariffs have been harmonised by the EAEU, moving decision-making from sovereign states to the union level. Additionally, it has lowered restrictions on capital and labour mobility and eliminated internal customs barriers.

Recent accomplishments by the European Association of Economic Unions (EAEU) include the creation of a unified energy market and a common market for pharmaceuticals. The union wants a common market for gas and oil by 2025, as well as a common market for electricity by 2019. Operators inside the EAEU would then be free to access energy networks in other EAEU member states. By 2025, the EAEU wants to remove all barriers to land, air, and sea transport, establishing a single transit zone and a single internal market for transport services via a standard electronic transport control system.

In order to guarantee united financial markets, the European Economic Area (EAEU) has decided to establish a common supranational authority on financial market regulation by 2025. Over 2000 people work for the bureaucratic apparatus of the EAEU, which is led by former prime minister of Armenia Tigran Sargsyan and is in charge of a growing number of laws. A more integrated EAEU with positive economic outcomes and ongoing trade agreements with other nations and organisations is the most likely scenario. The EAEU zone's economy is beginning to recover, which increases the project's appeal to both existing members and outside parties. As Uzbekistan aligns its import tariffs with EAEU regulations, Moldova became the first nation to be officially recognised as an observer in 2017. The EAEU and more than a dozen states have reached cooperation agreements, as well as various international organisations.

The integration process of the European Economic Area (EAEU) is beset by difficulties because member states frequently align themselves with Russia, which makes up 80% of the union's population and 87% of its GDP. Russia spends twenty times more on its military each year than all the other members of the EAEU combined. The member nations' expenses in breaking away from Russia may be substantial due to these geographical imbalances. The case of Ukraine has demonstrated that quitting the union may come down to a question of war or peace. Aware of the Kremlin's sensitivities, the new leaders who took over after Armenia's "velvet revolution" in 2018 handled relations with Russia cautiously.

They do, meanwhile, also have a lot of leeway and a strong negotiation position with Moscow. For instance, if Russia doesn't give in to Belarus' demands, Belarus, Russia's closest friend, threatens to boycott integration initiatives. Russia typically tries to accommodate Belarusian interests by cutting energy costs or writing off debts because it is not interested in continuing the fight.

With the European Union, Kazakhstan and Armenia have signed the Comprehensive and Enhanced Partnership (CEPA) Agreement, which is a "light" version of the EU Association Agreement and places trade policy responsibilities under the purview of the EAEU. In addition, Kazakhstan keeps negotiating agreements with China and has played a significant role in reviving the post-Soviet Central Asian states' union movement.

But as evidenced by the refusal of other union members to abide by Russia's sanctions in reaction to EU sanctions against Russia for its aggressive actions in Ukraine or Turkey's sanctions in 2015, Russia has occasionally put its economic interests ahead of the union's. Russia has a tendency to ignore limitations put in place by a shared rule if it feels that its interests are at danger.

9.7   RUSSIA'S EURASIAN VISION AND UKRAINE WAR

Russia is aware that its neighbours are increasingly vulnerable to political and economic pressure, especially in light of the Ukraine situation. All heads of state agree on important choices within the EAEU, despite its impact. In an effort to allay concerns about Russian domination, Moscow portrays the EAEU as an organisation that looks out for the interests of all members. Russia wants to prevent integration from becoming a burden on its own economy because it views coercion as having the potential to backfire. But Russia must also guarantee the union's prosperity and avoid being perceived as a Russian-led initiative with solely Russian objectives.

Since the present union only makes up around 6% of Russia's total trade, Putin is more concerned with the political than the economic parts of the project—deeper integration amongst the former Soviet republics. Rather, in order to improve its own standing in international affairs, Russia aims to make the union a significant player on the international stage and an economic powerhouse. The majority of trade and economic concerns might be resolved bilaterally between Russia and the various states in the region, given Russia's significance to each and every one of the member states. Belarus does not trade with other EAEU members; it mostly trades with Russia.

With only 14.6% of total trade among member states in 2017, domestic trade is generally at a relatively low level. Even if the majority of the members have higher levels of external commerce, there is reason to encourage closer cooperation because of powerful historical legacies like energy linkages, common technical standards from the Soviet era, and integrated rail and road transportation networks.

The individual member states of the regional integration bloc usually see it favourably, notwithstanding its modest economic achievement. The accommodating character of the nations' interests—such as Kazakhstan's external commerce with Europe and foreign direct investment coming from sources in the US, Europe, and China more and more—is mostly to blame for this.

With only 14.6% of total trade among member states in 2017, domestic trade is generally at a relatively low level. Even if the majority of the members have higher levels of external commerce, there is reason to encourage closer cooperation because of powerful historical legacies like energy linkages, common technical standards from the Soviet era, and integrated rail and road transportation networks.

The individual member states of the regional integration bloc usually see it favourably, notwithstanding its modest economic achievement. The accommodating character of the nations' interests—such as Kazakhstan's external commerce with Europe and foreign direct investment coming from sources in the US, Europe, and China more and more—is mostly to blame for this. The necessity to increase their tariffs to keep up with increased Russian tariffs initially put a strain on these economies. The expectation of a swift economic recovery was quickly dashed when lower oil prices and Western sanctions hit not just Russia but also other EAEU members. Benefits of integration were not always felt since Kyrgyzstan's local market was competitive with businesses from Kazakhstan, Russia, and Belorussia. Deals struck through the EAEU with third parties, however, may benefit all members as the union supervises economic and trade relations.

Free trade agreements are sought after by the European Economic Area (EEAEU) with nations including China, Iran, India, Egypt, Israel, Singapore, and Serbia. Seven nations have been given priority for free trade agreements by the EAEU Supreme Council following the signing of the first FTA with Vietnam in 2016. Comprehensive economic agreements have previously been inked by China and Iran, while Singapore has a Memorandum of Understanding. Memoranda of cooperation with the EEC have also been signed by Jordan, Morocco, the Faroe Islands, Cuba, Mongolia, South Korea, Cambodia, Ecuador, Chile, Peru, and Thailand.

Additionally, negotiations are underway for the EAEU to form partnerships with international organisations such as Mercosur, ASEAN, APEC, the Andean Community, and the CIS.

Although it has not yet formalised its relationship with the European Union, the EAEU is requesting official observer status at the WTO. With the goal of creating a comprehensive free trade area, the EAEU and Iran inked a preliminary free trade agreement in May 2018.

Given that it seeks to advance economic ties and foster reciprocal trade, the agreement with China may prove to be essential to the development of a complete free trade agreement. Both China and the Eurasian Economic Union acknowledge the significance of the Belt and Road project and the Eurasian Economic Union in fostering stable commercial relations within the region. The agreement intends to coordinate strategy with other EAEU members and limit Chinese influence in post-Soviet Central Asia. It could be advantageous for all EAEU members to come to a consensus on a stance on China.

Over the previous seven years, China has spent close to $100 billion in 168 projects in EAEU members, mostly in Central Asia, with Kazakhstan being the biggest beneficiary. Smaller and less diversified economies have been significantly impacted by China's direct discussions with each EAEU member; most of this investment is a component of Beijing's Belt and Road project.

Small economies in Kyrgyzstan are concerned about China's increasing influence, as it accounts for 28% of total trade turnover and 37% of foreign direct investment in the country. 41% of the nation's external debt is held by major project loans. Larger nations, like Kazakhstan, are also concerned about China because of the counterbalance provided by their partnership with Russia. Cheap Chinese goods and the increasing number of Chinese migrant labour undermine domestic producers. Although China provides financial support and investments to Central Asian governments, there is a chance that these states would develop projects that serve China's economic interests rather than those of the concerned states. The EAEU member states sell their goods on terms that are largely advantageous to China, especially natural resources and agriculture, given China's economic might and the need for investment. The EAEU may benefit from reaching a consensus on a shared policy.

9.8   Impact of Russia's War in Ukraine on Post-Soviet Space

The Russian invasion of Ukraine represents a dramatic expansion of Russia's territorial takeover of Ukraine since 2014 and raises concerns for post-Soviet security, the economy, energy, humanitarian crisis, logistics, and democracy. Fundamental concerns concerning the survival of Ukraine as a cohesive state, its independence as a nation, and the democratic underpinnings of its political institutions were brought up by the 2014 occupation of Crimea, Donetsk, and Luhansk. The EU and much of the globe were unprepared to respond to this unjustified onslaught that challenged the fundamentals of international order (Ordukhanyan 2023). The conflict in Ukraine is also profoundly altering the post-Soviet environment.

D. Trenin notes that a new policy of selective expansion based on Russia's national interests has begun, marking the end of Russia's geopolitical retreat. Due to concurrent developments in Belarus and Ukraine in Eastern Europe, the South Caucasus, and Central Asia, Russia's approach to its geographic boundary has recently experienced significant modifications (Trenin 2022).

Strengthening its geopolitical position, utilising military might to thwart NATO in Eastern Europe, encouraging Belarus's integration, controlling the situation in the South Caucasus, and incorporating the CSTO in its special military operation are all among Russia's national objectives. Traditional ideas of geopolitics, areas of influence, and the balance of power have a significant impact on Russia's policy.

Putin's claims that Ukraine has no right to exist as a sovereign nation with an independent society are consistent with Russian colonialist and imperialist practices. When taken as a whole, it may be assumed that Russia opposes both international law and the international order by threatening democratic ideals and independent post-Soviet states via a variety of coercive measures, including military, political, economic, and energy ones (Meister 2022).

Russia's war in Ukraine is the biggest military confrontation to occur on European soil since World War II, with repercussions for post-Soviet nations as well as all of Europe. The war has enormous effects on the economy, energy, humanitarian relief, logistics, geopolitics, and values because it jeopardises the territorial integrity and sovereignty of other post-Soviet nations that have chosen to pursue democracy.

The purported military triumph of a despotic nation has the potential to erode optimism for the establishment of democracy in the post-Soviet era and destroy endeavours to preserve their national identities.

The result of this conflict, which is not just about promoting geopolitical interests and gaining territorial dominance but also about the political ideals of authoritarian and democratic governance, will define the future of post-Soviet space. Russia's aggressive tactics pose a threat to Ukraine, which is the frontline of democracy in Eastern Europe that borders the Russian Federation. Due to the political activation of the 5th columns and internal political units financed and supported by Russia, other post-Soviet governments will fail in their democratic provisions even in the absence of a Russian invasion if Russia is successful in its aggressive tactics in Ukraine.

Russia's aggression endangers not only the security of Europe but also democracy's appeal as a safe haven for a sustainable, prosperous, and peaceful existence. Azerbaijan's recent attacks on Armenia's sovereign territories in September 2022 serve as an illustration of how other autocrats could imitate Russia's unjustified actions in Ukraine. The West needs to focus on the requirements of post-Soviet nations that are facing the greatest threat of the spread of authoritarian rule since the end of the Cold War in order to counter these negative tendencies. These needs include economic, security, and energy-related ones.

9.9   Conclusion

The EAEU framework has the potential to streamline bureaucratic red tape, encourage industry collaboration, and harmonise standards. Improved bargaining stances and improved ties between the EAEU and China could result from direct communication. Open markets and less reliance on China could result from free trade agreements with India. Each nation may gain if Russia persuades the EAEU's members to adopt similar policies towards China and other third countries, but doing so would also necessitate increased cooperation and commitment from all of the members, bringing them closer to Moscow. Since the European Union is the EAEU's largest economic partner, accounting for 40% of its imports and over half of its total exports, the EAEU's prosperity is dependent on how the EU views the region.

One of the EEC's foreign policy objectives is the negotiation of a free trade deal, which Moscow has been pushing for formal connections between the EAEU and Brussels. For political reasons, Brussels has refused formal talks with the EAEU, unwilling to give credibility to an organisation run by autocratic governments and unwilling to forge ties with a union that it perceives as being dominated by Russia. Increased collaboration with Russia, a nation that the EU and other Western states have sanctioned because of Moscow's hostile actions against Ukraine, would result from formal recognition of the EAEU. Brussels continues to view the EAEU as a geopolitical tool of Russia and is working to establish bilateral relations with the governments in the region.

In addition, the Russian invasion of Ukraine in February 2022 signalled a dramatic shift in the geopolitical environment. Russia is losing ground in nations outside of Ukraine that it still views as being within its sphere of influence as a result of the war. The need for a cohesive "post-Soviet" territory with Russia as its centre of gravity and a common identity has been highlighted by the war. Russia's position in security policies has changed in Belarus, Moldova, Armenia, Azerbaijan, Georgia, Kazakhstan, Kyrgyzstan, Tajikistan, Turkmenistan, and Uzbekistan. Moscow has used military cooperation and presence to exert control over the former Soviet empire, with the Collective Security Treaty Organisation (CSTO) acting as a conduit for Russian influence.

But in order to further its objectives, Russia has also resorted to violence and pressure, especially against nations that have decided to follow the West. These nations have had to consider the security footprint that Russia's political and military backing of irredentist regions has created when making decisions about their foreign policy. Primarily on Russian terms, the Eurasian Economic Union (EAEU) and the Commonwealth of Independent States (CIS) have played a pivotal role in advancing economic and political union.

REFERENCES

Cerutti, Eugenio, Gita Gopinath, and Adil Mohommad. 2019. *The Impact of US-China Trade Tensions*. International Monetary Fund, May 23.

Gotz, Elias. 2022. Near Abroad: Russia's Role in Post-Soviet Eurasia. *Europe-Asia Studies* 74 (9).

Hunter, Robert. 2016. NATO in Context: Geopolitics and the Problem of Russian Power. *Prism* 6 (2). Retrieved from: NATO in Context: Geopolitics and the Problem of Russian Power Geopolitics and the Problem of Russian Power on JSTOR.

Legucka, Agnieszka. 2023. Russia Turns towards Eurasia in New Foreign Policy Concept. *PSIM*. Retrieved from: https://pism.pl/publications/russia-turns-towards-eurasia-in-new-foreign-policy-concept.

Meister, S. 2022. A Paradigm Shift: EU-Russia Relations after the War in Ukraine. November 29, 2022. Retrieved February 10, 2023 from: https://dgap.org/en/research/publications/paradigm-shift-eu-russia-relations-after-war-ukraine.

Ordukhanyan, Emil. 2023. The Impact of Russia's War in Ukraine on Post-Soviet Space. *International Journal of Progressive Sciences and Technologies (IJPSAT)* 38 (2), May.

Pant, Himani. 2022. The Growing Relevance of Eurasian Economic Union for Russia. Indian Council of World Affairs. 22 December. Retrieved from: The Growing Relevance of Eurasian Economic Union for Russia—Indian Council of World Affairs (Government of India) (icwa.in).

Perovic, Jeronim. 2019. Russia's Eurasian Strategy. Centre for Security Studies. 10 May. Retrieved from: News Article – Center for Security Studies. ETH Zurich.

Pieper, Mortiz. 2020. The linchpin of Eurasia: Kazakhstan and the Eurasian Economic Union Between Russia's Defensive Regionalism and China's New Silk Roads. *International Politics* 58.

Stronski, Paul. 2020. *There Goes the Neighborhood: The Limits of Russian Integration in Eurasia*. Carnegie Endowment for International Peace, September 16.

Trenin, D. 2022. *Mapping Russia's New Approach to the Post-Soviet Space*. Carnegie Endowment for International Peace. Retrieved Mars 15, 2023 from: https://carnegiemoscow.org/commentary/86438.

Wani, Ayjaz. 2023. *Amid Russia-Ukraine Conflict, Advantage China in Central Asia*. Issue Brief. Observer Research Foundation. November 23.

Weinstein, Adam. 2007. Russian Phoenix: The Collective Security Treaty Organization. *The Whitehead Journal of Diplomacy and International Relations*. Winter/Spring.

Xue, Y. 2021. Twenty Years of the Shanghai Cooperation Organization: Achievements, Challenges and Prospects. *Open Journal of Social Sciences* 9 (10), October.

CHAPTER 10

Conclusion

Abstract In the 21st century, security is a crucial area in international politics. The Collective Security Treaty Organisation (CSTO) being an international organization, believes in securitizing post-Soviet nations from terrorism, religious fundamentalism, extremism, regional tension, and drug trafficking due to power vacuum after the Soviet disintegration. CSTO established in 1992 to fill the vacuum created by the collapse of the Soviet Union primarily manage new threats and challenges in soft security, such as drug trafficking and illegal cross-border migration. It works as a subsystem level organization, targeting traditional security issues of military. However, in recent years CSTO's integration is moving towards a traditional military-bloc like OSCE, EU, and NATO.

Keywords CSTO · NATO · Post-Soviet Space · Russia · Eurasia

Security is an important area to venture in international politics in the twenty-first century. How the modern states frame their security in an increasingly insecure world, what really becomes a security concern, the issues they identify, key importance they attaches to specific problems, and the extra ordinary measure they adopt to protect their valued object from specific threats are even interesting to deal with. If the constructivist theory of Barry Buzan, Ole Weaver and Jaap De Wilde to be analysed as they have outline in Security: A New Framework for Analysis by distinguishing between levels and sectors of security through the process of securitization as differentiated from politicisation. For them CSTO is one such organisation which believes in the process of securitization of the nations of the post-Soviet space from terrorism, religious fundamentalism, extremism, regional tension and drug trafficking has resulted due to power vacuum after the Soviet disintegration in the region. This probably answers the level and sector classification of Buzan and others in the security field. CSTO is an international organisation at a subsystem level and the units of the commonwealth are found firmly at this regional level. As far as the sectors of security are concerned, the Copenhagen School has provided for five sectors of security threats, such as: military, environment, economic, societal and political (Buzan et al. 1998). CSTO again fits well into this category targeting the traditional security issue of military. Hence, the selection CSTO for study and investigate into the matters of security in general and collective security of a specific region in particular fits with the framework of this book.

Collective Security Treaty (CST) signed in May 1992 was set up to fill the vacuum created by the 2002–2003 sudden demise of the largest political landmass on earth the great Soviet Union. In ten years' time the security cooperation evolved into the Collective Security Treaty Organisation (CSTO) in encompassing seven post-Soviet states including: Russia, Belarus, Armenia, Kazakhstan, Kyrgyzstan, Tajikistan, and Uzbekistan. From its inception, the CSTO has stressed that its primary function is to manage "new threats and challenges" in the sphere of "soft security," such as drug trafficking and illegal cross-border migration and is currently the primary framework for the politico-military integration of the Newly Independent States (NIS) (Nikitin 2007). With the transition to a joint air defence, three integrated army formations, horizontally integrated military systems, and collective peacekeeping forces, the CSTO's integration is also heading in the direction of a traditional military-bloc like OSCE, EU and NATO. However, it is yet to achieve the height and scale of NATO when it comes to collective security, military might and integration among the member states. Nevertheless, CSTO is newly origined and in a different situation to that North Atlantic Treaty Organisation. Further, the Commonwealth does not including powerful countries like US, UK, France the equal partners of NATO. It has only big powerful country called Russia having numerable issues of difference with its neighbours since it shares border with the regional countries unlike the NATO counterparts. Hence, it absolute comparison with NATO will not do justice to the existence and functions of CSTO. However, CSTO doesn't go unnoticed by other international organizations and forces engaged in the region. This speaks for CSTO's significance in the region and reflects the objectives for which it should work endlessly. In addition, the crisis of nation-states in the contemporary times, the plights of states such as Afghanistan and Syria in news has time and again put a question mark over the security of a single nation from that of a mightiest power. In this connection a collective security organisation like CSTO definitely has purpose to serve for the impoverished but energy rich nations of the region not just to secure their traditional security concerns but to maintain their good health.

But in order to fulfil its mandate for collective security, CSTO needs to prioritise the growth of political institutions, handle conflicts on member soil, monitor conflicts before they start, build a stockpile of sanctions and warning signals, lead peace talks, and implement agreements reached after the conflict. One step in this direction is the adoption of the "Agreement on Peacekeeping Actions and the State of Collective Peacekeeping Forces" by the CSTO. The CSTO's mandate has to be expanded to cover every facet of security for each member state if it is to continue in this direction. For instance, in Central Asia, this entails addressing delicate matters pertaining to water resources, water supply, energy redistribution, and resolving severe electricity shortages, all of which are seen as regional national security concerns.

In the lights of NATO as USA treats Europe as its breath knell. Russia can do the same for its partners as it has overcome worries of the past and emerged again as a super power in the world politics. If the CSTO is to become an organization which specializes in 'soft security,' then Russia has a larger role to play in tandem with other partners of the commonwealth. Given the recent activities of Russia, other Commonwealth members and the structures of CIS, it can be said that the CSTO is evolving into the primary structure through which the NIS might undergo politico-military integration. The CSTO is performing increasingly important functions for the collective security of the post-Soviet space. Such a trend of cooperation is likely to be continued into the long term future. With this hope and aspiration this book is written with the following objectives in the mind to be achieved.

The book begins with the five pertinent assumptions: *First*, deep-rooted linkages between regionalism and International politics and its unprecedented rise under globalization. *Secondly*, the idea of Eurasianism deeply entrenched in Russian socio-economic, political and civilizational values making Moscow the unchallenged flag bearer of the Eurasianism taling place in the wider region in the Post-Cold War era. *Thirdly*, The voluntary withdrawal of Russia from Central Asia and the Caucasus after the disintegration of the Soviet Union led to a security vacuum that created fertile grounds for the rise of terrorism, religious fundamentalism, extremism and drug trafficking; *Fourth*, CSTO's growing role in the post-Soviet space has led to the reduction of tension and conflict resolution, strengthening regional stability and security; and *Fifth*, The Russia-led CSTO has emerged as a counteracting force against the US particularly after latter's growing military presence in and around Afghanistan to keep Russia's natural role as an arbiter and defender intact.

To prove these hypotheses this book has been divided into ten different chapters. *The introductory chapter* dealing with the idea and concept of Eurasianism focuses on Eurasianism as a quasi-political and intellectual movement, emerged in the 1920s as an anti-Bolshevik movement. It emphasized Russia's unique blend of Slavic and non-Slavic cultures and ethnic groups, and the corporate nature of the Russian state. Eurasianism was a precursor to post-Soviet Russia's ideology, blending Marxism with nationalism. Historians have considered alternative options for the Soviet regime, including Trotsky, Bukharin, Mensheviks, and Peter B. Struve. The past is dependent on the present, with historians examining the past to understand the present political trends.

The second chapter "Regional Integration and Eurasianism" offered a theoretical framework. It advocates regionalism as an international political effort by nations to increase collaboration and support in various governmental operations, including military, political, economic, and social-cultural exchanges. It often results in regional integration among governments within a specific region. A process or a situation, driven by historical experiences, economic circumstances, geographic proximity, cultural similarity, or a common sense of threat from a dominant power, regionalism has been seen from various theoretical perspectives in this chapter.

Third chapter "Concept of Security" throws light upon the intellectual prominence of the issue of security studies in general and collective security in particular. Further it selects the post-Soviet space in order to examine the security integration process and collective security model in the post-Soviet space. The theoretical perspective and the scope are provided in the study and also the existing literature has been considered in the introductory chapter. It further gives a broad account of the aims and objectives of the work, the gap it tries to fill up and the research methodology adopted.

The Fourth chapter attempts to study the regional integration of the post-Soviet states to maintain friendly relations with each other in the framework of the Commonwealth of Independent States (CIS). It further focuses on the organization's formation, institutions and other bodies developed under it, such as EurAsEC, Common Economic Space and Common Monetary Zone and their role in strengthening the regional security paradigm. It also discusses the CIS' performance in dealing with security issues, including Collective Security Treaty providing an emerging new model of security at an international subsystem level encompassing several structures such as military, political, economic and social.

The fifth chapter looks onto the patterns of security environment in the post-Soviet space. It sets out to explain the nature of Russian foreign and security policy in the CIS region, more specifically in the Central Asian region and the Caucasus. It basically deals with the nature of Russian foreign policy just after the disintegration of the Soviet Union in 1991. Since then there has been spectacular shifts in the contours of Russian foreign policy. Since the collapse of USSR, Russia as a state had to find meanings and answers of its new existence and identity and also its relations with the post-Soviet states and the post-Cold war world system. It gives a theoretical framework of the Russian foreign policy and traditional principles of Russian security thinking. It further focuses on the themes and patterns that Russia followed while pursuing its security and foreign policy after 1991 in the CIS space. Russia refocused its foreign policy interest towards the post-Soviet states since the coming of Putin. It explains the nature of Russian foreign policy and the way Russian foreign policy drifted from its ideological base to pragmatism. Russia has taken many significant steps regarding the maintaining of security in its sphere of influence. The CSTO has been one of the most successful and useful attempts amongst it. Russia has been a guiding light to the newly independent states with less or no experience in overcoming the sudden problems persisting just after the disintegration of Soviet Union. The chapter also explains Russia's attempts in security integration and military cooperation with the post-Soviet states. It further explained the motive for security integration as to how a process of security integration is so very vital for both Russia and the other post-Soviet states. This process is mutually beneficial. The chapter further analyses Russia's efforts while cooperating with each CSTO member independently.

The sixth chapter focuses on the security integration process of the post-Soviet space in general and that of the role of CSTO in particular. This employs the method of descriptive analysis of the creation and evolution of the CSTO and the legal basis of its foundation. It also lays down an analysis of the successes and failures of this Russian-led organisation in countering the soft and hard security threats of the post-Soviet space.

The seventh chapter mainly centres on the security scenario in the post-Soviet space after the demise of the Soviet Union. The cardinal points of discussion are focused regarding the backdrop of the post-Soviet space, the relation between the newly independent states and the role that radical Islam plays in the wider regional security context. It is here that the chapter focuses on the symbiotic reply by the post-Soviet states against the threats posed and the founding of the Tashkent treaty as a consequence.

The eighth chapter deals with comparison between CSTO and to that of SCO and NATO. In the spirit of these organisations created with the purpose of securing the security of their member states, this chapter makes a valiant attempt not to make a comparison rather to understand each organisation against the background it was created. CSTO unlike NATO and SCO is an organisation created after a massive security vacuum created in the aftermath of the Soviet Union with a responsibility to ensure political integration and collective security to its members. While other organisations are discussed at length, the CSTO has been mentioned proudly as an evolving organisation not just to provide collective security to its regional members but also to grown into an organisation of far reaching implication in international politics with a positive note.

The *Ninth chapter* "Russia's Eurasian Strategy" discusses Russian aims to contain Chinese influence in Central Asia and develop a coordinated approach towards other powers. While European-Russian economic relations have suffered due to political tensions, trade between the EAEU and Asia has increased significantly. Russia's policy towards its immediate neighbors has evolved, with Russia focusing on rapprochement with the West and broadening trade and economic ties with Europe. The EAEU was officially established in 2014.

While the *Conclusion chapter* provides a brief analysis of the reach find-ings, the other chapters are used as an instrument to prove the hypotheses formed in the research design of the book. The second chapter has tried to answer the first hypothesis. It sets out to explain the nature of Russian foreign and security policy in the CIS region, more specifically in the Central Asian region and the Caucasus and as to how Russia emerged out from the ashes of the broken Soviet Union and how during the early years Russia had no clear Central Asia policy. Since the second half of the 1990s, Russia's foreign policy has been evolving much because of the rapid changes in Russia's domestic situation which gave birth to a different kind of phase of Russia's foreign policy. As the 'Primakov Doctrine' suggests Russia makes attempts to get back its lost great power status and as such gives prominence to the post-Soviet space and revives relations with these newly independent countries (Blank 2010). Till then the security scenario in the post-Soviet space was a disaster being a very volatile zone by creation of a security vacuum that led to the rise of concerns regarding terrorism, religious fundamentalism, extremism and drug trafficking and most of all nuclear arms proliferation.

After its disintegration of the Soviet Union in December 1991, it left behind an enormous arsenal of nuclear weapons and a vast nuclear weapons complex which was before the disintegration controlled by authoritarian government and hence it was under tight scrutiny and control. However after its demise, the collapse of the Union led to a condition where nuclear weapons coexisted in such unstable and insecure atmosphere. Nuclear leakage is not a hypothetical danger. It was one of the grave and immediate dangers of that time not only for Russia but the entire post-Soviet complex.

During Yeltsin's reign there was no apparent policy for Central Asia but with the coming of Putin in power, Russia had two major concerns with regard to Central Asia, firstly it had strategic concerns about the growing engagement of foreign actors in Central Asian Countries, and secondly it had security concerns about the threats to the security of the region. Economic concerns were intrinsic to both the issues. The increasing influ-ence of the Taliban in 1996 in Afghanistan, their further influence in Tajikistan and Uzbekistan border in 1998 and the fact that it gave support to Chechen separatists which was regarded as a major internal security threat, posed several problems for Russia. The growing "Islamic threat" posed as the major internal and external security threat. Along with this, the growing influence of the United States added to the problems of

Russia. Russia had to manage both its domestic economic priorities and also had to secure its neighbourhood. Russia's new focus on economic and energy cooperation became the central theme of its foreign policy towards Central Asia. Russia's response to US influence was of special interest as it was away from the zero sum perspective. There was a clear reflection of a cooperative perspective in Russia' approach.

The 9/11 terrorist attack was a major occurrence which influenced the Russian foreign policy. Rather than taking rhetoric steps to oppose US presence in the Central Asia, Russia actually cooperated with US and gave consent to a US military presence in 2001 (Wu 2011). However, Russia always wanted to be the big brother in this region. Furthermore, Russia in order to actively participate in the promotion of regional integration in the post-Soviet states made its attempts through the CIS Collective Security Treaty and the Shanghai Cooperation Organisation (SCO). This concern of Russia was seen in its various steps taken in order to revive relations with these countries that Russia considers to be under its 'sphere of influence'. While taking this measure, Russia through the CSTO sought to manage trans-border security problems that were emanating right from the borders. It also sought to prevent proliferation of terrorist groups and terrorist activities that would breed from neighbouring Afghanistan and threaten the whole of Russia, Central Asia and the adjoining areas. The main motive behind security integration is however mutual. Security integration and collective security benefits all the parties involved. As the post-Soviet states specifically the CSTO members in this context, benefits from being a part of the Russia-led CSTO, similarly Russia also draws benefits by engaging with these states be it in security dimensions or economic benefits.

10.1   RUSSIAN HEGEMONY, UKRAINE WAR AND THE FUTURE OF CSTO

Six post-Soviet nations have joined forces to form the CSTO, a military alliance aimed at ensuring mutual security. The Collective Security Treaty (CST), which was signed on May 15, 1992 by Russia and five other newly independent republics (Armenia, Kazakhstan, Kyrgyzstan, Tajikistan, and Belarus), was the result of the fall of the Soviet Union. As a means of allaying their concerns, the parties joined the CST in order to avoid the possible risks of a regional security vacuum, which may have resulted in intraregional wars and the intervention of foreign powers.

Russia saw the CST as a key tool for preserving its hegemony in the area and defending its so-called "privileged interests" zone. Nonetheless, the weaker governments saw their alliance with Russia as a way to assure Moscow that they posed no threat to national security. Consequently, these CST republics followed the maxim "keep your friends close, but your (potential) enemies closer" in an effort to avert any military involvement by Russia.

This security architecture was improved into the CSTO in 2002, creating a formal institution and a new international organisation to carry out the 1992 manifesto. At first, the CSTO essentially functioned as a paper entity, mainly for the purpose of formalising Russian armament shipments and training. It also functioned as a means of providing a multilateral façade—as opposed to a unilateral or bilateral one—to justify the Kremlin's military bases outside of the Russian Federation.

Nevertheless, the CSTO was more akin to a network of spokes that all emanated from Moscow than it was a truly multilateral alliance, and nothing would have remained to hold it together had Moscow failed in its obligations. But in the 2010s, the CSTO made a number of changes to become a more robust and effective security apparatus. Still, it remained relatively weak and reliant on Russia for survival.

However, the world appears to be fully immersed in the conflict in Ukraine since February 24, 2022 causing shockwaves throughout the rest of Europe, the Russian invasion of Ukraine has destroyed the widely-held notion that the atrocities of World War II had been forgotten. Since then, the new view of the security issues of the twenty-first century has been influenced by strong undercurrents of change. Few people in the West could have predicted that Russia's annexation of Crimea in 2014 would permanently alter the structure of the international system, turning it into a bipolar conflict between newly formed armed blocs. Fewer few nevertheless strongly cautioned against giving in to the notion that everything was returning to normal.

Fewer people cautioned even more forcefully against giving in to the notion that the world had returned to the previous Cold War logic. Former communist nations in Central Asia have pursued rather distinct paths in terms of security concerns and military ties since the fall of the Soviet Union. In terms of economic, energy, and security cooperation, Uzbekistan and Tajikistan have increasingly moved closer to the United States, while Kazakhstan maintains close connections with its aspirational and extraordinarily wealthy neighbour, China. Russia is losing the upper hand over its former dominions, as evidenced by the large influx of Chinese investments into Kazakhstan's oil and natural gas production and the 2001 establishment of a US military post in Uzbekistan (Umarov 2020).

For these reasons, the Organisation for Collective Security Treaty (CSTO; Organizatsiya Dogovora o kollektivnoi bezopasnosti; ODKV), which was founded at the initiative of the leaders of the Commonwealth of Independent States (CIS), has quickly developed into a potent tool that Russia might use to revert to the conditions of 1991. This research aims to investigate the extent to which the consequences of the ongoing war in Ukraine have had a significant impact on the CSTO as a major military bloc.

This book while providing an overview of the ways in which Russia has benefited greatly from post-1991 Central Asian regional institutions, including the CIS, SCO, and the CSTO, in maintaining and expanding its sphere of influence over the past several decades explains the key features and purposes of the CSTO, a military stronghold commanded by Russia that has progressively grown to oppose the NATO alliance, which is dominated by the US. However, Russia's assault on Ukraine and Moscow's hegemony in the wider region may in short term allow it to have its sway in the region but certainly in long term jeopardise the security organization's future while offering a thorough examination of the CSTO Member States' disparate security interests.

Even well before the Ukraine war the credibility of CSTO was under serious question due to predominant position enjoyed by Russia vis-à-vis other countries of the grouping. For instance, the institution's irrelevance began in 2010 when it failed to comply with Kyrgyzstan's request to counter ethnic clashes in its southern part of its country. This failure was due to the alliance's claim that its mandate only extended to external aggression, not domestic instability. Russia's 2014 annexation of Crimea and its open support for the secession of ethnic Russians in Ukraine's eastern Donbas region further undermined the foundations of the CSTO. Belarus and Kazakhstan sought to distance themselves from the CSTO by taking concrete steps to secure their sovereignty through changes to their national security doctrine, rhetoric, and policy.

Nevertheless, Russia's 2022 invasion of Ukraine has been costly for the Russian armed forces, causing a redirection of state resources from domestic projects and affecting Russia's military network in Eurasia. The Collective Security Treaty Organization (CSTO), a military alliance of six post-Soviet states, appeared to be at its zenith in its relevance and cohesiveness. No doubt, among the CSTO members only Belarus has extended open support to Russia in the Ukraine war yet the silence among the other member countries or unchallenged opposition to Russian hegemony somehow put the credibility of CSTO under litmus test. In addition to the Ukraine war, CSTO's coherence is also challenged by the Armenian-Azerbaijani dispute over Nagorno-Karabakh and border tensions between Tajikistan and Kyrgyzstan. The Nagorno-Karabakh conflict escalated in 2022, leading to Armenia's request for support. The CSTO responded with a special observation mission, but remained concerned and urged caution. Armenia withdrew from CSTO exercises and the Deputy Secretary General position. Border disputes between Tajikistan and Kyrgyzstan have worsened Central Asia's security situation. The CSTO's lack of clear actions indicates weak inertia, especially when Russia lacks the will to intervene and end conflicts. The Russian position on recently held mass protest in Kazakhstan and critical Russian position on democratic polity of Kyrgyzstan certainly exhibits the dominant position Russia has been enjoying in the grouping putting the peace, order and security of the region at the mercy of Kremlin and reduces the security of other countries to the convenience of Moscow.

To conclude, the invasion of Ukraine has certainly weakened Russia's ability to respond to crises in its southern and eastern neighbourhoods and hampered its involvement in large-scale CSTO operations. This may lead to the CSTO becoming marginalized in the coming years, resulting in additional changes in the post-Soviet area's security system. Some CSTO members may seek military support from other countries, especially China, Türkiye, and the U.S. The weakening of the CSTO may also lead to a greater terrorist threat in its area of responsibility and Europe. The U.S. may declare arms supplies and support in the fight against terrorist organizations with Afghanistan and organize regional exercises to limit China's influence in the region. A definite vacuum in the security apparatus in the Eurasian region if CSTO fails to capitalise the situation will certainly allow the major powers to play the role of security manager in the wake of Russian monopoly over the security interest of other stakeholders in the region.

REFERENCES

Blank, Stephen. 2010. International Rivalries in Eurasia. In *Key Players and Regional Dynamics in Eurasia: The Return of the Great Game*, ed. Maria Raquel Friere and Roger E. Kanet. Cham: Palgrave Macmillan.

Buzan, Barry, Ole Weaver, and Jaap de Wilde. 1998. *Security: A New Framework for Analysis*. Boulder: Lynne Rienner.

Nikitin, Alexander. 2007. Post-Soviet Military-Political Integration: The Collective Security Treaty Organization and Its Relations with the EU and NATO. *China and Eurasia Forum Quarterly* 5 (1): 35–44.

Umarov, Temur. 2020. China Looms Large in Central Asia, *Carnegie Russia Eurasia Center*. Carnegie Endowment. March 30. Available at: China Looms Large in Central Asia—Carnegie Endowment for International Peace.

Wu, Yu-Shan. 2011. Russia and the CIS in 2010. *Asian Survey* 51 (1): 64–75.

Bibliography

(* Indicates Primary Sources)

Bektour Iskender, Kyrgyzstan Flirts with Democracy, Al Jazeera, 13 October 2011.

*Bordyuzha, Nikolay. 2007. Speech delivered on 13th February 2007 at the Meeting of the OSCE Permanent Council.

*Bordyuzha, Nikolay. 2011. Transnational Threats and Challenges: Strengthening the Coherence of the OSCE Response and Interaction with Other International Actors. Speech Delivered on 30th June 2011 at the 2011 Annual Security Review Conference: Vienna.

*Government of the Republic of Kazakhstan. 2011. *Astana Calling, Ministry of Foreign Affairs, Astana.*

*Govt of the Russian Federation. 2011. Submitting to the President of the Russian Federation of the Agreement on the Creation of the System of Control of the Forces and Assets of the Collective Security Treaty Organisation System. Discussion at the Government Presidium meeting on August 4, 2008: Dushanbe.

*Informal Meeting of the Collective Security Treaty Organisation. 2011. Transcripts of the Informal Meeting of the CSTO Member-States Leaders, 2011 (Astana). President of Russia Website, 2 November 2011. http://eng.kremlin.ru/visits/2722.

*Informal Summit of the Collective Security Treaty Organisation. 2010. Transcripts of the Informal Meeting of the CSTO Heads of States, 2010 (Yerevan). President of Russia Website, 2 November 2011. http://eng.news.kremlin.ru/transcripts/811.

*Kristensen, Hans M. 2006. New and Traditional Security Threats to Russia, and the Utility of Nuclear Weapons. Meeting Paper on 12–13th October, 2006 on Emerging Nuclear Weapons Policies: An Opportunity to Increase Dialogue, FAS: Washington DC.

*Medvedev, D. 2008. Press Conference Following the Collective Security Treaty Organisation Summit, Moscow (5 September 2008). President of Russia Website [Online Web]. http://archive.kremlin.ru/eng/speeches/2008/09/05/2125_type82912type82914type82915_206180.shtml. Accessed on March 13, 2012.

*Medvedev, D. 2009. Press Conference following CSTO and EurAsEC Summits, Moscow, 4 February 2009. President of Russia Website [Online Web]. http://www.kremlin.ru/eng/speeches/2009/02/04/1956_type82914type82915_212504.shtml. Accessed on March 13, 2012.

*President of Russia Website "Press Statements Following the Shanghai Cooperation Organisation Council of Heads of States Session", 15 June 2006.

*Russian President, 'Otvety prezidenta ...' [Replies by the President], 11 February 2003 [Online Web]. http://194.226.82.50/text/appears. Accessed on March 19, 2003.

*Russian President, 'Vystuplenie prezidenta ...' [Speech by the president], 28 May 2002 [Online Web]. http://www.president.kremlin.ru/events. Accessed on May 31, 2002.

Adomeit, H. 1998. Russian National Security Interests. In *Security Dilemmas in Russia and Eurasia*, ed. R. Allison and C. Bluth. London: Royal Institute of International Affairs.

Adomeit, H. 2009. Inside or Outside? Russia's Policy Towards NATO. In *The Multilateral Dimension in Russian Foreign Policy*, ed. Elana Wilson Rowe and Stina Torjesen. USA and Canada: Routledge.

Akbarzadeh, S. 2004. Keeping Central Asia Stable. *Third World Quarterly* 25 (4): 689–705.

Akiner, Shirin. 2005. Political Process in Post-Soviet Central Asia. In *Central Eurasia in Global Politics*, ed. M. Amineh and H.Houweling. Netherlands: Brill Academic Publishers, Martinas Nijhoff Publishers and VSP.

Allison, R. 2004a. Regionalism, Regional Structures and Security Management in Central Asia. *International Affairs* 80 (3): 463–483.

Allison, R. 2004b. Strategic Reassertion in Russia's Central Asia Policy. *International Affairs* 80 (4): 277–293.

Allison, R. 2008. Russia Resurgent? Moscow's Campaign to Coerce Georgia to Peace. *International Affairs* 84 (6): 1145–1171.

Allison, R., and C. Bluth. 1998. *Security Dilemmas in Russia and Eurasia*. London: Royal Institute of International Affairs.

Andreev, Yuri. 2012. *Former Soviet Space: Ukraine's NATO Membership Could Provoke Global Catastrophe*. Strategic Culture Foundation, January 19.

Aris, S. 2011. *Eurasian Regionalism: The Shanghai Cooperation Organisation.* UK and USA: Palgrave Macmillan.

Aurel, Braun. 2008. Russia's Backyard: The Place of the Near Abroad in Russian Foreign Policy, p. 41.

Averre, Derek L. 2003. Transborder Security and Regionalism. In *Russian Regions and Regionalism: Strength Through Weakness*, ed. Graeme P. Herd and A. Aldis. USA and Canada: RoutledgeCurzon.

Babus, Sylvia W. 2004. Democracy Building in Central Asia Post September 11. In *The Tracks of Tamerlane: Central Asia's Path to the 21st Century*, ed. D. Burghart and T. Sabonis-Helf. Washington, DC: NDU CTNSP.

Baev, Pavel K. 1996. *The Russian Army in a Time of Troubles.* Oslo: PRIO.

Baev, Pavel K. 2003. Military Aspects of Regionalism. In *Russian Regions and Regionalism: Strength Through Weakness*, ed. Graeme P. Herd and A. Aldis. USA and Canada: RoutledgeCurzon.

Baylis, John. 2007. International and Global Security in the Post-Cold War Era. In *The Globalisation of World Politics: An Introduction to International Relations*, ed. John Baylis, Steve Smith, and Patricia Owens. Oxford: Oxford University Press

Bergman, J. 1998. Was the Soviet Union Totalitarian? The View of Soviet Dissidents and the Reformers of the Gorbachev Era. *Studies in the East European Thought* 50 (4): 247–281.

Berryman, J. 2010. Russia and China in Eurasia: The Wary Partnership. In *Key Players and Regional Dynamics in Eurasia: The Return of the Great Game*, ed. Maria Raquel Friere and Roger E. Kanet. UK and USA: Palgrave Macmillan.

Blagov, S. 2008. Kremlin Backed Security Grouping Exerts Greater Role in Eurasia. *Jamestown Foundation* 5 (9).

Blank, S. 2010. International Rivalries in Eurasia. In *Key Players and Regional Dynamics in Eurasia: The Return of the Great Game*, ed. Maria Raquel Friere and Roger E. Kanet. UK and USA: Palgrave Macmillan.

Bohr, A. 2004. Regionalism in Central Asia: New Geopolitics, Old Regional Order. *International Affairs* 80 (3): 485–502.

Boland, Julie. 2010. Learning from the Shanghai Cooperation Organization's 'Peace Mission-2010' Exercise. Brookings, October 29. Available at: http://www.brookings.edu/research/opinions/2010/10/29-asia-war-games-boland.

Bowker, M. 2007. *Russia, America and the Islamic World.* Great Britain: Antony Rowe Ltd.

Brannon, R. 2004. Regional Security Cooperation and Foreign Policies in Central Asia: A 21st Century 'Great Game'? In *The Tracks of Tamerlane: Central Asia's Path to the 21st Century*, ed. D. Burghart and T. Sabonis-Helf. Washington, DC: NDU CTNSP.

Bridge, R. 2011. CSTO Talks Tough on NATO. RT, December 20 [Online Web]. http://rt.com/politics/csto-nato-russia-medvedev-kazakh stan-257/. Accessed on June 16, 2012.

Buszynski, L. 2005. Russia's New Role in Central Asia. *Asian Survey* 45 (4): 546–565.

Calleo, David P. 2003. Reflections on Eurasian Security. In *Limiting Institutions? The Challenge of Eurasian Security Governance*, ed. James Sperling, Sean Kay, and S. Victor Papascoma. Manchester and New York: Manchester University Press.

Casier, T. 1999. The Shattered Horizon: How Ideology Mattered to Soviet Politics. *Studies in East European Thought* 51 (1): 35–59.

Charter of the Shanghai Cooperation Organisation, SCO Charter, Article 1, 2001. Available at: http://www.hrichina.org/content/5207.

Chausovsky, Eugene. 2011. The CSTO and Russian Strategy [Online Web]. http://www.stratfor.com/analysis/20110706-dispatch-csto-and-russian-str ategy. Accessed September 17, 2011.

Checkel, J. 1993. Ideas, Institutions and the Gorbachev Foreign Policy Resolu-tion. *World Politics* 45 (2): 271–300.

Choo, J. 2003. The Geopolitics of Central Asian Energy. In *Limiting Insti-tutions? The Challenge of Eurasian Security Governance*, ed. James Sperling, Sean Kay, and S. Victor Papascoma. Manchester and New York: Manchester University Press.

Chung, Chein-peng. 2004. The Shanghai Cooperation Organisation: China's Changing Influence in Central Asia. *The China Quarterly* 180: 989–1009.

Cimbala, Stephen J. 2010. *Nuclear Weapons and Cooperative Security in the 21st Century: The New Disorder*. USA and Canada: Routledge.

Clunan, Anne L. 2009. *The Social Construction of Russia's Resurgence*. USA: Johns Hopkins University Press.

Colton, Timothy J. 2008. Post-Communist Russia, the International Environ-ment and NATO. In *NATO-Russia Relations in the Twenty-first Century*, ed. Aurel Braun. New York and London: Routledge.

Erkomaishvilli, David. November 2008. Collective Security and Unilateral Deci-sions—Security Prospects for the Post-Soviet Space. *CEJISS* 2 (2): 33.

Deyermond, R. 2008. *Security and Sovereignty in the Former Soviet Union*. Colorado and London: Lynne Rienner Publishers Inc.

Duffield, John S., C. Michota, and S. Miller. 2008. Alliances. In *Security Studies: An Introduction*, ed. Paul D. Williams. Oxon, USA and Canada: Routledge.

Embassy of Tajikistan to Pakistan. 2012. Tajikistan Holds CSTO Anti-terror Drills [Online Web]. http://www.tajikembassy.pk/m-news21.aspx. Accessed April 14, 2012.

Evan Feigenbaum. 2007. The Shanghai Cooperation Organization and the Future of Central Asia. Delivered to the Nixon Center, November 6. http://dushanbe.usembassy.gov/sp_09062007.html. Accessed December 21, 2010.

Everett-Heath, T. 2003. Instability and Identity in a Post-Soviet World. In *Central Asia. Aspects of Transition*, ed. T. Everett-Heath. London: Routledge.

Fawcett, L. 2008. Regional Institutions. In *Security Studies: An Introduction*, ed. Paul D. Williams. Oxon, USA and Canada: Routledge.

Fawn, R. 2003a. Realignments in Russian Foreign Policy: An Introduction. In *Realignments in Russian Foreign Policy*, ed. Rick Fawn. London and Portland: Frank Cass & Co. Ltd.

Fawn, R. 2003b. Russia's Reluctant Retreat from the Caucasus: Abkhazia, Georgia and the US After 11 September 2001. In *Realignments in Russian Foreign Policy*, ed. Rick Fawn. London and Portland: Frank Cass & Co. Ltd.

Flynn, Gregory, and Henry Farrell. 1999. Piecing Together the Democratic Peace: The CSCE, Norms. *Construction of Security in Post-Cold War Europe: International Organization* (53): 505–535.

Frederking, B. 2003. Constructing Post-Cold War Collective Security. *The American Political Science Review* 97 (3): 363–378.

Friere, Maria R. 2010. Eurasia at the Heart of Russian Politics: Dynamics of (In)dependence in a Complex Setting. In *Key Players and Regional dynamics in Eurasia: The Return of the Great Game*, ed. Maria Raquel Friere and Roger E. Kanet. UK and USA: Palgrave Macmillan.

Friere, Maria R., and Roger E. Kanet. 2010. Russia in Eurasia: External Players and Regional Dynamics. In *Key Players and Regional Dynamics in Eurasia: The Return of the Great Game*, ed. Maria Raquel Friere and Roger E. Kanet. UK and USA: Palgrave Macmillan.

Frost, Alexander. 2009. The Collective Security Treaty Organisation, the Shanghai Cooperation Organization, and Russia's Strategic Goals in Central Asia. *The China and the Eurasia Forum Quarterly* 7 (3): 83–102.

Fumagalli, M. 2007. Alignments and Re-alignments in Central Asia: The Rationale and Implications of Uzbekistan's Rapprochement with Russia. *International Political Science Review* 28 (3): 253–271.

Fyodorov, Y. 2005. Do We Need Reform of Russian Foreign Policy? In *Russian Foreign Policy in Transition: Concepts and Reality*, ed. Andrei Melvill and Tatiana Shakleina. Budapest: Central European University Press.

Gibler, Douglas M., and Jamil A. Sewell. 2006. External Threat and Democracy: The Role of NATO Revisited. *Journal of Peace Research* 43 (4): 413–431.

Giustozzi, Antonio, and Anna Matveeva. 2008. The SCO: A Regional Organisation in the Making Crisis States. Working Papers Series 2, 39. Crisis States Research Centre, London School of Economics and Political Science, London, UK.

Gleason, G. 2010. Russia and Central Asia's Multi Vector Foreign Policies. In *After Putin's Russia*, ed. Stephen K. Wegren and Dale R. Herspring. UK: Rowman and Littlefield Publishers, Inc.

Godzimirski, Jakub M. 2005. Russia and NATO: Community of Values or Community of Interests. In *Russia as a Great Power: Dimensions of Security Under Putin*, ed. Jacob Hedenskog, Vilhelm Konnander, Bertil Nygren, Ingmar Oldberg, and Christer Pursiainen. Oxon, USA and Canada: Routledge.

Goldgeier, James M., and Michael McFaul. 2003. *Power and Purpose: US Policy Toward Russia After the Cold War*. Washington, DC: Brookings Institution Press.

Gorenburg, D. 2011. Why NATO Won't Recognise the CSTO [Online Web]. http://valdaiclub.com/near_abroad/27800.html. Accessed on April 24, 2012.

Haas, Marcel de. 2007. The Shanghai Cooperation Organization and the OSCE: Two of a Kind? Helsinki Monitor: Security and Human Rights, No. 3. http://www.clingendael.nl/publications/2007/20071100_cscp_art_haas.pdf. Accessed on February 11, 2011.

Haas, Marcel de . 2010. *Russia's Foreign Security Policy in the 21st Century Putin, Medvedev and Beyond*. USA and Canada: Routledge.

Habibe Ozdal, 2010. Putting the CSTO to the Test in Kyrgyzstan, October 4. *The Journal of Turkish Weekly*. Available at: http://www.turkishweekly.net/columnist/3383/.

Hayrumyan, N. 2012. CSTO to Armenia-I Am Declaring War [Online Web]. http://www.lragir.am/engsrc/comments25210.html. Accessed on March 29, 2012.

Herd, Graeme P. 2003. Russia's Demographic Crisis and Federal Instability. In *Russian Regions and Regionalism: Strength Through Weakness*, ed. Graeme P. Herd and A. Aldis. USA and Canada: RoutledgeCurzon.

Herspring, Dale R. 2010. Putin, Medvedev and the Russian Military. In *After Putin's Russia*, ed. Stephen K. Wegren and Dale R. Herspring. UK: Rowman and Littlefield Publishers, Inc.

How Capitalism Was Built: The Transformation of Central and Eastern Europe, Russia, and Central Asia . Cambridge University Press, 2007.

Hughes, James, and Gwendolyn Sasse. 2001. Comparing Regional and Ethnic Conflicts in Post Soviet Transition States: An Institutional Approach [Online Web]. https://docs.google.com/viewer?a=v&q=cache:Erkdm5DPA1MJ:www.essex.ac.uk/ECPR/events/jointsessions/paperarchive/grenoble/ws2/hughes_sasse.pdf+&hl=en&pid=bl&srcid=ADGEESgMQ5ycYDBG9EdQD FO7fP6PDWZhrBJlPctRHknlK1x1pmTTReY_U0TdEVzU1fW8gvqEocX r093oRY_Mqq4seeuCUVdAQdAH07r0XHMTQuVFk4HJkC76IwZkLkXMl 5UdJ06Idx&sig=AHIEtbR4bCbaUMwFNEmq1RjiUQ0UZwpI7g&pli=1. Accessed September 14, 2011.

Isakova, Irina. 2005. *Russian Governance in the Twenty-First Century.* NewYork: Frank Cass.

Itar-Tass News Agency. 2011. Tajikistan Hopes to Sign a Military Coop Agreement with Russia, July 21 [Online Web]. http://www.itar-tass.com/en/c154/189540_print.html. Accessed March 25, 2012.

Ivanov, S. 2005. On the New Version of the National Security Conception of the Russian Federation. In *Russian Foreign Policy in Transition: Concepts and Reality*, ed. Andrei Melvill and Tatiana Shakleina. Budapest: Central European University Press.

Jackson, N.J. 2003. *Russian Foreign Policy and the CIS. Theories, Debates and Actions.* London: Routledge.

Johnson, Rebecca. 1999. Post Cold War Security: The Lost Opportunities [Online Web]. http://www.unidir.org/pdf/articles/pdf-art257.pdf. Accessed September 9, 2011.

Jonson, L. 2004. *Vladimir Putin and Central Asia. The Shaping of Russian Foreign Policy.* London, New York: I.B. Taurus.

Jonson, Lena. 2005. Understanding Russia's Foreign Policy Change: The Cases of Central Asia and Iraq. In *Russia as a Great Power: Dimensions of Security Under Putin*, ed. Jacob Hedenskog, Vilhelm Konnander, Bertil Nygren, Ingmar Oldberg, and Christer Pursiainen. Oxon, USA and Canada: Routledge.

Kanet, Roger E. 2010. Russia and the Great Caspian Basin: Withstanding the US Challenge. In *Key Players and Regional Dynamics in Eurasia: The Return of the Great Game*, ed. Maria Raquel Friere and Roger E. Kanet. UK and USA: Palgrave Macmillan.

Karatnycky, Adrian. 2005. Ukraine's Orange Revolution. *Foreign Affairs*, April.

Kay, S. 2003. Geopolitical Constraints and Institutional Innovation: The Dynamics of Multilateralism in Eurasia. In *Limiting Institutions? The Challenge of Eurasian Security Governance*, ed. James Sperling, Sean Kay, and S. Victor Papascoma. Manchester and New York: Manchester University Press.

Kazakhstan Today. 2006. Returning of Uzbekistan to CSTO with Strengthen the Role of the Organization [Online Web]. http://engnews.gazeta.kz/art.asp?aid=280829. Accessed March 14, 2012.

Kembayev, Zhenis. 2009. *Legal Aspects of the Regional Integration Processes in the Post-Soviet Area.* Verlag Berlin Heidelberg: Springer.

Khushqadamov, H. 2012. Tajikistan as the CSTO Member to Provide Humanitarian Aid to Kyrgyzstan [Online Web]. http://khovar.tj/eng/archive/1072-tajikistan-as-the-csto-member-state-to-provide-humanitarian-aid-to-kyrgyzstan.html. Accessed on March 6, 2012.

Kobrinskaya, Irina. 2007. The Post-Soviet Space: From the USSR to the Commonwealth of Independent States and Beyond. In *The CIS, the EU and Russia: Challenges of Integration*, ed. Katlijn Malfiet, Lien Verspoest,and Evgeny Vinokurov. New York: Palgrave Macmillan.

Kudenko, A. 2012. US Attack on Iran Will Shake Everyone—CSTO Chief [Online Web]. http://rt.com/politics/us-attack-iran-csto-835/. Accessed March 21, 2012.

Kumar, Rama S. 2002. Impact of US-Led War on Terrorism. *Economic and Political Weekly* 37 (33): 3414–3419.

Kurdiukov, G., and K. Malfliet. 2007. Integration by Absorption: New Subjects for the Russian Federation. In *The CIS, the EU and Russia: Challenges of Integration*, ed. Katlijn Malfiet, Lien Verspoest, and Evgeny Vinokurov. New York: Palgrave Macmillan.

Kuzio, T. 2000. Geopolitical Pluralism in the CIS: The Emergence of GUUAM. *European Security* 9 (2): 81–144.

Lanteigne, M. 2006–2007. In Medias Res: The Development of the Shanghai Cooperation Organisation as a Security Community. *Pacific Affairs* 79 (4): 605–622.

Legvold, R. 2009. The Role of Multilateralism in Russian Foreign Policy. In *The Multilateral Dimension in Russian Foreign Policy*, ed. Elana Wilson Rowe and Stina Torjesen. USA and Canada: Routledge.

Legvold, R. 2011. Russia's Unformed Foreign Policy. *Foreign Affairs* 80 (5): 62–75.

Libman, Alexander. 2007. Regionalization and Regionalism in the Post-Soviet Space: Current Status and Implications for Institutional Development. *Europe-Asia Studies* 59 (3): 401–430.

Lo, Bobo. 2002. *Russian Foreign Policy in the Post Soviet Era: Reality, Illusion and Mythmaking*. New York: Palgrave Macmillan.

Lowry, Ritchie P. 1970. To Arms: Changing Military Roles and the Military Industrial Complex. *Social Problems* 18 (1): 3–16.

Lucas, E. 2008. *The New Cold War: Putin's Russia and the Threat to the West*. New York: Palgrave Macmillan.

Lurer.com. 2012. Armenia to Get Necessary Assistance as CSTO Full Member-Nikolai Bordyuzha [Online Web]. http://lurer.com/?p=13017& l=en. Accessed March 13, 2012.

MacFarlane, Neil S. 2004. The United States and Regionalism in Central Asia. *International Affairs* 80 (3): 447–461.

Malik, Mohan J. 2002. Dragon on Terrorism: Accessing China's Tactical Gains and Strategic Losses After 11 September. *Contemporary Southeast Asia* 24 (2): 252–293.

Mankoff, Jeffrey. 2009. *Russian Foreign Policy: Return of the Great Power Politics*. New York: Rowman & Littlefield Publishers Inc.

Mankoff, Jeffery. 2011. *Russian Foreign Policy: The Return of the Great Power Politics*, 2nd ed., 340–352. Lanham, MD: Rowman & Littlefield.

Manoli, P. 2003. The Black Sea Economic Cooperation: What Contribution to Regional Security? In *Limiting Institutions? The Challenge of Eurasian Security Governance*, ed. James Sperling, Sean Kay, and S. Victor Papascoma. Manchester and New York: Manchester University Press.

Marlène, Laruelle. 2008. Russia's Central Asia Policy and the Role of Russian Nationalism. Central Asia-Caucasus Institute and Silk Road Studies Program, April: 17.

McCauley, Martin. 2002. *Afghanistan and Central Asia: A Modern History*. Great Britain: Pearson Education Limited.

Melville, Andrei. 2005. Foreign Policy Therapy 'a la Dr Putin'. In *Russian Foreign Policy in Transition: Concepts and Reality*, ed. Andrei Melvill and Tatiana Shakleina. Budapest: Central European University Press.

Merry, Wayne E. 2004. The Politics of Central Asia: National in form, Soviet in Content. In *The Tracks of Tamerlane: Central Asia's Path to the 21st Century*, ed. D. Burghart and T. Sabonis-Helf. Washington, DC: NDU CTNSP.

Mishra, A. 2007. *Security in New Russia*. Delhi: Kalpaz Publications.

Moroney, Jennifer D.P. 2004. Building Security in Central Asia: A Multilateral Perspective. In *The Tracks of Tamerlane: Central Asia's Path to the 21st Century*, ed. D. Burghart and T. Sabonis-Helf. Washington, DC: NDU CTNSP.

Mowchan, John A. 2009. The Militarisation of the Collective Security Treaty Organisation. *Centre for Strategic Leadership* 6 (9): 1–6.

Neumann, Iver B. 2005. Russia as a Great Power. In *Russia as a Great Power: Dimensions of Security Under Putin*, ed. Jacob Hedenskog, Vilhelm Konnander, Bertil Nygren, Ingmar Oldberg, and Christer Pursiainen. Oxon, USA and Canada: Routledge.

Neumann, Peter R. 2008. NATO, the European Union, Russia and the Fight Against Terrorism. In *NATO-Russia Relations in the Twenty-First Century*, ed. Aurel Braun. New York and London: Routledge.

Nieuws. 2011. Tajikistan Calls for CSTO to Strengthen Fight Against Cybercrime, December 20 [Online Web]. https://www.cpni.nl/index.php/nieuws/tajikistan-calls-for-csto-to-strengthen-fight-against-cybercrime/. Accessed February 16, 2012.

Nurshat, Ababakirov. 2008. The CSTO Plans to Increase Its Military Potential. *CACI Analyst Bi-Weekly Briefing* 10, 18, September 17. http://www.cacianalyst.org/?q=node/4942. February 18, 2009.

Nygren, B. 2003. Russia's Immediate Security Environment Under Putin, Before and After 11 September. In *Russian Military Reform and Russia's New Security Environment*, ed. Y. Fedorov and Bertil Nygren. Stockholm: The Swedish National Defence College.

Nygren, B. 2005. Russia's Relations with Georgia Under Putin: The Impact of 11 September. In *Russia as a Great Power: Dimensions of Security Under*

Putin, ed. Jacob Hedenskog, Vilhelm Konnander, Bertil Nygren, Ingmar Oldberg, and Christer Pursiainen. Oxon, USA and Canada: Routledge.

Nygren, Bertil. 2008. *The Rebuilding of Greater Russia: Putin's Foreign Policy Towards the CIS Countries.* New York: Routledge.

Nygren, B. 2010. Russia and the CIS Region: The Russian Regional Security Complex. In *Key Players and Regional Dynamics in Eurasia: The Return of the Great Game*, ed. Maria Raquel Friere and Roger E. Kanet. UK and USA: Palgrave Macmillan.

Oldberg, Ingmar. 2005. Foreign Policy Priorities Under Putin: *A Tour d'horizon*. In *Russia as a Great Power: Dimensions of Security Under Putin*, ed. Jacob Hedenskog, Vilhelm Konnander, Bertil Nygren, Ingmar Oldberg, and Christer Pursiainen, 14. Oxon, USA and Canada: Routledge.

Oldberg, Ingmar. 2009. Russia's Great Power Strategy Under Putin and Medvedev. *Eurasia Daily Monitor (EDM)* 6 (108): 2–23.

Oliker, O. 2004. Friends Like These: Defining US Interests in Central Asia. In *The Tracks of Tamerlane: Central Asia's Path to the 21st Century*, ed. D. Burghart and T. Sabonis-Helf. Washington, DC: NDU CTNSP.

Papayoanou, P. 1997. Great Powers and Regional Orders: Possibilities and Prospects After the Cold War. In *Regional Orders. Building Security in a New World*, ed. D. Lake and P. Morgan. University Park, PA: Pennsylvania State University Press.

Pradhan, Ramakrushna. 2010. Geopolitics of Central Asia: China-US Engagement, VDM Dr. Muller Publication (Published in Germany, US and UK) (Monograph).

Ponsard, L. 2007. *Russia, NATO and Cooeprative Security: Bridging the Gap.* Oxon, USA and Canada: Routledge.

Pop, Irina. 2009. Russia, EU, NATO and the Strengthening of the CSTO in Central Asia. *Caucasian Review of International Affairs* 3 (3) (Summer): 278–290.

President of Russia Website "Press Statements Following the Shanghai Cooperation Organisation Council of Heads of States Session", 15 June 2006.

Pursiainen, C. 2003. Regionology and Russian Foreign Policy: Identifying the Theoretical Alternatives. In *Russian Regions and Regionalism: Strength Through Weakness*, ed. Graeme P. Herd and A. Aldis. USA and Canada: RoutledgeCurzon.

Radyuhin, V. 2011. CSTO Tightens Foreign Base Norms. *The Hindu*, December 21 [Online Web]. http://www.thehindu.com/news/international/article27 35791.ece. Accessed on June 10, 2012.

Radyuhin, V. 2012. And Then There Were Five. *The Hindu*, July 11.

Reuters. 2008. Factbox: Ukraine-Russia Relations [Online Web]. http://www.reuters.com/article/2008/02/12/us-russia-ukraine-relations-idUSL1282 952720080212. Accessed on January 26, 2009.

Roeder, P. 1997. From Hierarchy to Hegemony: The Post-Soviet Security Complex. In *Regional Orders. Building Security in a New World*, ed. D. Lake and P. Morgan. University Park, PA: Pennsylvania State University Press.

Rosefielde, S. 2004. *Russia in the 21st Century: The Prodigal Superpower*. New York: Cambridge University Press.

Roskaya Bersnya. 2012. CSTO Suffers from Artificial Anti-Azerbaijani Policy— Expert [Online Web]. http://vestnikkavkaza.net/news/politics/23397.html. Accessed on March 27, 2012.

Rowe, Elana W., and S. Torjesen. 2009. Key Features of Russia's Multilateralism. In *The Multilateral Dimension in Russian Foreign Policy*, ed. Elana Wilson Rowe and Stina Torjesen. USA and Canada: Routledge.

Rozanov, Anatoliy A., and Dovgan, Elena F. 2010. *Collective Security Treaty Organisation 2002–2009*. Geneva/Minsk: Procon Ltd.

Rupert, J. 1992. Dateline Tashkent: Post Soviet Central Asia. *Foreign Policy* 87: 175–178 and 180–195.

Sakwa, R. 2010. Senseless Dreams and Small Steps: The CIS and CSTO Between Integration and Cooperation. In *Key Players and Regional Dynamics in Eurasia: The Return of the Great Game*, ed. Maria Raquel Friere and Roger E. Kanet. UK and USA: Palgrave Macmillan.

Samarkhan, K. 2011a. SCO RATS to Improve Anti-terror Work Through Joint Efforts of Its Member States, Dzhumanbekov [Online Web]. http://www.inf orm.kz/eng/article/2349905. Accessed on February 14, 2012.

Samarkhan, Kurmat. 2011b. SCO RATS to Improve Anti-terror Work Through Joint Efforts of Its Member States, Dzhumanbekov. *Kazinform*, February 9. http://www.inform.kz/eng/article/2349905. Accessed on February 9, 2011.

Savranskaya, S. 2011. Gorbachev and the Third World. In *The End of the Cold War and the Third World*, ed. M. Kalinovsky, Artemy M., and S. Radchenko. Oxon. USA and Canada: Routledge.

Selezneva, L. 2003. Post-Soviet Russian Foreign Policy: Between Doctrine and Pragmatism. In *Realignments in Russian Foreign Policy*, ed. Rick Fawn. London and Portland: Frank Cass & Co. Ltd.

Sergounin, A. 2003a. Russia and the World: Changing Paradigms of Russian Foreign and Security Policy Under Yeltsin and Putin. In *The Russian Federation—Ten Years of Statehood: What Now?*, ed. Godzimirski. Oslo: Norwegian Institute of International Affairs.

Sergounin, A. 2003b. Russia's Regionalisation: The Interplay of Domestic and International Players. In *Russian Regions and Regionalism: Strength Through Weakness*, ed. Graeme P. Herd and A. Aldis. USA and Canada: RoutledgeCurzon.

Sheilfer, A., and D. Triesman. 2005. A Normal Country: Russia After Communism. *Journal of Economic Perspectives* 19 (1): 151–174.

Sheives, K. 2006. China Turns West: Beijing's Contemporary Strategy Towards Central Asia. *Pacific Affairs* 79 (2): 205–224.

Simon, J. 2008. NATO Enlargement and Russia. In *NATO-Russia Relations in the Twenty-First Century*, ed. Aurel Braun. New York and London: Routledge.

Skak, M. 2005. The Logic of Foreign and Security Policy Change in Russia. In *Russia as a Great Power: Dimensions of Security Under Putin*, ed. Jacob Hedenskog, Vilhelm Konnander, Bertil Nygren, Ingmar Oldberg, and Christer Pursiainen. Oxon, USA and Canada: Routledge.

Smith, G. 1999. Russia, Geopolitical Shift and the New Eurasianism. *Transactions of the Institute of Britain Geographers, New Series* 24 (4): 481–494.

Smith, Martin A. 2003. A Bumpy Road to an Unknown Destination? NATO-Russia Relations, 1991–2002. In *Realignments in Russian Foreign Policy*, ed. Rick Fawn. London and Portland: Frank Cass & Co. Ltd.

Socor, V. 2007. Organizational Setbacks at OSCE's Year-End Ministerial Conference. *Jamestown Foundation* 4 (225).

Socor, V. 2009a. CSTO Summit: Rapid Deployment Forces Advance at a Snail's Pace. *Jamestown Foundation* 6 (24).

Socor, V. 2009b. The CSTO: Missions, Capabilities, Political Ambitions. *Jamestown Foundation* 6 (25).

Speech by Russian Minister of Foreign Affairs Sergey Lavrov at SCO Council of Foreign Ministers Meeting, Bishkek, July 9, 2007. Available at: http://www.mid.ru/brp_4.nsf/0/6348382D9C12B077C3257314001B98B8.

Sperling, J. 2003. Eurasian Security Governance: New Threats, Institutional Adaptations. In *Limiting Institutions? The Challenge of Eurasian Security Governance*, ed. James Sperling, Sean Kay, and S. Victor Papascoma. Manchester and New York: Manchester University Press.

Spirova, Maria. 2008. Corruption and Democracy the "Color Revolutions" in Georgia and Ukraine. *Taiwan Journal of Democracy* 4 (2): 75–90.

Stepanova, E. 2005. Russia's Approach to the Fight Against Terrorism. In *Russia as a Great Power: Dimensions of Security Under Putin*, ed. Jacob Hedenskog, Vilhelm Konnander, Bertil Nygren, Ingmar Oldberg, and Christer Pursiainen. Oxon, USA and Canada: Routledge.

Stockholm International Peace Research Institute. 2007. SIPRI Yearbook.

Swanstorm, Niklas. 2010. Traditional and Non-traditional Security Threats in Central Asia: Connecting the New and Old. *China and Eurasian Forum Quarterly* 8 (2): 35–51.

Swiderski, Edward M. 1998. Culture, Contexts and Direction in Russian Post-Soviet Philosophy. *Studies in East European Thought* 50 (4): 283–328.

Times.am. 2012. CSTO 'Cooperation 2012' Military Exercises Will Be Held in Armenia [Online Web]. http://times.am/?l=en&p=5199. Accessed on February 30, 2012.

Tolipov, F. 2012. CSTO Summit Raises Ambiguity Regarding Uzbekistan's Membership. *CACI Analyst* [Online Web]. http://cacianalyst.org/?q=node/5694. Accessed on March 14, 2012.

Torjesen, Stina. 2009. Russia as a Military Great Power: The Uses of CSTO and SCO in Central Asia. In *The Multilateral Dimension in Russian Foreign Policy*, ed. Elana Wilson Rowe and Stina Torjesen. USA and Canada: Routledge.

Troitskiy, Mikhail, Pan Guang, et al. 2007. The Shanghai Cooperation Organization (SIPRI Policy Paper No. 17). Stockholm International Peace Research Institute, May, p. 208.

Tsygankov, Andrei P. 2010. Russia's Foreign Policy. In *After Putin's Russia*, ed. Stephen K. Wegren and Dale R. Herspring. Lanham, MD: Rowman and Littlefield Publishers, Inc.

Valovaya, Tatyana. 2005. The Post Soviet Space in the Era of Pragmatism. *Russia in Global Affairs* 3 (2): 112–125.

Vinokurov, Evgeny. 2007. Russian Approaches to Integration in the Post-Soviet Space in the 2000s. In *The CIS, the EU and Russia: Challenges of Integration*, ed. Katlijn Malfiet, Lien Verspoest, and Evgeny Vinokurov. New York: Palgrave Macmillan.

Wallander, Celeste A. 1989. Third World Conflict in Soviet Military Thought: Does the New Thinking Grow Prematurely Grey? *World Politics* 42 (1): 31–63.

Weinstein, Adam. 2007. Russian Phoenix: The Collective Security Treaty Organization. *The Whitehead Journal of Diplomacy and International Relations* VIII (1): 167–178.

Weitz, Richard. 2006. Terrorism in Eurasia: Enhancing the Multilateral Response. *China and Eurasia Forum Quarterly* 4 (2): 40–42.

Weitz, Richard. 2009. Growing Pains. *The Journal of International Security Affairs* 17 (Fall).

Weitz, R. 2010. Why Is the CSTO Absent in the Kyrgyz Crisis? *Central Asia-Caucasus Analyst* 12 (11): 6–8.

Willerton, John P., and Mikhail A. Beznosov. 2007. Russia's Pursuit of Its Eurasian Security Interests: Weighing the CIS and Alternative Bilateral-Multilateral Arrangements. In *The CIS, the EU and Russia: Challenges of Integration*, Katlijn Malfiet, Lien Verspoest, and Evgeny Vinokurov. New York: Palgrave Macmillan.

Willerton, John P., and G. Cockerham. 2003. Russia, the CIS and Eurasian Interconnections. In *Limiting Institutions? The Challenge of Eurasian Security Governance*, ed. James Sperling, Sean Kay, and S. Victor Papascoma. Manchester and New York: Manchester University Press.

Wilson, Jeanne L. 2009. Colour Revolutions: The View From Moscow and Beijing. *Journal of Communist Studies and Transition Politics* 25 (2,3): 369–395.

Wu, Yu-Shan. 2011. Russia and the CIS in 2010. *Asian Survey* 51 (1): 64–75.

Xuequan, Mu. 2012. CSTO Opposes Using Force Against Iran. English.xinhuanet.com, April 13 [Online Web]. http://news.xinhuanet.com/english/world/2012-04/13/c_122970617.htm. Accessed on April 27, 2012.

Zagorski, A. 1998. Regional Structures of Security Policy Within the CIS. In *Security Dilemmas in Russia and Eurasia*, ed. R. Allison and C. Bluth. London: Royal Institute of International Affairs.

Zagorski, A. 2009. Multilateralism in Russia's Foreign Policy Approaches. In *The Multilateral Dimension in Russian Foreign Policy*, ed. Elana Wilson Rowe and Stina Torjesen. New York: Routledge.

Ziegler, Charles E. 2008. Russia and the CIS in 2007: Putin's Final Year? *Asian Survey* 48 (1): 133–143.

Zwick, P. 1989. New Thinking and the New Foreign Policy Under Gorbachev. *Political Science and Politics* 22 (2): 215–224.

INDEX